THE YIN AND THE YANG OF IT ALL

THE
YIN AND THE YANG

OF IT
ALL

ROCK 'N' ROLL MEMORIES
FROM THE CUSP
AS TOLD BY A MIXED-UP,
MIXED-RACE KID

JOHN KIM FAYE

Advantage | Books

Published by Advantage, Charleston, South Carolina.
Member of Advantage Media.

ADVANTAGE is a registered trademark, and the Advantage colophon is a trademark of Advantage Media Group, Inc.

Printed in the United States of America.

10 9 8 7 6 5 4 3 2 1

ISBN: 978-1-64225-743-4 (Hardcover)
ISBN: 978-1-64225-742-7 (eBook)

LCCN: 2022919658

Cover design by Michael Leavy.
Layout design by Matthew Morse.

In loving memory of Mom and Papa

When I let go of what I am, I become what I might be.
—Lao Tzu

They lived and laughed and loved and left.
—James Joyce

Happiness is not a state of mind
It's more a collection of flashes in time
Appreciate them while they shine.
—IKE

CONTENTS

PART IV: SALAD DAYS

PART V: THE A&M YEARS

PART VI: UNSIGNED AGAIN, NATURALLY

PART VII: IT KEEPS EVOLVING

A PROLOGUE

ere's a question I ask myself all the time: Where the hell was K-Pop when I needed it? Or *Kim's Convenience*? Or *Parasite*? Or *Pokémon*, or *Squid Game*, or *any* of the things that have come to signify "Asian cool"? I watched this cultural transformation unfold long after my fading youth made it impossible to see the pair of "Gangnam Style" socks my sister sent me one Christmas as anything more than a slap in the face. In the 1970s, America had none of these things, or anything that would make growing up Asian, or even part Asian, seem remotely appealing. Sometimes people fantasize about who they would get to play themselves in the movie based on their best-selling memoir. The only person I would have been able to come up with at the time is Pat Morita, "Arnold" from *Happy Days*, and later, the somewhat hipper Mr. Miyagi from *The Karate Kid*. He was the only Asian I knew of in show business. And he wasn't exactly what you would call "cool." Bruce Lee was cool, but he was already dead.

Nobody called me cool. They called me a lot of other things, though. Chink, Chinaman, Chinee, Jap, Jappy Eyes, Slope, Boat Person, Someone Whose Idea of a Joke Is to Go Pee Pee in Your Coke. That last one never really bothered me. I mean, hey, they were the ones drinking my urine. And as much as the other terms may have stung the sensitive boy I was, few, if any, actually applied. It was pretty clear that none of the name-throwers in this mash-up of epithets had the slightest desire, maybe not even the ability, to distinguish between Chinese and Japanese and Burmese, as if all of the Far East was just a monolithic swarm of dog eaters. I found it weird, though, that I hardly knew of any insults aimed specifically at Koreans. I was occasionally called a "gook," which I only later found out was used during the Korean War. And what about Irish Koreans? No one would even know what to do with that. I sure as hell didn't.

To be honest, I wasn't making a lot of distinctions either. Not that I remember any other squinty-eyed kids running around in Newark, Delaware in the post-Vietnam era, but even in principle I wanted to keep my distance. The month I spent in Korea with my mom when I was thirteen would be no help in that regard, as all I'd be able to think about for years after the trip wasn't my exposure to a culture I felt no connection to but the exposure of my chubby, soaped-up, naked body after my two teenage cousins pulled the shower curtain to one side, interrupting my bathroom rendition of "Funky Town" or whatever it was I was trying to sing, and I shrieked at the top of my lungs for them to "get the fuck out" while they laughed and one of them said his first words to me that I could actually understand: "You have breast like woo-mon." This comment turned out to be quite the zinger, as it combined both emasculation and fat-shaming in one tidy burst of broken English. It was all I could do just to fling suds in their general direction. I guess it would be safe to say that I was no stranger to being laughed at, whether by kids hurling ethno-disparagement or by relatives I barely knew or even my sister's future husband, who took great pleasure in saying, "I am a mesomorph. You are an endomorph." That's a fancy word for "fat kid," in case you were wondering. I know because when I asked Mom what it meant, she told me to look it up.

With all that baggage packed away in my childhood-self-esteem closet, I probably should have known from the get-go that when most people picture a rock musician in their heads, that image doesn't look anything like me. As much as I was fascinated with the world of music growing up, it appeared—through my starstruck eyes, anyway—like an exclusive club that I could only dream of being part of. So, I dreamed.

And listened. And mimed. And mimicked—until lip-syncing morphed into whispers, which morphed into murmurs, which morphed into something that sounded like singing. I still remember the first backhanded compliment I ever got for my voice: "Wow, I would *never* have expected *that sound* to come out of someone like *you*." Well, we're both stuck with that, aren't we?

So where do *I* fit into all this? Rock 'n' roll is supposed to be an oasis for the outsider, a refuge for the rebel, a sanctuary for the unsatisfied. Is there not a place for *me* on a musical continuum that seems inclusive of every conceivable shade of provocateur, libertine, politician, and crier for help under the sun?

It's been said that rock 'n' roll is "all things to all people," and, if I can borrow a line from a song of mine you've probably never heard, *that's my definition of God.*

Sometimes I imagine I'm in a fugue state and wander into a greenroom to find all my own rock gods and goddesses simultaneously immersed in their much-talked-about pre-show rituals, like making sure there are no brown M&M's in the candy dish or having a friend pinch your nipples.

Hey, it's Keith Richards eating a shepherd's pie and doing blow cut with his father's cremains!

So what's *my* pre-show ritual?

Transcendental meditation? A stiff drink? A prayer to the Almighty? No. I'll tell you what I do. *I* … cut up a pineapple. OK, I know this does not sound very rock 'n' roll *at all*, but I have to tell you, it's actually a pretty savage act. When I twist off that sharp, waxy crown of leaves, it evokes the grinding crunch of the best limb-avulsion scenes from B horror movies like *The Toxic Avenger*. Follow that with a serrated stainless steel blade sawing through the rough golden skin into fragrant tropical flesh, leaving a puddle of pulpy juice and another thin groove on the face of a well-worn cutting board.

These overlapping knife lines, etched by a now-decades-old Ginsu (one of the few things I took after my divorce), are the untidy hash marks that keep count of innumerable gigs, from thankless three-set shows in stick-to-the-floor dive bars, where rowdy, fluffy-bearded bikers put you in a headlock while demanding you play something by Bob Seger, to surreal rock star experiences in sold-out concert venues with backstage catering and lighted marquees with the name of the band spelled correctly.

By the time the whole grisly process is over, an eavesdropper like me might reasonably assume I'm disposing of a body rather than prepping a Tupperware container of fruit. I won't get into the wonky details about its anti-inflammatory properties or how it stimulates the salivary glands. All you really need to know is this: pineapple is to my vocal cords as a quart of 5W-30 is to an oil-burning fifteen-passenger touring van with two hundred thousand miles on it, bald tires, and "wash me" written in the dust that coats the rear windows. It's not as pretty as it once was, but it still gets me where I'm going. Run into me on any given night when I'm singing, and you'll find me carrying that Tupperware around like it's the baby Jesus. Or maybe the nuclear football.

Why all this talk about rock 'n' roll and pineapples anyway? The answer is simple: *Music gave me my voice*—not just the transmitter of lyrics and melodies from the songs I write but my place in the world, my sense of belonging somewhere and believing in something. The intersection of my singing voice and my capital-*V* Voice is at the epicenter of everything I've ever accomplished, every ounce of validation I've ever received. And I wasn't always able to use my voice—or my Voice—in the way that I do now. It took me well into adulthood to truly find them and an even longer time to muster the courage to exercise them like an inalienable right. Their mercurial character reflects my own, with all the complexities and contradictions inherent in the unlikely union between the parents who made me. It's a fusion of two seemingly disparate worlds that still sometimes leaves me feeling like a minority of one.

I heard somewhere that it takes a village to raise a child. In my case, it was a *very small* village. My parents had me, and they were all I had, along with my three older sisters from Mom's first marriage. Papa died without my having met a single relative from his side of the family, and as I've told you, things did not get off on the best foot with the other side. From the time I was six, it was just me and four older women. While my sisters were wonderful to me, they were more like indentured babysitters than siblings I would grow up alongside and share new experiences with. And while I thought for a time that I was no different from any other American kid—I loved the shit out of apple pie, I can tell you that—enough ignorant people planted enough seeds of doubt in me that I became convinced I was different, and not yet in a good way. But what the hell *was* I?

"Sex, drugs, and rock 'n' roll"? That's never been me. Well, unless you substitute "dessert" for "drugs." I'm one of a handful of musicians I know who's never had any interest in smoking pot or playing for drink tickets. I don't imbibe. Once in a blue moon, maybe. I'll politely sip an adult beverage because someone at the bar insists on buying me one and in that moment I'd rather not explain for the millionth time that I'm kind of allergic to alcohol. Apparently, I'm one of those Koreans who lacks a certain enzyme that breaks down booze in the bloodstream. I get drunk off one shot and, therefore, am a very cheap date. When I do accept someone's kind gesture, I always go for the hard stuff—Jack Daniel's or Jameson. Apparently, I'm one of those Irish who needs to prove to myself and others that I can hold my liquor, my single gulp of what my countrymen call "the drink."

I have one tattoo. It was a post-divorce-slash-early-midlife-crisis kinda thing, but the general consensus among the people I know who enjoy getting "inked" is that it was a bold first move. I guess I could have asked my tattoo artist, a guy called Bird, for a tasteful treble clef on my ass cheek or something else "musician-y," but instead I walked into Philadelphia Eddie's just off South Street and asked him to tattoo the entire width of my upper arm with a black-and-green yin-yang symbol, substituting clovers where the small circles would usually be.

"First tattoo," I said, just to break the silence while Bird took out a sketch pad. "I'm half Korean, half Irish, so …"

Bird whipped up a drawing in about twenty seconds, mercifully eliminating any further opportunity for me to speak.

"Something like this?" he asked, showing me the pencil outline.

I told him I thought it looked great but then asked him, "Instead of four-leaf clovers, could you knock it down to three?"

I wanted my shamrocks to have realistic expectations.

Bird offered a caveat that although the upper arm is one of the least painful places to get tattooed, much of the surface area of the piece would need to be solid black and solid green and that this might be the source of some discomfort. But there was no turning back for me. After about three hours and what must have been thousands of needle pricks to the dermis, Bird took my $300 in cash, covered my arm in Saran Wrap, and sent me back out into the world with a tattoo that sums up who I am better than just about any of the more than 150 songs I've recorded over the span of fifteen or so releases. The seemingly incongruous and contradictory forces within me were now joined together, in Technicolor ebony and emerald. I walked around the block to the TLA—Theatre of Living Arts—and bought a ticket to see Tinted Windows, an unlikely supergroup consisting of the lead singer from Hanson, the bass player from Fountains of Wayne, the drummer from Cheap Trick, and the guitarist from Smashing Pumpkins—the Asian one. I hiked my shirt sleeve up toward my shoulder to make sure my tat was visible. It felt so *relevant.*

Taken individually, the yin and yang and the shamrock are the visual clichés of each side I inherited, but together, they represent something unique. My songs have always been more complicated, reflecting duality as turmoil, my two halves in conflict, full of lines to read between. I want my voice and my songs to be as true and honest as this tattoo, my symbol of self-acceptance, with the power to persuade a short, stocky, shy kid that he's good enough, lovable as is, with his warped sense of humor and racial makeup as random as a mix tape that segues "Close to You" by the Carpenters into "Holiday in Cambodia" by Dead Kennedys.

In the sunset years of her life, my mother was on a path to cracking the code to her own enigmatic existence. Watching me struggle to discover myself, she would often summon me to her den to share a quote from the philosophies of the Dalai Lama or Lao Tzu. As a parent of two children of my own, I can only now fully appreciate what must have been Mom's frustration as the words of these great thinkers fell on my deaf ears.

What do they know? I thought. I had been living by my own "philosophy" cobbled together from songs of my youth with titles like "Birth, School, Work, Death," "I Wanna Be Sedated," and a song by the Violent Femmes that I related to so deeply I quoted the entire chorus in my 1984 yearbook layout, a full page, which every senior in the graduating class of the private school I had attended since seventh grade had been given to express who we thought we were. In addition to telling everyone they could just "Kiss Off," I cited other topical song lyrics, which made references to barbecued iguanas and the brain impulses of severed limbs. It was all just a big private joke to me. A few pages later in that same yearbook, Mike Neiger, my classmate and first real bandmate, did me the honor of quoting one of my early lyrics.

I've got nothing to say
But I write it anyway

Of course, there was plenty to say; I just didn't quite know how to say it yet.

Luckily for me, I got the chance to learn and bloom late. I never felt more humbled than when I stood in the wings at a radio festival in Milwaukee, still sweating from the set I had finished earlier with my band, the Caulfields, watching the Ramones unleash a punk rock tornado in front of a bunch of kids who had no idea how privileged they were to bear witness. Though it was only a year before he would play his last show, Joey Ramone, even skinnier in person than on the cover of *Rocket To Russia*, left strewn onstage the blueprint of everything I aspired to be as a performer. For me, he was as rock 'n' roll as they come.

Experiences like that appear throughout my musical landscape, but they often get balanced out with the consequences of bad decisions, bad timing, bad advice, and bad luck, when the even-keel wisdom of those Dalai Lama quotes Mom was offering up could have come in handy, had I been listening. Even if I wasn't ready to adopt Eastern philosophies, she knew how to get through to me in other ways. Savvy psychiatrist that she was, Mom sometimes quoted my own lyrics back to me from a song called "Figure It Out," which was the lead single on the Caulfields' second and final album on A&M Records. All she needed to say was the title of the song in her quietly dignified voice for me to pause and begin to recalibrate my thinking and, above all, try to live by my own words.

Both before and after the Caulfields' fifteen minutes in the spotlight, I've had some pretty profound highs and lows, submerged in the all-hustle-all-the-time, almost-middle-class existence of a working musician—a "lifer," as we call ourselves. I'm always just one song, one soundtrack, one viral anything from being able to put my kids through college *or* one unforeseen dry patch from having to play "Wagon Wheel" in front of an eighty-inch plasma TV that the bar owner refuses to turn off during my set. So where *do* I fit in, man?

Each one of us has to figure that out on our own, the hard way. Like that unpredictable mix tape, we never know what's coming up next, the playlist just rolls on, as we do our best to reconcile the contradictions, the dualities, the space between black and white, something and nothing, the yin and the yang of it all.

LETTER TO AN 8 ⋆ 10

There's a song I sing in the shower sometimes. I wrote it for you. Actually, I wrote it for us.

Everything that you went through, mama
You know it made me what I am
It's good to finally have that conversation
I finally feel like I'm a man
Now I'm starin' down the truth in the mirror
Naked and brutal in the sun
And my reality is so much clearer
I know there's nowhere left to run

I know. Heavy subject matter, a far cry from the Bee Gees' falsettos I used to ape while shampooing my hair when I was a kid. That innocent voice, falling flat and cracking on the edge of puberty, is now a distant echo reverberating off bathroom tiles of old.

The last time I heard *your* voice is nowhere near as remote, but an awful lot has happened since then. The little flame that kept my man-childhood burning well into my forties just sort of flickered out amid the pressures of raising teenagers and the flurry of unsolicited mail from AARP. I do have to say that a 15 percent senior discount at Denny's holds a certain appeal, but I always tear those envelopes in half and throw them in the trash, the same way you did with your junk mail.

A newly heightened state of forgetfulness often finds me fighting the temptation to coin your old phrase "that's me these days," which was your catchall defense for the dates you forgot, words you misinterpreted, or situations you mishandled, like any other imperfect human being might. But you were never like any other human being to me, imperfect as we all were. In spite of the more frequent sputtering of my own now-over-half-century-old brain, there are days when it feels like you never left.

In my one-bedroom apartment, where I've deliberately left the walls undecorated to replicate the soothing blankness of staring for hours at the tray table directly in front of me, at peace in its locked position in the twenty-fifth row on a cross-country flight, the only framed 8 × 10 on display is this photograph of you. You are the picture of calm, silver-haired contentment, all decked out in your traditional Korean *hanbok*. Your arms, enveloped in vibrant purple sleeves, meet in a symmetrical lock of your hands at the center of a white cloud of silk, shaping a serene heart. You only wore this dress on special occasions, and if memory serves, you struck this distinguished pose in the early 2000s, right around the time Natalie was born.

You played along and used the nickname "Goosie" that Lisa and I imposed upon her soon after we brought her home from the hospital. And when she could eventually talk, she gave you your own nickname: "Gaga."

Yours is also the smiling face—still youthful in your eighties—cropped into close-up in the photo on my iPhone lock screen. It's the first face I see at the beginning of the day, other than my own puffy countenance in the bathroom mirror. You're wearing that straw hat you put on pretty much any time you ventured out into nature, which was, through your viewfinder, a never-ending panorama of wonder. You were drawn to things most people would disregard—if they even noticed them at all.

You once took a snapshot of the decaying trunk of a fallen tree and presented it like a Rorschach test to anyone you could get to scrutinize it, asking "What does this look like to you?" No one else could really see the face you saw emerging from the splintered wood, even after you pointed out the serendipitous splat of bird shit shaping the white of its eye. No matter what the subjects of your fascination were, they always brought you to the same wide-eyed conclusion: "Isn't that beautiful!"

And yet, even when sharp-shooting, gazillion-pixel cameras became affordable and prevalent, your preferred photographic butterfly net was a Fujifilm QuickSnap disposable, sold in multipacks at Costco, where I would drive you once a week, sometimes to pick up your prints and stroll the aisles salivating over the party-size barrels of Utz cheese balls, or just to eat a dollar hotdog and get you out of the house. It was mind-boggling to me why you refused to upgrade to a better 35mm machine, but I think I get it now. *Point, click, wind.* Simplicity. In a digital wasteland, you were defiantly analog.

The soft focus of those pictures is how you wanted to look at the world by then, and I think I inherited that inclination from you. The thing is, this avoidance of higher definition, the sidestepping of greater clarity, the cataract blur of the pores and the moles and the nose hairs, can make the unpleasant and the uncomfortable come back to haunt us—or worse, haunt us by never going away in the first place. This is why I feel I have to look at all of it again through a more candid, unflinching lens.

The fewer than ten years that passed between those two pictures of you, around the time the mini strokes began, had to have been lonely. You were practically quarantined in your own home, all three of your daughters living on the opposite coast—one completely estranged—and me, over an hour away near Philadelphia. My attention was all over the map, playing stay-at-home dad to two little kids, my marriage slowly calcifying, my music career a metaphorical boulder that I was pushing uphill for the umpteenth time. Natalie and Sean were your last grandchildren, the ones you had to wait for until I was practically as old as you were when you had me. Other than the mutual joy we felt in their company, you and I found it hard to connect. I'm not sure there was ever a time when it was easy.

It sounds funny to say, but I think I felt closest to you when you would yell at me in Korean. To this day, when people ask me if I speak the language, my answer is that I don't, but I can tell when I'm being cussed out. Most of the time, I knew it wasn't serious, because you were fighting back a wry smile as you reprimanded me. You always covered your mouth whenever you felt a smile coming on, like you didn't want anybody to see you do it.

I liked it when you let your guard down a little. Your short bursts of Korean profanity could be downright playful, as playful as you can get with a word like *deongtanji*, which you told me translates to "bucket of shit." You also liked to call me *nom*, which means "boy," but your tone veered a little more toward "punk." You always put a "Yey" at the front of it, basically "Hey, you," winding up into the word not unlike the ring announcer who says, "Let's get ready to rummmmmmble."

"Yeyyyyyyyyynom!" Even in the form of mild castigation, these exchanges felt intimate, even warm, welcome breaks between more difficult moments. Détente.

So much of our long struggle to see eye to eye occurred in your den, Tae Im's old bedroom. This is where I called you out for being "overemotional" on the night before I was to move twelve minutes away into my freshman dorm at the University of Delaware, one of the two colleges I got into. Though it was never said, we both knew I chose Delaware not for the business administration major I nearly failed out of before switching over to English, but for a much more practical reason: to keep the band together.

I was taking inventory of the laundry I had forgotten overnight in the dryer by the back door. You didn't care much for my fashion choices and interrogated me on why I was holding on to what you often referred to as "that awful shirt." After all, you had just bought me a substantial new collection of fall clothes.

You pointed to my ripped, already rewrinkled army-green tee, emblazoned with a skull and crossbones and the endearing phrase "Kill 'em all, let God sort 'em out."

"I didn't ask you to buy me anything," I chirped at you, making a halfhearted attempt to fold the shirt I had bought at Zipperhead on South Street in Philly and proving myself the ingrate you may have been waiting to accuse me of being.

"I just don't want you going to class dressed in rags," you said. "Look at these holes."

I told you that the holes were intentional and that my days of following a dress code were over. This was in snide reference to the no-jeans-no-T-shirts-no-sneakers rule of the button-down private school I had just graduated from that summer.

"Is this really how you want to act on your last night in this house?" you said.

"Look, Mom, I'm *literally* moving down the block," I said, with a still-tenuous grasp on how to use "literally" in a sentence.

Things degenerated badly when I said, "Don't worry, I'll be back for band practice and to do my laundry."

What other response could I have expected than the teary one you gave: "Don't bother coming back at all!"

Watching you cry was one of the lowest moments of my life. It was just not something you did. Your brand of stoicism, which I had become so used to, which I always thought of as cold-hearted disinterest, was really your fiercest defense mechanism, and somehow I had broken through it. It had served you well, the protective shield that allowed you to bear the challenges of your life, not to mention those of your kids. Each of us battled hardships that you often took to heart as though they were your own. I never took the time back then to wonder where it all came from.

> EACH OF US BATTLED HARDSHIPS THAT YOU OFTEN TOOK TO HEART AS THOUGH THEY WERE YOUR OWN. I NEVER TOOK THE TIME BACK THEN TO WONDER WHERE IT ALL CAME FROM.

I'm sure part of it came from watching North Korean soldiers break into your house and drag your cousin away because they suspected him of being an agitator. I'm sure part of it came from the knowledge that he had been tortured and killed. The same thing happened to your sister's husband.

I'm sure part of it came from growing up in Korea under Japanese occupation, being forced to take a Japanese name in school, having to read, write, and speak in a language that wasn't your own. During one of our many recent sibling powwows, Tae Im told me that when you were in your twenties you took to the streets in protest and got thrown in jail for days. If I had the guts to do that, I would make sure I told my kids about it, but you never said a word to any of us. Tae Im wasn't even supposed to know. I guess your family didn't really see it as something to be proud of, so you learned not to bring it up.

There were always little clues of how you kept the world at arm's length.

You signed your checks with initials "J. S. K."—short for Jung Sook Kim, a name you never allowed *anyone* to call you directly. Except for a short-lived stint as "J. S." to appease Tae Hyun's in-laws sometime in the '80s, your friends and colleagues addressed you only as "Dr. Faye." I remember your friend Dr. Winston found a little loophole and somehow got away with calling you "Kim," like Kimberly.

I came to learn that "Kim" is basically the Korean surname equivalent of "Smith," but your particular bloodline of Kims is traceable back to the highest royals of the Silla Dynasty. These ancestors appear as the top branch of a family tree that your brother Suk Joo researched and drew up for you as a gift. Seeing it now, beautifully framed at Tae Im's house, it's crazy to see all the indecipherable names of relatives I never knew and never will know sprawling through the centuries before dropping down to where your brother's calligraphy commingles with his angular Western penmanship to include the names that appeared once you married an American.

There was no mention of Ralph, your beloved first son-in-law, whom you loved up to the very end, only Tae Kyung's second husband, Gus, whose name you expunged using a box cutter with extreme prejudice, sometime around their nightmare divorce. It was an ordeal that hit you so personally, it threw you into a serious depression. Perhaps it transported you back into memories of your own split from the father of your girls. That wasn't so much a parting of ways as it was a case of total abandonment and betrayal. You were the last to know. Your husband began an affair with a nurse while the two of you were still in medical residency. After you went to the Korean embassy to try to have him deported back to Daegu, he tried to have you declared "mentally incompetent" and even drugged you with tranquilizers before skipping town and settling in Saskatchewan.

Of all the Korean words you never taught me, one seems to be the most fitting to describe your complex pain: *han*. There's no English equivalent for it. It's a state of lament, an ache of resentment, a hope for resolution. It's supposedly distinctly Korean, but it sounds like it applies to the Irish, too, which I guess means it fully applies to me.

On the night I made you cry, all I could see was a nagging mother lashing out at her son for simply not wanting to dress like a preppie anymore. When I replay it now, I see you grappling with the realization that your last child was leaving home, and it made zero difference if the distance was three miles or three thousand.

Years later, in the same den, you created an artistic space for yourself. Over the course of thousands of hours in solitude, your arthritic hands crafted dozens of meticulously embroidered quilts and pillows. These were the embodiment of the very appreciation for beauty and persistence you wanted to pass down to everyone you loved. On one occasion, which mirrored several others like it, I barged in to find you shrouded in another work in progress, an ornate bedspread spilling off the couch onto the small wooden coffee table, which, itself, served mostly as a footrest and a repository for discarded Stim-U-Dents, the dental plaque removers you went through like a pack-a-day smoker would a box of Marlboro Reds. I yelled at you to turn your TV down, like a curmudgeonly neighbor about to call the cops with a noise complaint. I berated you for watching Fox News after you said, "They have such a lovely family," when footage of the Georges Bush and their Kennebunkport clan flashed on-screen.

Of course the TV was loud. You put up with nearly ten years of high-decibel band rehearsals in your basement, first with No Excuse, which begat the Beat Clinic, which begat the Caulfields, resulting in the default volume of your television being as loud as or louder than the PA system I practiced through. I'm so sorry for the hearing loss that we caused you.

I know you did your best to understand and support my pursuit of a life in music, dutifully driving out to the Logan House with the other band moms during my "theatrical front man" years. I opened my shows dressed in a bathrobe, reading an upside-down newspaper while seated on the shadily acquired American Standard I had lifted from the curb in front of the Holloways' house. I just took it, like someone would snatch an old recliner discarded during a home remodeling. You complained only occasionally that I was storing it behind your hedges between gigs, and you marveled at how I was able to wedge it into the back seat of the maroon two-door Mustang I inherited as my first car. You also bore witness to and provided the screwdriver for my removal of the toilet seat as part of my plan to dance with it around my neck on the occasion of the first really big show of my life, at the classiest venue in Wilmington, of all places—the Grand Opera House.

You never indicated one way or another whether you found these antics entertaining or embarrassing. More often than not, any feedback you had for me came in the form of a question: "Is that *good*?" Well, that's what I was asking *you*. I took the fact that you always listened to any song I played for you, and came to most every performance for as long as your health allowed, as tacit approval of what I was doing. But I don't think I realized how much your sense of obligation played into it. In the time and place you were raised, obligation to family always trumped the individual. So when you chose to join the first generation of Korean women to attend medical school over the recommended study of "home economics," I wonder how conflicted that must have made you. I wonder if you felt the same weight of your parents' expectations as I felt, always wondering if I had failed to live up to yours.

And what about your own expectations for yourself? Could you have expected that the nuns who ran the hospital where you first arrived for your residency would hand you a nurse's uniform because they were as sexist as any man, and you not capable of speaking up for yourself in a new language just yet? Could you have expected you would never remarry after Papa died, choosing to go it alone in the same house you bought as the only doctor in our blue-collar neighborhood? Could you have expected that when you absolutely couldn't make it on your own any longer, your daughters would have forty years of your life packed up and in a moving van before you could blink? Could you have expected that a woman born into an aristocratic Korean family, which, in spite of years of occupation and war, still claimed an entire mountain in which to bury their dead, would end it all the way you did, in a hospice bed somewhere in suburban Oregon?

I guess neither one of us was partial to the path of least resistance. Then again, did we really have a choice? We can't control the things that swerve into our crosswalks. We can only control what we do once they hit us.

PART I

FIGURE IT OUT

Once, I woke up
And nothing was good enough
So I tried
To make what I couldn't buy
No one knows whether to come or go
So they grow in any direction
Look back through all the years
Then ask me how I wound up here
Sometimes I figure it out again
Then something begins to change my mind

—THE CAULFIELDS, "FIGURE IT OUT"

SPEAK UP

wanted to speak up, but I didn't quite know how. You can't just piss in your label rep's cornflakes by saying, "Uh, I don't think this is an appropriate outlet for my artistic vision," without sounding like a complete brat. Especially after they call in God knows how many favors and stroke God knows how many egos just to get you booked on the show. Even if there had been some flickering opportunity to lodge such a concern—some break in the dizzying strobe of the early-morning *in*continental breakfast, and the *what-band-are-you-again* chitchat with the bell hop in the hotel lobby, and the black Lincoln Town Car blasting 1010 WINS like a white noise machine while slithering and honking its way past sidewalk preachers and what appeared to be Charo standing on the corner in tight white jeans with her fly completely down—I didn't feel I had the right. I knew that our "tab" for tour and promotional support was pretty close to $100,000 by this point, so I reminded myself that I was lucky to even have the opportunity to be performing on live TV.

It was late summer in 1995, and the Caulfields had just cleared a hurdle most major-label "baby bands" never even reach in the first place. We got a *second* single off of *Whirligig*, our debut album for A&M Records. You didn't get a second single unless the first one had the label smelling money—*hit-record money*—and another platinum victory just like the ones they had orchestrated for Gin Blossoms and Blues Traveler and Sheryl Crow in recent fiscal quarters. We could be next, right?

"Devil's Diary," the first single off the album, had cracked the modern rock top-40, gaining initial momentum on WDRE and Y-100 in Philadelphia, eventually hitting number one for a week in Niagara Falls, generating "great phones" in Grand Rapids, "testing" with eighteen-to-thirty-four-year-olds in Milwaukee and Madison, and catching fire down south in Atlanta, appealing to postgrunge kids with a chorus hook that was equal parts irony and blasphemy:

I'm bigger than Jesus now.

The song also appeared to be generating a little backlash in certain conservative quarters, or so we thought about forty minutes before we were due onstage at a small club in Slidell, Louisiana. It was a fill-in date on the night before a huge radio festival in New Orleans, which was a little less than an hour away, driving on I-10 around Lake Pontchartrain.

While most of the band was digging into the "meat platter" provided in the office doubling as our dressing room, I was trying to rest my eyes and save my vocal cords. My voice was in nightly danger of crapping out from a touring schedule that regularly included sleepless fifteen-hour drives originating somewhere near the Canadian border for seemingly every show we played in the southern half of the country.

The venue booker knocked on the door and let himself in, saying something like, "Hey y'all, um, David Duke is here and, um, he'd like to talk to ya."

While the others probably didn't hear this over the sound of their own ravenous chewing, I immediately snapped to attention, as did our manager, Doron Segal. Leave it to the half-Asian and the Jew in the room to know all about former Grand Wizards of the KKK.

"*The* David Duke?" we asked simultaneously, in the weirdest "jinx, you owe me a soda" moment of our lives.

"Only one that I know." The booker laughed.

"Uh, could we have a minute, please?" Doron asked in the polite manager's voice he had used to charm many a hotel receptionist into early check-ins and complimentary meals for us.

The second the booking agent left the room, both our voices went up about an octave in pitch, and before long the entire band was fully engulfed in panic, as was our tour manager, Tony, who was already dressed in the Elvis jumpsuit that just happened to be hung up in the corner of the room, waiting for him like an open invitation.

I believe all of us were thinking the same thing: *Why the hell did we take this gig?*

Certain that I was going to die that night, I could feel my pulse racing toward tachycardia. Before any of us could coagulate our thoughts into a plan of action, the booker came back into the room again, this time with David Duke in tow, all smiles.

"I'm sorry to barge in on you," he said before turning toward Doron. "You must be the manager." While no one in the room would ever be mistaken for Brian Epstein or Peter Grant, I suppose Doron looked the most *managerial*, with a healthy collection of laminated backstage passes connected to a black lanyard around his neck.

David Duke leaned in toward him with a toothy grin.

"How's *business?*" he asked, in a tone that implicitly tacked on the phrase "in the Jew-run media."

"I can't stay for the show, but my daughter's a big fan, and I was hoping to get the band's autographs for her." He offered each one of us a handshake, in the manner of the slick politician he had become by then. His forced grin turned to mild confusion when he came around to shaking my hand. I can only speculate as to why. Maybe he thought I was in charge of dry-cleaning the Elvis jumpsuit.

I'd like to say I told him where to shove it on behalf of all the minorities over whom he had claimed superiority, but I was completely taken aback. We all were. I was a walking example of the race mixing that was still illegal in his home state the year I was born, and I was pretty sure David Duke would have wanted to keep it that way. All I knew was that I was scared shitless and didn't want any trouble. Doron shuffled Tony toward the merch tub to grab some Sharpies, and before we knew it, our signatures were drying on a copy of *Whirligig*, which, who knows, may to this day be sitting in a dusty shoebox of teenage memorabilia on a closet shelf belonging to David Duke's daughter.

Our second single, "The Day That Came and Went," bore little resemblance to "Devil's Diary" and stemmed from a different place entirely. The grungy guitars and the snide, quintessentially "alternative" lyrics on the debut single, which contained the oft-quoted line "it's never good to be understood by a girl in acid wash," were nowhere to be found on the jangly E-minor elegy written to my long-deceased father. It was a song of loss so completely devoid of snark that it wouldn't be out of bounds to question if it was actually performed by the same band or written by the same songwriter. It was. If "Devil's Diary" was my cold-blooded, ice-in-the-veins north pole, "The Day That Came and Went" was my equator, my emotional center where my heart stayed warm. It was also the exact point on my songwriting continuum where my lyrics finally got real. Sure, "Devil's Diary" was clever, but "The Day That Came and Went" was the biopsy of a cataclysm.

With the same 24-7 caffeine buzz emanating from most of the other New Yorkers I had met on tour, a small coterie of production assistants hurriedly ushered me and the other members of the Caulfields—Sam Musumeci, Ritchie Rubini, and Mike Simpson bringing up the rear—into the "fX Apartment," which was the fX

> IF "DEVIL'S DIARY" WAS MY COLD-BLOODED, ICE-IN-THE-VEINS NORTH POLE, "THE DAY THAT CAME AND WENT" WAS MY EQUATOR, MY EMOTIONAL CENTER WHERE MY HEART STAYED WARM.

Network's production set, located smack-dab in the heart of Manhattan's Flatiron District. I tuned my guitar with just a few chaotic minutes remaining before we were to go live on *Breakfast Time*.

About a decade before the fledgling network started broadcasting shows like *It's Always Sunny in Philadelphia*, *Breakfast Time* was the flagship program on fX.

And here I was, sinking into a love seat, hugging my Taylor acoustic like it was some kind of security blankie, about to sing the most personal song I had written in my life. Television cameras on dollies were locked and loaded as I sat in their crosshairs.

Sitting beside me was our drummer, Ritchie, the only other band member who could fit on the couch. He had, by now, logged dozens of live radio performances with me, tapping gently on a tambourine and singing harmonies, but this was our first time on live television. We had appeared on *Live from the House of Blues* earlier in the year and had seen our sweat-soaked photo-op with announcer Dan Aykroyd, dressed in full Elwood Blues regalia, appear a month later in *Billboard* magazine, but the title of that prerecorded show was a little misleading.

We were flanked by co-hosts Laurie Hibberd and Tom Bergeron, who was just at the beginning of his ascent to mainstream ubiquity, well before he became the face of *America's Funniest Home Videos* and *Dancing with the Stars*. And just behind the couch, close enough to whisper in my ear, was Bob. Bob was in charge of the comic relief, frequently cracking jokes with the hosts throughout the show. He had a disheveled, jaundiced look about him—unkempt hair, big, unfocused googly eyes. One might have thought he was high on something, but it turns out that's just the way he always looked.

One other thing about Bob: he was a puppet, not just in the sense that he was totally under the control of his producers—which he was—but an *honest-to-God-arm-up-the-neck-mother-fucking puppet*, lurking behind me like Oscar the Grouch's stoner cousin. As I played "The Day That Came and Went," I could see Bob out of the corner of my eye, cheerily swaying back and forth. I swear I could almost feel his faux-fur whiskers brushing my face. It was a situation far better suited to a Jimmy Buffett impersonator in a Hawaiian shirt and khaki shorts singing "Cheeseburger in Paradise" than to some '90s alt-rock front man baring his soul about his dead father on national TV.

Slinking off the set after the segment was over, I spoke to no one, ignoring pats on the back from *Breakfast Time* staffers. Sam, who'd watched the whole thing from just outside the shot, simply smirked and said, "Nice puppet." I was pretty sure that would sum up the reaction of anyone else who might have seen this. I secretly hoped no one else had. I wondered if I was really prepared to do whatever it took to be heard by a wider audience. I wondered if Papa was rolling over in his grave, like Beethoven in that Chuck Berry song. But it was no wonder at all that the kid whose pain is so apparent in the lines

They never let me say goodbye to you
They thought I was too young
and wouldn't know what to do

was still there just beneath the surface of my supposedly thickened skin, still trying to make sense of it all, still trying to figure it out.

THE MULLIGAN

If I could do it all over I'd make it right
I would make it right

—IKE, "WHERE TO BEGIN"

O n a warm night around Papa's birthday, twenty-one summers after he was gone, Mom, without explanation, emerged from her bedroom closet and presented me with a black document bag, which amounted to a dossier on Papa.

"Here, honey. Learn about your father," she said to me as she gently pushed the bag against my chest.

With some trepidation, I sat down on the bed in my old room, directly across the hall from Mom's. I hadn't really been in there since before leaving for California to record my first album on a major label. I ran my fingers along the jagged brass teeth of the zipper that had long protected the contents of the black bag.

Why now? I wondered.

Was this a belated attempt at a do-over for having kept me in the dark about so many things where Papa was concerned? Was she asking for a mulligan? As I began to sift through items that had been untouched for decades, I soon found myself transported into the early life of my father, a young man I instantly recognized, though I had only ever seen him in the body of someone well into their sixties.

Timeworn newspaper clippings dating back to the Great Depression—a few laminated, most exposed and delicate—contained blurbs from his days as a semi-pro second baseman for the Philadelphia Angels and other sandlot teams from Kensington to East Falls. They cited great defensive plays or game-winning hits by Johnny Faye, or his occasional alias, Eddie Faye. Sepia-tone photos of Papa striking a fighter's pose or taking a knee in an old-time leather helmet revealed stints in regional boxing and semi-pro football circuits under a mysterious nom de guerre: "Chick McKinney."

In addition to the sports clippings, there were oddball human interest stories. In one article, Papa had to think fast when the drive-shaft of the New Jersey Public Service bus he was driving snapped on a steep incline, sending him and his passengers back downhill in reverse. The reporter attributed the relative lack of injury and property damage in the accident to the "coolness of John Faye, driver of the bus, in guiding the heavily loaded vehicle backward through motor traffic."

Another clipping, circa 1930, contained the headline "Milk Bottle Used to Ward Off Bandits." Somewhere near West Orange, New Jersey, where he worked in one of Thomas Edison's labs, Papa encountered three would-be thieves who told him to "stick 'em up." According to the report, Papa grabbed a milk bottle from the front step of a nearby house, and I can only imagine the ensuing slapstick.

Although his athletic prowess and general bravery seemed to have skipped over my generation, I recognized a similar attraction to the spotlight in these memorabilia. In the same way I had been saving almost every casual mention of me or my band in the local papers, here was everything from box scores for games in which he went two for four to full columns dedicated to the baseball wunderkind who was granted a tryout for the Chicago White Sox at the age of fifteen, or the "former Knute Rockne protégé," who was part of the Notre Dame football program that produced the legendary Four Horsemen. I had no idea what his aspirations for himself were, but it was clear he was pretty damn good at doing what he loved, and he reached heights very few people ever achieve, even if he never became a household name. Maybe this was our closest connection of all.

It felt like an archaeological dig, almost an academic exercise, exhuming documents like his birth certificate, which listed his first home as Oak Ridge, Tennessee. I learned, for the first time, the names of my paternal grandparents, Edwin and Ida May, as stated on Mom and Papa's marriage certificate, which I noticed was dated the year after I was born.

The bittersweet thrill of these discoveries left me ill prepared for the emotional Mack truck that blindsided me after I discovered Papa's official autopsy report, which detailed twenty-one points of diagnosis and a list, longer than I could bear, of every internal organ where the malignant cells had metastasized.

Now, suddenly, I felt like I knew too much.

While he was alive, we made the most of my first six and a half years. He brought me along on his travels every chance he got, passing down the same unabashed smile I found in the center photo of his 1918 collage, mounted on thin cardboard, surrounded by the cutout faces of his uniformed Little League teammates and his handwritten caption: "Great oaks from little acorns grow."

I can't imagine the fresh-faced fourteen-year-old in that collage would ever see himself in the twilight of his life as a retirement-age father to an accidental son and three Korean stepdaughters, with whom his new role as a caretaker, cook, and chauffeur brought along challenges he probably never bargained for. Some days, he spent his waking hours fulfilling requests that probably felt more like demands, carting Tae Kyung to friends' houses to accommodate her budding social life or delivering Tae Hyun to the library or shuttling Tae Im back and forth to doctor's appointments, notably carrying her up and down long flights of stairs as she lay immobile in a full body cast, a by-product of her battle with polio.

These were the same girls whose maladroit attempt at building a snowman, some years earlier, provided the serendipitous circumstance for Mom and Papa to meet. Our family folklore says that Papa was out walking on a snowy day in the Pennypack section of Philadelphia and saw my sisters out in front of their apartment building creating a monstrosity that looked more like the Elephant Man than the character voiced by Burl Ives from the Christmas special they had recently watched on TV. After he helped them avoid leaving an eyesore on the lawn, they presumed to invite this stranger into their home for hot chocolate, where he first exchanged hellos and sidelong glances with Mom. A little more than a year later, he brought Mom home from the hospital with a baby boy, the improbable love child of a forty-year-old working mother and a sixty-two-year-old ex-cop, many decades removed from when he dove competitively with Johnny Weissmuller from the Tarzan movies.

At the very bottom of the black bag sat a tiny envelope with a handful of wallet-size photographs. There was a young man with Papa's eyes in a military uniform. There was a shot of Papa beaming with pride in a fetching white suit, standing next to a young bride in a wedding dress. I flipped the snapshot over. There was writing on the back in fading pencil.

Daddy, love you always.
—Dana

It was dated 1962. I tapped on Mom's door, holding the photographs, and asked her to tell me about the people I realized were my half siblings. She didn't have much to say. Apparently, Papa's relationship with his other children had been strained well before I came into the picture. I couldn't imagine that his pivot into a new life with us did anything to alleviate that. Regrets, I'm sure he had a few.

I asked Mom what my brother's name was. She told me his name was John. In that moment, it dawned on me. Maybe I was the do-over. The Mulligan.

BESIDE THE ONE SHE LOVES

I think she was trying just to give this place some joy
A sun for her son
A life for a death
A meaning for her boy

—THE CAULFIELDS, "BESIDE THE ONE SHE LOVES"

T he car lurched through the black wrought iron gates at All Saints, and having cheated death yet again, I heaved a heavy sigh of relief. I don't know how many Cheat Death cards you get in a lifetime, but I was making a considerable dent in my allotment coming to this place. While I had long since grown used to our frequent visits to Papa's grave, the left turn into the main entrance off Kirkwood Highway was invariably hair raising.

Our blinker flashed impotently as we sat through the bulk of Joan Jett's "I Love Rock 'n Roll" on the radio while we waited for traffic in the oncoming lane to whiz by. Yielding to impatience, Mom took a quick swat at the volume knob, inadvertently turning the song up, as she cut across the grain of the almost impenetrable convoy of economy cars. I pulled my seat belt tighter across my shoulder as I heard the squeal of rubber on pavement during the instant she floored it. It seemed like an act of blind faith—faith that the Creator, whoever that was, lacked the kind of dark sense of humor that would allow us to get T-boned while trying to enter a Catholic cemetery.

At least that's how I saw it. I fantasized about barging into the offices at DelDOT demanding a stoplight with a left-turn arrow be installed and making my case for financial restitution, estimating that each ten-minute drive from our house took a year off my life. I was too damn young to be graying at the temples. Fucking left turns.

Mom pulled over and parked the Audi 5000, a vehicular indulgence she'd allowed herself after the Pontiac was totaled, left tires on the grass, right tires on the narrow asphalt ribbon that split off into several arteries throughout the sprawling acreage that surrounded us. The dread that I felt coming here when I was eight or nine had transformed into something else, a kind of psychic time-out. I could lose myself here, feel small in a good way, take in hundreds of granite memorials adorned with everything from plastic plants to American flags to tragic teddy bears for infants and children taken too soon. I could contemplate the untold stories of the people beneath the surface in a strange and unlikely serenity, follow the road back past mausoleums and virtually unpopulated sections of freshly mowed green grass, uninterrupted by the markers of death, until the rear property line butted up against the south end zone of the football field at St. Mark's High School, snapping me back to the hierarchy I came from, pulling me from the afterlife haze of the great equalizer, returning me to stark reality.

At sixteen, I had been coming here for a decade, and I had already lived more years without him than the almost seven I got. But it was still hard for me to zero in on Papa's exact coordinates as I ran ahead while Mom was still gathering her things. Even with the exalted beacon of the statue of Jesus, Mary, and Joseph as my north star and the green industrial trash cans I tried to use as visual landmarks, I spent a mind-fucked eternity fast-walking between rows of stones, my eyes scanning left to right for Papa's name until I finally located the grave.

Mom walked up, took a moment to admire the statue, and, with gravity and sincerity in her voice, said: "Look, honey. Mother, father, and son."

"I *know*, Mom. You say that every time," I huffed.

This was my standard reaction whenever she pointed out that Papa had been laid to rest in the shadow of these bronze figures, the son standing piously, bookended by his parents. The inscription at the base of the statue read: "Did you not know that I must be about my father's business?" I had zero interest in digging into the meaning behind Luke 2:49, although I wondered what kind of parallels Mom could possibly be seeing between ourselves and the towering likenesses before us. She certainly was not comparing me to Jesus and herself to the Virgin Mary, but I think she wanted me to get the message that I was special and that I would be reminded every visit that I had two parents who loved me very much, even if Papa could no longer show me and she was only capable of showing me in her own mysterious ways.

As was her ritual, Mom came armed with a brown paper grocery bag containing gardening gloves, large-handle scissors, and a glass gallon jar of Newark's finest tap water. Before either of us engaged in any kind of moment of reflection, she began to remove fallen leaves and snip away any overgrown grass that threatened to cover even the slightest corner of Papa's in-ground memorial. She pulled every last clump of crab grass within a five-foot radius, deciding to clean up a couple of the neighboring plots, their unkempt appearance betraying the truancy of their survivors. After grooming Papa's stone, Mom placed homegrown lilies into the small built-in vase, and we both knelt at the foot of it and thought our thoughts for about sixty seconds.

Typically, when our moment of silence was up, we would head back to the car, without a word, and drive across the highway for lunch at Friendly's, where I would drown my sorrows, or whatever they were, in food. I usually went with a grilled ham-and-cheese sandwich marketed as a "Supermelt" and a "Friendly Cola," which I only drank because I got a kick out of the server having to say "Friendly Cola OK?" as the management-dictated response required whenever someone ordered a Coke. I always thought it was kind of charming, the quixotic stand that Friendly's took against the corporate sugar-water empire that would eventually infiltrate their operation, but my Cheshire cat smile would soon morph into nostril-flaring disgust as I sank into the cool, hard vinyl on my side of the booth, embarrassed that Mom had ordered liver and onions again.

Lunch was delayed on this day, because I had negotiated an assurance that I would be allowed to take the car for a practice spin around the cemetery to prepare for my driver's exam that coming fall. Though there were no posted speed limit signs, I drove like I was in a school zone, clenching my fists at ten and two around the steering wheel, slamming on the brakes at the slightest bump or bend in the road. Mom had a bemused look on her face that insinuated, "You drive like a pussy." I know she would never have used that word at the time, because it wasn't until a couple of years later, after the parade of young musicians she allowed into her house tracked the mud of anatomical slang onto the welcome mat of her consciousness, that I remember her asking me, "Honey, what is a 'pussy' on a woman?"

As I looped back around toward the cemetery gates, I got out to look for the grave of Gary Michael Celeste. I hadn't known him personally, but I felt a strange connection to the guy. He had made local headlines six or seven years earlier when he died in a freak accident while attending the University of Delaware around the same time Tae Hyun was there. A bullet fired at birds, shot by a fifteen-year-old boy from over a quarter mile away, struck him in the head at his hairline just in front of his left ear. I was, quite figuratively, blown away by the whole thing. You're just minding your own business, trying to get to a lacrosse game, and you walk right into the trajectory of something that isn't meant for you. And just like that, nothing is ever the same.

Leaving the cemetery with Gary Celeste at the forefront of my thoughts made visiting Papa feel almost incidental. The last thing I would want is for a sense of rote normalcy to infect my remembrance of the man who helped bring me into the world. I hadn't spent my minute with him thinking fondly of our many trips to the Newark branch of Wilmington Trust, where he would use his weekly transactions as an excuse to show me off to the young bank tellers, but instead ruminating on the fact that Mom had purchased the adjacent burial plot for her own. I wondered if she found it unsettling or comforting to be able to touch the very spot where she expected she'd be laid to rest someday. I looked down at the stone and read Papa's name over and over again. There was no epitaph, just "John Daniel Faye, 1904–1973." It felt a little like I was staring at my own grave, and I wondered if my future children might someday visit me at my final resting place. Would they be any better than I was at showing some emotion? I imagined that if they could see Mom and me, stone faced and off in our own little contemplations, they would see that such temperamental restraint is an armor built over time, the flexing of a muscle that grows on the dark bones of moments past that strike tense and dissonant chords in our hearts.

MINOR KEY MOMENTS

JOHNNY WILL HELP YOU

Dot Kelley, the school nurse at E. Frances Medill Elementary, plucked me out of my first-grade classroom, drafting me to volunteer to help administer polio vaccines to kindergarteners. This was to be my first experience helping others, although the irony of such strong-armed recruitment made the whole situation feel pretty damn *in*voluntary. I wondered, initially, "Why me?" but then I thought about my oldest sister Tae Im, the one who made my favorite comfort food when Mom was working late at the hospital—Oscar Mayer wieners and ketchup on white bread, canned corn topped with a melting pat of butter, and whole milk sweetened with heaping teaspoons full of sugar. I had no idea that the rollout of Jonas Salk's breakthrough vaccine just a generation earlier had been a little too late to help her, stricken as she was at the age of twenty months in postwar Korea. I felt protective of her when I saw her struggle every day with her crutches and orthopedic leg braces. Maybe ol' Dot just knew empathy when she saw it and simply thought I was the best man for the job. It felt nice to have someone's confidence.

My homeroom teacher was Mrs. Wieczorek—"it rhymes with 'historic'" was how I remembered the pronunciation. Mrs. W. released me into Dot's charge, and I was out the door, led by the arm in what might appear to a casual observer to be some sort of juvie perp walk, down the dim corridor, the walls decorated with scores of Easter bunnies rendered in the medium of construction paper and crayon, the stick figure masterpieces of grade school minimalists. We turned the corner, and I caught a strong whiff of sawdust and vomit. I spotted our school janitor cleaning up another gastric mess left by another kid, who probably should have just waited a couple of minutes after lunch before going full bore into a game of recess kickball and shaking his insides like a dirty martini. It looked like he'd *almost* made it to the boys' room.

I arrived at the nurse's office, greeted by a set of different smells— disinfectant, rubbing alcohol, fear perhaps. My job was to arrange sugar cubes on a flat metal tray while Dot released tiny beads of light-pink liquid from an eyedropper onto each one.

Destination: the waiting baby-bird tongues of five-year-olds who had probably never heard of polio but excitedly received the sweet inoculating eucharist. Other children, for reasons I can't recall, had to go the old-fashioned route of a big-ass needle in the upper arm. My second job was to help these kids roll up their shirt sleeves high enough to expose the injection spot on their deltoid, where I applied a light circular swirl with a nostril-tickling alcohol pad.

Dot addressed the children in a monotone that drew little attention to itself, but every now and then, I overheard snippets of more expressive phrases like "Oh, let *her* do that" and "Do you want her to hold your hand?" *Wait a second*, I thought. *Does she think I'm a girl?* Granted, I was playing "house" with my female classmates when she came calling, and my hair was a little longer than the average boy's. My parents had been AWOL for weeks, and it had been a while since my last trip to Papa's barber. Then, just as I caught a glimpse of the next nervous kid fumbling with his shirt sleeve, I heard Dot proclaim with certitude: "Johnny will help you; *she'll* help you."

My face burned with the crippling of whatever masculinity a six-year-old boy is capable of, and each successive, clearly enunciated feminine pronoun aurally bitch-slapped me from side to side. By the time the last sugar cube dissolved and the final Band-Aid stretched over a tender needle mark, more than a handful of kids from Mrs. Brown's kindergarten class had borne witness to my humiliation. They could all kind of tell I was a boy, but I guess they figured if I wasn't speaking up, why should they? Despite my real-time revenge fantasies, which involved pulling out my pecker to prove my manhood, I said nothing—nothing audible, anyway. Not then, not when I got home, not until I met Lisa as a junior in college and found I could make her laugh by laughing at myself.

NO FURTHER THOUGHT

In the soupy summer humidity of the year I turned thirteen, my middle older sister, Tae Kyung, recommended me to a young couple she knew from college. Her friend Alison, who, years later, I would realize was a dead ringer for Kevin Cronin from REO Speedwagon, needed someone to feed her cat while she and her boyfriend, Jed, escaped our hometown for a few days. Tae Kyung was the one who'd changed my diapers when I was barely out of my bassinet and soon after made me her dress-up partner, bouncing me in my crib as her infant sidekick while she'd played the mod cosmopolitan girl straight out of the hippest shop on Carnaby Street. Now she was vouching for me in hopes of getting me my first paying job. I appreciated the gesture, my *women's intuition* telling me that she'd convinced her friend to give me the opportunity, realizing that my Slurpee and Bubble Yum lifestyle didn't come cheap, although I had been cutting down on the Bubble Yum because of some rumor that it was made with spider eggs.

With a key and a list of instructions, I walked the mile toward the back of our development to a complex of drab rectangular buildings, passing the innocuous "No Through Traffic" street signs that were there to create a de facto separation in the neighborhood between the "house people" and the "apartment people." I used to come back here all the time to do a whole lot of nothing with a couple of kids from school. I wondered if I'd run into Rodney and Maurice.

Rodney, a paunchy white kid with a mid-Atlantic drawl, used to traffic in crude sexual humor, often derailing his dirty jokes midsetup, interrupting in a conspiratorial whisper: "You know they're fuckin', right?" This rendered any eventual punchline a complete anticlimax, but that's what I found funny about him. What no one seemed to find very funny was his wake-the-dead body odor. On summer days like this, to get closer to him than three feet felt like walking unwittingly into a parmesan sauna. Even his all-season crew cut offered little relief from a state of perpetual perspiration, his overworked eccrine glands barely providing the briefest detectable respite, antifreeze for the pubescent soul.

Maurice, a kid so black even the Black kids made fun of his blackness, was on my baseball team, the Expos. I could sometimes see him smile all the way from his position in center field. His plus-size teeth, yellowed from neglect and barely reined in by his retainer, resembled the butter-coated marshmallows that my sisters would melt down to make Rice Krispies Treats. Most games, I found myself on the pitcher's mound, boasting the league's slowest fastball. Sometimes I'd strike out the side, whiffing batters who were so far out in front of my pitches that they finished swinging before the ball even crossed the plate. And sometimes I kept Maurice very busy tracking down doubles and triples once the hitters adjusted to my slower-than-molasses lobs. How things turned out in any given game was as much a head-scratcher as why I was the only pitcher in Newark PONY League history to use a first baseman's mitt. It was a gift that my Korean uncle bestowed upon me during one of his handful of visits to the States, and I did not want to offend him, or Mom, by saying anything.

I missed my friends. I missed feeling like part of something, even if that something was a ragtag diversity rainbow with kids who had yet to discover the benefits of deodorant or a toothbrush. I remembered the three of us doubled over in hysterics, stomach muscles cramping like we had all done fifty sit-ups, upon hearing Rodney's rendition of the classic playground rhyme "Milk, milk, lemonade, 'round the corner fudge is made," pointing to the requisite body parts of the person

I MISSED MY FRIENDS. I MISSED FEELING LIKE PART OF SOMETHING, EVEN IF THAT SOMETHING WAS A RAGTAG DIVERSITY RAINBOW WITH KIDS WHO HAD YET TO DISCOVER THE BENEFITS OF DEODORANT OR A TOOTHBRUSH.

of the corresponding color as he went, taking it to dizzying allegorical heights. "Get it, Faye? You're the lemonade."

On this day, the milk and the fudge were nowhere to be found. I hadn't seen them in a long time. I told myself that maybe we'd just drifted apart. I told myself that kids get tired of each other sometimes, recalling that it only took forty-eight hours for Cindy Cole to pretend I never existed and start holding another boy's hand during assembly in the second grade. I told myself everything but the truth. They'd stopped talking to me because Mom had put me in private school the previous fall, but that wasn't *my* decision. Nothing was. I was fed crumbs of information on a need-to-know basis. Mom told me the new school would be better for me, and it was no secret she was scared of where I'd end up in the public-school desegregation that began that September. I should have known that if I was going to have to get on a bus every morning to go to school in another town, Mom was damn well going to pick the bus.

A few kids on bicycles rode toward me as I approached Alison and Jed's building.

One of them blurted out "Ching Chang Chong!" as he rolled past me, the ensuing laughter from his friends seeming to trail off in a Doppler effect. I felt a familiar hot blush in my face and braced for him to turn his bike around and ride by to say it again, maybe in a different order, but he was gone in a flash, giving me no further thought. I wished I could just invoke that old platitude about "sticks and stones," but his little helium-voiced insult chimed on a loop inside my head, oddly attaching itself to the three-note melody I heard on NBC after episodes of *The Rockford Files*, making it all the more sinister and impossible to forget.

Ching Chang Chong.

I regretted not standing up for myself—again—but I just as quickly recalled why I wasn't one to pick fights, rewinding to the day when I scrapped with that kid Doug back in kindergarten, not quite sure if it was a lesser or greater insult that he'd called me a fart on the playground. All I really remember from that kerfuffle is that I wound up with a big clump of his sandy hair in my fist and a dent in my shin from the toe of his Buster Browns.

When asked what word he had called me, I squirmed with such discomfort that I could only manage to sound out the first of the four letters for what felt like five minutes, my teacher trying to coax it out of me like Annie Sullivan trying to get Helen Keller to say "water" in *The Miracle Worker*.

"He called me a fffffffffff."

"A what?" my teacher asked.

"A fffffffff. Fffffffffffffffffff."

"A fart? Did he call you a fart?"

I nodded in the affirmative, so relieved that the word was completed for me. I promised myself never to come that close to fisticuffs again, if only to avoid having to provide any explicit testimony in the aftermath.

I made it into the building and dragged myself up two flights of stairs and into the apartment, where I immediately searched for the bathroom. I looked at myself in the mirror and pried my eyelids apart with my fingers, wishing I could stretch the *ching-chang-chong* right out of them, but they snapped back into place. I felt nothing like the all-American boy dragging a baseball bat and wearing red, white, and blue swim trunks in the photo that Papa took of me so long ago.

I shooed away these thoughts like I would a swarm of gnats and got to the job at hand. I reached into the back pocket of my "husky"-size Toughskins and produced the page of brief instructions, the green ink having blurred slightly from exposure to the near-tropical temperatures that are generated in boys' pants of a certain polyester blend. With the Tender Vittles poured and the water bowl refreshed, I went off in search of the cat.

Having seen no sign of the feline, I moved toward the bedroom and pushed open the door, the slow creaking reminding me of the sound of a poorly rosined bow skipping across the strings of the violin that Mom rented for the aborted lessons I took in third grade. Maybe she thought I wasn't quite Asian *enough*.

The unmade bed looked inviting. For a quick moment I entertained the thought of lying down, but just then the closet to the right caught my eye. The sliding door was completely open to one side, displaying Jed's half of the wardrobe space. There wasn't much there beyond the requisite selection of slacks and button-downs, and a few shiny disco shirts hung on wire hangers. It wasn't a walk-in closet, but I walked in anyway and sat cross legged on the floor with barely enough room to slide the door closed without hitting my knees. Though the air was somewhat stifling, I felt like I could breathe again, comforted by the confined space.

A thin ray of light hit a small pile of magazines on the carpet, and tucked beneath a few issues of *Sports Illustrated*, the first copy of *Playboy* I would ever hold in my hands washed away the ethnic slur that had been echoing in my head. The cover held me spellbound—Farrah Fawcett, perfectly tanned with feathered blond hair, wearing nothing but high heels and an oversized dress shirt. She had a classy-looking drink in her hand and a cocktail toothpick raised to her blinding pearly whites. It was the best argument for white supremacy I had ever seen. I turned right to the centerfold and scanned each panel, thinking maybe there is a God, but if there is, I hope he's not watching and judging me a pervert. Besides, what kind of pervert is *he* to be watching *me* right now?

I was not unacquainted with the sensation between my legs—I had been dry humping the living room furniture since I was five—but I never experienced it with such a sense of salaciousness. This was nothing like scanning the pages of back issues of *National Geographic*, giggling at the slightest glimpse of Pygmy tits. Nor was it anything like loitering with a bunch of neighborhood kids alongside 7-Eleven, sipping a Slurpee that tasted of the phenol that contaminated the local water supply that summer, listening to Mike Crossan recount his supposed dalliance with an eighth grader. Our jaws collectively dropped when he gloated, "And then I licked her pussy hair," not one of us knowing enough about the female anatomy to ask, "Just the hair?" No, this sweltering closet was nothing short of the true incubator of my adolescence. The bulge in my drawers was like a tortoise of hope poking its head out of its shell to dream big, even for a fleeting moment.

A hot flash of self-consciousness crept into my head, and I started to feel paranoid and dirty. I put the magazine back exactly the way I found it—my initial arousal replaced with the thought that women like this are not meant for "ugry duckring" boys like me. Blue balls be damned, I slid the door back open and reentered the world, as though simultaneously emerging from the confessional booth I would never enter again and the peep show booth I would grow to know intimately. The cat finally appeared from underneath the bed and yawned a casual meow. I reached out to pet her, but she walked right out of the room, giving me no further thought.

MARIONETTE

I was a trembling eleven-year-old on the side of the highway reaching out for a tentative, almost reluctant embrace from a bystander as we waited for the arrival of ambulances. The gentleman was older, perhaps the age that Papa was the last time I saw him, and he was at a loss as to how to console me. The pleated sleeves of his brown suit jacket that I clung to were cold comfort, as he scanned the now-bottlenecked traffic for any sign of an emergency vehicle. I could breathe only through my mouth, not fully aware that I had broken my nose. The force of the collision had thrown my face directly into the unforgiving passenger seat in front of me. I was the only one in the bland-yellow Pontiac Astre to remain conscious, but I have no recollection of being pulled from the mangled sedan. Deflecting my panicked pleas for action, the man told me the others couldn't be helped until the professionals arrived.

My youngest older sister, Tae Hyun, was not moving. She was the one who would become my staunch advocate when my musical interest morphed into passion. She would also, much later on, make the decision to leave our family, after another in a long line of Christmastime spats proved to be her last straw. Her boyfriend, Keith, who had suggested the afternoon drive to Jack in the Box, convincing Mom to let him borrow the car and inviting me to tag along, was also unconscious, hunched over in the driver's seat, his open mouth drooling a viscous mixture of blood and saliva from having bitten his tongue close to clean off upon impact.

Almost, but not quite, completing an ill-timed left turn at the intersection of Kirkwood Highway and Duncan Road, he never saw it coming, but for a split second, I did. There was no time to brace myself, and the other car had no time to stop, hurling the Pontiac about sixty feet down the road before it skidded to a halt. The rapid-fire symphony of sounds, the crescendo of the approaching car horn, the desperate screech of brakes, the dissonant shattering of steel and glass, gave way to a momentary rest of eerie quiet. I stared at the others, mute. I couldn't help but think they were dead, both of them motionless, their bodies in limp repose, like two marionettes whose wires had been dropped suddenly by their puppet masters. My fingers curled tighter around the sleeves of the old man's blazer, watching helplessly as emergency rescue teams, equipped with the Jaws of Life, arrived to pull my sister and her boyfriend out of the wreckage. As the ambulances raced against time to the hospital, I feared this might be the last I would ever see of Tae Hyun.

Treated in the ER with nothing beyond a Tylenol with codeine for my newly deviated septum, I was on track to spend my adolescence snoring loudly and looking like I'd lost multiple bar fights.

Keith was released from the hospital later in the evening of the accident, the bandage wrapped around his head reminding me of an injured Revolutionary War soldier playing the fife in a painting I saw on the Bicentennial Freedom Train the year before. I spent the night in Keith's apartment instead of staying at home, while Mom and Tae Kyung were still mired in the touch-and-go at Tae Hyun's bedside in the ICU. I stared up at the ceiling above Keith's bed, unable to sleep, my mind going a mile a minute.

I thought of how different things had been since Keith started dating my sister, whose last boyfriend, Jerry, with his long unkempt hair, tight bell-bottoms, and Fu Manchu mustache, lasted about as long as could be expected in the spotlight of Mom's white-hot disapproval. Jerry, whom Mom would only refer to as "Jingus Khan," never said much to me, but that might have been because I was too scared to make eye contact. He looked menacing, like a member of Lynyrd Skynyrd. Keith himself was mustachioed with a fairly high blond afro, not the cleanest-cut guy in the world either. His was a hairstyle I envisioned for my own, having suffered several consecutive yearbook photos with my face framed by straight, coarse locks. Tae Hyun had even offered to give me a home perm to make my hair more like Keith's until Mom put the kibosh on that idea.

Afro or not, Keith had Mom's endorsement, in part because of how kind he was to me. We spent hours together on the basketball court near his parents' house, where he helped me hone a decent bank shot, though it was almost always comically blocked when playing two-on-two against a couple of tall teenage kids, Chris and Gene. I liked it a lot better when we played H-O-R-S-E. The precision of my uncontested trick shots off the backboard made me a more formidable opponent. The sound of that basketball swishing through the bottom of a steel chain net at the playground was music to my ears.

Keith knew a lot about music, and I looked to him for guidance. He had steered me out of my AM Gold comfort zone, playing *Aja* by Steely Dan, and declaring, "This is how a *real* record should sound." He instructed me on how to handle the album, pouring it like water from its inner sleeve, directing my thumb to the outside edge, then balancing the platter with my middle finger over the hole in the center label. He gave me strict warning never to touch my fingers to the grooves. The vinyl was thick, sturdy, nothing like my flimsy "as seen on TV" compilations at home. I treated its weight with respect as I lowered it gently onto the spindle of his turntable, which had glowing green lights that pulled me like a tractor beam onto a sonic spaceship, there to launch me into a new galaxy of high fidelity.

Such pleasing sounds whirling around in my head stood in sharp contrast to the violence of the car crash and the harshness of its audio track, which interrupted at regular jarring intervals. Keith tapped on the door and entered the room, nudging me over to one side of the bed, and sat with his back against the headboard, eventually pulling me by the armpits into his embrace, manipulating my limbs like I was the marionette, enveloping me, silently expressing his guilt and sorrow, rocking me gently into sleep, the way a parent would do when a child needs it the most, the way Mom did when she finally told me Papa was gone, the way she hadn't done in all the years since.

THE DAY THAT CAME AND WENT

SUMMER, 1973

"**M**ama, when is Papa coming home?" I directed this inquiry more into the air than at Mom, probably not quite trusting I'd get an answer. Days of not seeing him around the house had stretched into weeks, and the sneaking suspicion that something was not right colored my question. My little frame was curled up in a fetal ball on Papa's side of the king-size bed, while Mom seemed lost in the pages of a *Time* magazine, her reading glasses barely clinging to the tip of her nose.

I was still at that age when little kids call their mother "Mama" or "Mommy." It was a signpost of my innocence. My life up to that point had been like a nursery rhyme, evoking images of baseball, birthday cakes, and day trips to Seaside Heights, where I once colluded with my sisters and stood on the boardwalk to pose for a clandestine photo, my fingers in a V, raising an invisible cigar to my lips, mimicking Papa smoking on the sand a few feet in front of me. As he sat alongside Mom, his beautiful raven-haired bride, he was clearly enjoying the second act that my unlikely existence had handed him. I couldn't possibly know that the easy, unforced smiles captured on my parents' faces in that photo were the hard-won momentary flashes of relief that those who have truly lived truly live for.

Unwilling or unable to look up from her magazine to make eye contact, Mom said something close to, "Honey, the doctors tried everything they could, but Papa wasn't getting any better."

"Maybe they just need to try everything again until it works," I said, unaware that I had basically just proposed a version of what some people refer to as "the definition of insanity."

She couldn't keep it from me any longer. "Honey. Papa already died."

I paused in the way someone who is waiting to sneeze might pause, feeling an intense need to suspend time and block out all sight and sound to fully focus on expelling the stunned emotion that immediately welled up within me.

"Mama. I think I'm gonna cry."

Mom didn't speak. She just gave me the subtlest of nods along with a blink of her sad eyes, which might have been imperceptible to anyone else, but I know I saw it because I had to, and I took it to mean "OK, just this once." Her glasses fell onto the comforter as she dropped her magazine and rolled toward me, cradling me as my tears began to flow, their salty taste quickly creeping into the corners of my mouth. I buried my face in Papa's pillow, which still smelled of the pilfered spritzes of Aqua Net he sprayed on the remaining wisps of his once-full head of blond hair. Though my anguish was begging for her to speak comfort, Mom seemed to know that there was not much she could say. Instead, she hummed the tune to "Arirang," a wistful Korean folk song, which I'll forever consider a lullaby. The circular melody came out as an airy whisper, barely squeezing past what must have been the lump in her throat, but Mom persisted and calmed me down until exhaustion put a period on the river of commas that flowed from my eyes. I would, years later, make it a point to teach myself how to play "Arirang" on the black keys of our piano.

The scent of hair spray in the tear-soaked pillowcase, which I probably more tasted than smelled, would be gone by the next time Mom could bring herself to do laundry again, and yet it stays with me always. It stays with me in the same way the sweet, thick air in late spring, when daylight is just beginning to fade, places me in the far corner of our backyard. Papa is showing me a trick with honeysuckle, his manly, weathered fingers gently pulling flowers off the plant, which grows wildly, weaving through the diamond-patterned wire of the chain-link fence. He pinches the bottom of the stem and pulls it straight through the bloom to yield the tiniest droplet of nectar, whose sweetness registers on my tastebuds for a split second, then fades away.

It stays with me in the same way Mom's term of endearment—"Honey"—takes me back to my first bee sting, the year we landed in

> I BURIED MY FACE IN PAPA'S PILLOW, WHICH STILL SMELLED OF THE PILFERED SPRITZES OF AQUA NET HE SPRAYED ON THE REMAINING WISPS OF HIS ONCE-FULL HEAD OF BLOND HAIR.

Red Mill Farms, our neighborhood in Newark. I'm caught unawares near my right earlobe while waving to our new neighbor, Tracy Galloway, as she smiles at me from her second-floor window. I can still hear the precise cadence of the buzzing in my ear just before the pinch of the stinger sends me crying back to Papa, who is waiting by our mailbox after encouraging me to go greet the girl next door. There's a long vibrating hum, followed by four rapid staccato stabs, so close to my ear drum that I would now compare the sound to the overdriven fuzzed-out guitar intro from "Revolution" by the Beatles. Papa brings me back inside where he wipes my tears with the linen handkerchief that he keeps in his back pocket. Perhaps trying to lighten the mood, he says something to Mom like, "That bee musta thought he was made o' honey, honey." I watch a smile break through her serious expression, as she applies a home remedy paste of water and meat tenderizer to my now-swollen ear and silently assimilates "honey" into her lexicon.

A handful of physical mementos spread throughout the house placed me in equally vivid moments of recollection and also served as little enablers of denial, which did wonders for a long time to allow me to feel like he was still there, still alive, still eventually coming home. I'm pretty sure they were serving the same purpose for Mom. In front of the mirror on their shared bureau sat the plaid fedora he likely wore on the day they met—its pristine red feather still tucked inside the hatband. Papa's wooden brush, with the words "for fine hair" branded into the handle, and a framed picture of him carving his last Thanksgiving turkey remained untouched for months. Even the half-used bottles of Old Spice cologne and Hai Karate aftershave lingered in the medicine cabinet all the way up to the day Mom left Delaware for good after the turn of the millennium.

I got into the habit of spending time in our downstairs hall closet, creating a little fort for myself among his belongings. His senior bowling league tournaments at Blue Hen Lanes sprang to life at the touch of the emerald-green shirt he'd worn when competing with his team, the Pick Ups, their name embroidered in bright yellow stitching on the back. I can smell crinkle-cut french fries, just pulled from a deep fryer of ancient cooking oil. I use two hands on a squeeze bottle of ketchup to make a red crisscross pattern over the fries to match the design on the flimsy paper tray. There's an echo chamber of bowling balls spinning down the surrounding lanes, crashing into pins, as a tiny fragrant cloud of talc floats from the tattered bag Papa flips repeatedly in his right hand to keep it dry as he waits for his ball to reappear from the mouth of the mysterious tube under the floor.

On an oppressive summer afternoon a few days after Papa died, one of my sisters walked me over to the Ostheimers' house, two doors up the street. The younger of the two sons who lived there, David, was a couple of years older than I was, but he was around fairly often for games of hide-and-seek or tag in our backyard, once stuffing handfuls of autumn leaves down the back of my shirt as a more emphatic way of saying "You're it!" I probably assumed that I was going over to his house to play, but he wasn't there when I arrived. I was greeted by David's grandmother, who simply offered me a seat on the couch in front of a small TV and left me alone to watch the holy trinity of *Sesame Street*, *The Electric Company*, and *Mister Rogers' Neighborhood* on Channel 12 for the next couple of hours.

These three shows were better company than I had known in a while. Fred Rogers was changing back to street shoes from sneakers when David walked in holding a bottle of Coke, appearing rather unsurprised to see me. Before either of us spoke, his grandmother appeared and playfully helped herself to a sip. "You like that, Grandma?" he asked with an inflection that suggested he thought this might be her first time drinking a soda.

"*David*," she said before pausing for effect. "I have been drinking Coca-Cola since I was a little girl."

Knowing what we know now about the early days of Coca-Cola, I like to think that the sass behind her statement contained a darker message than her propriety would allow her to relay to an eight-year-old kid:

I was drinking Coca-Cola when it still had cocaine in it, you little shit!

I like to make up little scenarios of what I think is going on in other people's heads. Sometimes it's easier than dealing with what's going on in mine.

David's parents came in, I supposed coming from wherever he had come from, and told me it was about time for me to go home. As I made my way toward the door to leave, David blurted out, "Your mom makes really good sandwiches."

When did my mom make you a sandwich? I wondered.

I didn't really care to pursue it; I just said, "See ya," and started the short walk home. A couple of cars were pulling away from makeshift parking spots on our side lawn as I walked up to the door.

Inside, Mom, Tae Im, Tae Kyung, and Tae Hyun were making busy bees of themselves, washing and drying tarnished silver platters, preserving the already-diminished freshness of leftover ham sandwiches in Alligator Baggies and collecting empty bottles, not unlike the one David was drinking from. I retreated to the living room, mainly to stay out of the way, and sat on the chair where Papa had taken what would become a cherished Christmas photo of me and the girls. All of them looked disinterested while I modeled a strange outfit of new acquisitions: snow mittens, a clip-on tie, a plastic whistle in my mouth, and the same yacht cap that would be made iconic by the guy in Captain & Tennille a few years later.

I moved over to the couch and curled up with my head next to the end table, where a nearly empty pouch of Carter Hall tobacco sat rolled up beside a small wooden stand that cradled Papa's pipe. I could picture him sitting there, every night after dinner, savoring each puff flowing from the briarwood bowl, sipping in the smoke, all the while dying from the cancer that took him away from me.

Strewn next to the pipe was a stack of envelopes, most of which remained sealed, like the lips of my three sisters and Mom, all still in the kitchen engaging in any menial task that would forestall their finally having to confront our new reality. On top of the envelope pile sat a solitary Hallmark greeting, seemingly the only card anyone was up to the task of opening. The front of it read "With Deepest Sympathy" in a flowery cursive script. I felt the same urge to cry as I had just days earlier in my parents' bed, but there were no tears this time. It would be years before I cried again, for Papa or anyone.

I heard an offer from the other room. "Honey, do you want a sandwich?" Swallowing a surging fury at why I hadn't been allowed to eat that sandwich earlier in the afternoon, among the people I now know were the mourners at Papa's funeral, I gave a measured response: "No, thanks, Mom."

Papa was gone forever. And "Mama" was too.

LETTER TO AN 8 × 10, PART 2

I drove past your house today. I know I should say it was our house, but let's be honest: everything about it went through you, your tastes, your permissions. You're the only one of us who was there from beginning to end—thirty-nine years. The mark you left on the place was apparent even today on my little drive-by, as I scanned the property from an open driver's side window with my right foot suspended between the gas pedal and the brake.

Even though the bamboo trees are gone—the ones that used to piss off the neighbors when they sprouted up into their yards— the Japanese maple you planted when I was a teenager is still there, standing as strong as I remember, although the current occupants don't seem to have the skill or desire to maintain it like you did. I shudder to think about how many hours you dedicated to trimming that thing, wearing those gardening gloves that were two sizes too big for your hands. I always felt like your secret dream job might have been as one of those topiary arborists at Longwood Gardens. I could see you spending your days transforming shrubs into zoo animals.

Whether you were in the front yard tending your azaleas and flower beds or in the garden picking perilla leaves to make *gaennip*, your green thumb was the outward identity of 17 Bisbee Road, and it pointed the way to some inner peace, which God knows you needed with all the racket I was making, even before I started a band.

I think I was around ten years old when I blasted my first true rock album in the dining room, on the Zenith stereo that jutted out from the wall in that immovable oak console. A gentle hum and an aura of warmth prompted me to open the lid to find the power left on and Tae Hyun's new copy of *A Night at the Opera* on the turntable. As soon as I heard the manic piano and the ominous guitar riff in "Death on Two Legs," that volume knob went up until the walls began to vibrate.

Tae Hyun completely overjustified her love for Queen, hyping up their classical influences and their musical sophistication. It was clearly just a red herring to divert attention from the fact that she had the hots for Freddie Mercury.

"He needs to do something about his teeth, but he's still *soooo* sexy," I overheard her say to Tae Kyung once.

Everyone had their little bubble of fantasy, their secret or maybe not-so-secret crushes. Even you. I would not necessarily have pegged you for the Tom Selleck type, but the fact that you never missed a single episode of *Magnum P.I.* speaks volumes.

"Oh, he's very handsome, honey," you would say without a shred of self-consciousness.

Maybe it was just easier to retreat into a more vicarious world. You never so much as went on a single date for the rest of your life after Papa died. I guess you just couldn't stand the idea of getting hurt even one more time.

I couldn't blame you. You suffered more than your share of heart-break in that house: Papa's cancer, those Christmastime fights with Tae Hyun that left both of us wanting to avoid the holidays for years, and then watching your kids, one by one, leave the nest that you had built for us. We'd all come back to visit, but it would never be the same. To your credit, and perhaps a bit to my chagrin, you never seemed to get bogged down looking in the rearview mirror at things that were, perhaps, closer than they appeared. You were more concerned with what was in front of you. Once something was done, it was done. Once *some of us* were gone, we were gone. Tae Kyung's room became your library. Tae Im's room became your den. Most every trace there was of me in the house had faded like disappearing ink by the time I was bringing my kids around to visit you on Sundays.

Painted over was the bedroom I had always just assumed you'd preserve as a shrine to my childhood. I remember walking in to find the outlines of the orange, yellow, and maroon stripes that once loop-de-looped across the four walls, trying in vain to break through already-forming cracks of what appeared to be a single coat of non-descript beige. I can still picture my Atlantis, a vibrant world now submerged beneath a sea of gray: drums taking up half the floor space, stereo on top of the bookshelf, speakers on top of the dresser, posi-tioned to blow out my right ear as I sat on my brown TAMA throne. I see myself practicing the syncopated beat to "This Is Radio Clash" and screaming "get off the streets" like Joe Strummer in "Know Your Rights." I can picture the grade school–era Elton John poster, later replaced by the high school–era Go-Go's poster. I can see the Johnny Rotten quote, torn from the pages of *Trouser Press* or some other rock monthly, clinging to the spot just to the right of the light switch, thanks to the single piece of rolled-up Scotch tape affixed to its back. The three lines read like a distorted haiku:

I ain't no communist.
You know what communists say—
I've got nothing, and I want you to have some of it.

These mental Polaroids are the keepsakes of my mind's eye, living alongside even more ancient snapshots: bright yellow kitchen walls decorated with twin tapestries of a carrot and a scallion, the black kitchen table with the wobbly legs, the old-timey newsprint curtains in the downstairs bathroom.

Above and to the right of the sink in this bathroom, there's a bumpy patch of plaster on the wall that probably should have been sanded down way back when but was simply whitewashed over. This tiny spot kept a secret that was just for me. I never told you or anyone else about it. A few years after Papa died, Tae Kyung and Ralph rescued an abandoned baby rabbit in the backyard. The gray little thing looked more like a mouse than a bunny, and I watched for days as Ralph kept it alive, feeding it milk and water through an eyedropper while it lay on its side, never once opening its eyes. I didn't expect it would hit me so hard when the rabbit didn't pull through. I remember touching its tiny rib cage with two fingers after it stopped breathing, and shortly after walking into the bathroom and touching those same fingers to the little plaster patch on the wall, saying quietly but out loud: "This is how I'll always remember you." That was the simple goodbye I never got to say to Papa. It might be the most important mark I ever left on that house and possibly the most indelible it ever left on me.

PART II

DOPAMINE

How many times can I paint this future
Without hanging up our past
Tell me how long I can make this picture last

—IKE, "MEMORY"

I WANNA GO HOME

There's always been something about melody. In my particular brain, it seems to pull right into the driveway of my recall, leaving the lyrics to circle the block a few times to find parking. Melody just rolls up like it owns the place and casually tosses me the keys like I'm the valet. Lyrics eventually make their way in and try a little too hard to be clever, but melody is the life of the party because it always brings the dopamine.

For some people, recollection begins as a quick subliminal flash, like the single frame of pornography that Brad Pitt's character in *Fight Club* splices into the family films showing at the movie theater where he works as a projectionist. It gives you pause for a split second, and your brain either pursues it further or you just go on with your life. Sometimes that single kernel, that inkling in the mind's eye, can kick down the door to a hoarder's paradise of long-dormant detail. In my case, memories are just as often triggered by sound as they are by sight. Something I hear can act as a sonic battering ram, breaking through in the way Ella Fitzgerald's voice could shatter a glass in an old Memorex commercial.

Play me the first nine notes of Beethoven's "Für Elise," and in an instant, that iconic piano motif hurls me back in time to the house at 17 Bisbee Road, where I watch and listen with curious ears. My sister Tae Kyung is seated at the cherrywood Wurlitzer upright in our living room. Backlit by remnant beams of light still peeking through the curtains at the end of the day, her nonstop black hair cascades down perpendicular to the floor. The outline of her posture traces a near perfect L. The tips of her fingers move between white and black keys as her hands fight to work independently. The right plays melody while the left arpeggiates the chords, and she lands on the changes with the split-second hesitation of someone still developing her muscle memory.

The *earliest* recollection I can conjure is also rooted in something I heard, but it's one whose very validity I have questioned, probably overquestioned, because if it really happened the way my mind tells me it did, it dates back to before I was even three years old. The high-speed tape rewind that first landed me in this primeval place came well beyond a decade later and left me feeling awestruck, then unsure, then convinced, then unsure, and so on, and so on, and so on.

But I'm a musician, goddammit. I have to trust my ears.

It all starts in 1984 when I purchase *Pet Sounds* by the Beach Boys, during my senior year in high school. I don't remember why I decide that I absolutely *must* own this album on this specific day, but I go to three different record stores in Newark, Delaware to find it. The third time's the charm at a place called Wonderland, which, depending on whom you ask, is either a vinyl shop that sells drug paraphernalia or a head shop that sells records.

The cover art for *Pet Sounds* is a straight-up play on the title, depicting the Beach Boys in what appear to me to be varying states of discomfort while feeding farm animals at a petting zoo. Carl Wilson is the only member of the group who truly seems into the whole concept. One look at his face and you can practically hear him saying, "Awwwwwwwww." The body language of his bandmates is considerably less enthusiastic. Brian Wilson appears to be telepathically communicating, "You're too close to my face." Dennis Wilson might be hallucinating, as he appears to be feeding an animal visible only to himself. Mike Love won't even get near the goats, making human shields of Dennis and guitarist Al Jardine. Love stands back, looking on with concern as Jardine offers up a piece of unidentifiable vegetation, probably hoping not to draw back bloody nubs where his fingers used to be.

The whole group looks pretty dorky, to be honest, but who am I to judge an album by its cover? For years, I've dedicated an unhealthy percentage of free time to creating amateurish mock-ups of my imagined future discography, comprising songs as yet unwritten. These look like the work of a second grader, but they're telling examples of my rich rock 'n' roll fantasy life. My drawing ability has seen little progress since the cover I made in the eighth grade for an album called *The Punk Revolution*, which features a pierced ear with a capital *P* dangling from its lobe and a nose with a giant bullring in its nostrils. Very punk rock, indeed.

In my adolescent bedroom, I listen to music on my new stereo, purchased at Radio Shack, where all teenage audiophiles go for their components. This year's model includes a turntable, a cassette deck, and an eight-track player all-in-one, a practically weightless unit. I put on my fresh copy of *Pet Sounds* and stretch out on my bed, excited to dive into an album that was released the year I was born. It begins on a familiar note, as the 45 of "Wouldn't It Be Nice" has been in my possession for some time now. It was the crown jewel of a long-since-abandoned box of my sisters' records in our basement. By the end of the second song, "You Still Believe in Me," I'm all-in with the album's orchestral leanings, which are nothing like the twangy surf guitar riffs I loved on their early hits. Track six, an instrumental called "Let's Go Away for Awhile," is so soothing, I almost nod off. Then the final song of side one begins, and within seconds I spring up from the mattress and hover over the turntable, watching the record spin, wide awake on the edge of an inkling exploding into a full-blown memory.

Of course, I have to have heard this song before—it's one of the Beach Boys' most famous—but hearing its melody on my record player in this specific instant catapults me into the past, backward though adolescence, through my entire childhood, and deposits me somewhere on the edge of potty training. It's about a year after the Summer of Love, and I'm propped up on the couch in a house on the grounds of the state hospital in Trenton, New Jersey, where my family moved shortly after I was born. It's a house that holds no sentimental place in my heart, except for this one sound bite in time.

My sisters, Tae Im, Tae Kyung, and Tae Hyun, are seated like a committee at the dining room table. All three of them go by "Tae," which must make answering phone calls in our house a unique challenge.

Uh, hello, is Tae there? … Which one? … I don't know … Tae.

Joining them at the table are Linda and Shelly, the teenage daughters of Mom's close friend, Dr. Choi, a fellow med-school grad from back home. Mom and Papa are nowhere in my field of vision. Here's hoping they were making out in the kitchen or something.

Dr. Choi is seated in a nearby chair. She pops the top on a green can, possibly a 7 Up. She's holding the can high above her head, which is tilted back as if she's looking up from a dentist's chair. She pours clear fizzy liquid into her wide-open mouth, not once letting her lips touch aluminum. Then she tightens her lips into a taut, puckered *O*, which an older, worldlier version of me would feel obliged to point out looks like an asshole. She maintains this shape, along with a constipated look on her face, for what seems to be an excruciating amount of time. Relief eventually washes over her, and after weathering the uncomfortable burn of carbonation, she finally swallows. It looks like a helluvalotta work just to get a drink down the hatch, especially to someone used to the simplicity of a bottle with a rubber nipple on it. If my mind works anything like it will when I grow up, I probably scan the room with a bewildered look in my eyes, asking, "Is anyone else seeing this?" It often seems to me like I'm the only person who even notices half the things I find bizarre.

The teenagers are oblivious to Dr. Choi's thirst-quenching techniques, caught up in their own effervescence, lighting up the room with infectious laughter, seeming to need nothing but one another's company to have a good time. Taking in their youthful, giggly chemistry from the couch across the room, I'm drawn to their energy, and I lock it into a primal place within myself. I'll try time and again throughout my life to recapture this feeling and hold it like a lightning bug in the palm of my hand. This very scene is probably why I would always rather hang out with girls than with a bunch of bros. It's possible, however, that at least part of their giddiness is fueled by the presence of a boy in the room, a boy with a guitar.

Jae Geon Oh, a friend of Linda and Shelly's, has a soft, reserved voice and seems a little intimidated by his rambunctious gal pals. I must have a precocious penchant for wise-assery, because even at this tender age, I can't resist calling this kid "Chicken Oh" from my little observation deck. His black-rimmed glasses are sliding down over the beads of sweat dotting his nose, but his confidence comes alive through the body of his six-string acoustic, as he fingerpicks the chord pattern to a bright, folksy tune, which the girls already seem to know. He leads the group with the first couple of lines of the verse, until they all lock in, creating a big unison vocal sound before one of my sisters veers into a spot-on harmony a few lines later. The words are in a language I don't understand, although one line sounds phonetically close to English—that is, if anyone would have a reason to write a lyric that states, "I'm gonna eat dog-doo, and Petey's sorry." Unintelligible as the lyrics may be, something in the melody acts like a hot brand on the hide of my long-term memory. It feels like it's always been there, like it came standard with my brain, deciding to connect the dots during this teenage moment in my room while I'm submerged in the depths of *Pet Sounds*.

> **AND AT THAT MOMENT, FOR ME, MUSIC WAS NO LONGER JUST A NICE PLACE TO VISIT. I LIVED THERE NOW. IT WAS MY HOME.**

"Sloop John B." It was a revelation. It was resonating evidence of what my sisters, through the osmosis of the soundtrack of their youth, had implanted into my musical DNA. If I could hear it sung so joyously in Korean by those teenagers gathered around the dining room table, while I was still in diapers, and unlock that memory on the brink of graduating from high school, with the Beach Boys as the conduit, there was only one conclusion I could reach. Melody was my queen. And at that moment, for me, music was no longer just a nice place to visit. I lived there now. It was my home.

> *So hoist up the John B's sail*
> *See how the mainsail sets*
> *Call for the captain ashore*
> *Let me go home*
> *I wanna go home*

THE K-TEL YEARS

ALLOWANCE

Standing at the kitchen sink, I giggled to myself as I glanced at the advertisement I had torn from one of Mom's psychiatric monthlies. Stuck to the freezer door with a single refrigerator magnet in the shape of a Hershey's Kiss, the ad, for an antipsychotic drug called Haldol, depicted a close-up of a young man with a furrowed brow and sullen eyes, the words "change upsets me" in quotes at the top of the page. There was just something about those words that struck me as funny. Funny because it was true. And it was way easier to laugh than to cry.

My waterlogged fingers were starting to turn pruney under the steady deluge of steaming hot water flowing from the faucet. The raggedy sponge in my hand finally smelled of the thick coatings of "lemon fresh" Joy I had liberally squeezed into its pores to neutralize its default olfactory setting. Packing the potent essence of garlic, soy sauce, and scallions from Mom's bulgogi marinade and the vinegary tang of her homemade kimchi, which fermented in a hole in the backyard for an entire season of the year, that sponge had seen better days. One unfiltered whiff was practically like having an entire meal repeat on you through a loud sustained belch. I immersed the remaining dishes pulled from the black Formica dinner table, as an abundant froth floated atop the gray dishwater, spume overflowing down the front of the wooden cabinetry. I was making a complete crime scene of the place, but there were no witnesses, so no one was complaining, least of all me.

I was almost done with the chore that was going to earn me the filthy lucre that Mom begrudgingly agreed to pay me for a task she felt should be the uncompensated contribution of any responsible family member. She probably caved because she was sick of my constant requests for money that invariably went toward 7-Eleven's bottom line in exchange for anything edible in either the sweet or savory category. She was also most likely getting wise to my five-finger expeditions into her change purse for coins I didn't think she would miss. At least now I'd be working for my spending money, and this week's allowance was earmarked for something beyond junk food.

The last of the dishwater gurgled down the drain, and I pounded the sink strainer against the inside of the trash can under the counter like I was playing a tom-tom. I dislodged several stray soybean sprouts, *kongnamul*, and the fragments of glass that had popped like an M-80 from the inside of my Fat Albert thermos, the one casualty of my now-daily after-dinner routine. I conveniently forgot to tell Mom about the thermos, fearing she might renege on forking over the $3.50 I had coming to me for a week of doing the dishes.

Mom pulled up in front of Woolworths in the Newark Shopping Center and let me jet from the car into the store before she went hunting for a parking spot. I sprinted past the luncheonette that, although closed for the day, still radiated a cloud of airborne animal fat. I ran up the escalator two steps at a time, extending my eight-year-old legs to the point of nearly splitting my pants.

Woolworths's "record department" consisted of a few rickety metal racks that were just large enough to hold a random sampling of the top-40, plucked from playlists I was hearing first on AM pop radio stations like WAMS in Wilmington and, whenever the signal carried into Delaware on a clear day, WFIL in Philadelphia.

I vetted each seven-inch single in the rack, examining the artwork of all the different record labels visible through the cutout paper sleeves, inspecting the vinyl, leaving fingerprints in the grooves like those I had stamped into so many of my sisters' 45s. Even if I couldn't afford to buy all of them, which I desperately wanted to do, just feeling them in my hands felt as if the songs could somehow flow directly into me.

I spotted a copy of "Sunshine on My Shoulders" by John Denver, the only song Mom ever told me to "make louder" when it was on the radio. Even then, I knew that if your mom liked a song, it was a nonstarter, and I continued perusing singles by Carly Simon, Roberta Flack, and the Carpenters. It was easy-listening nirvana in there, but it all just turned out to be window shopping when *Music Power* caught my eye in the album rack next to the singles. *Music Power* was the K-tel compilation album I had seen the commercial for on TV. "22 original hits. 22 original stars"—$4.99. Perfect for a kid on a dish-washer's income.

The problem was, I only had three crumpled dollar bills and two quarters in my pocket. The thought of three more days of dishwashing and probably another week of waiting to get back to the store with the full retail price in hand felt overwhelming to me. First-world third-grader problems, I know. Mom reached the top of the escalator and walked over to me. I had to have looked and sounded pathetic, because as soon as I started in about my financial predicament and the per-song value of the full-length over any given 45, she coughed up the difference I needed to buy the album without so much as an "*aigo*," a Korean word Mom used often when she was annoyed with me. I walked out of Woolworths carrying the first record I ever bought, if only partially, with my own money. Mom's mercy loomed large. For the price of just one seven-inch single, she had floated me a taste of what the future held. It was my first advance, and it felt like she had given me the keys to the world.

SHOW-AND-TELL

Music Power ran the gamut of sounds and styles in a way that Mom might diagnose as schizophrenic. There was rock 'n' roll, soul, folk rock, novelty songs, spoken word, even a Sonny & Cher lowlight that plagiarized a beer commercial. Dropping the needle onto the bluesy chromatic guitar intro of "Smokin' in the Boys Room," then following its thirty-three-and-a-third RPM spiral through memorable tracks like "Oh Girl" by the Chi-Lites and my first doses of power pop— "Tonight" by the Raspberries and "Little Willy" by the Sweet—was like taking the first few steps down a polyphonic yellow brick road.

"Keeper of the Castle" by the Four Tops was quite possibly the first song whose words I paid real attention to. The lyrics, imploring men to be good father figures to their children, often nudged me to play this song again and again. It felt like Papa's presence and absence rolled into one, and the voice of Levi Stubbs left me shaking like I was one of the leaves on the family tree he was singing about.

Eventually, deep into side two of *Music Power*, the stylus would reach Dobie Gray's soulful masterpiece "Drift Away," which was unjustly relegated to the penultimate spot in the running order at track twenty-one. No song I had heard up to that point made me want to escape into rock 'n' roll quite like this one. I loved the song so much that I brought the album in for show-and-tell to play "Drift Away" for my entire class. I went up directly after Michael Clifton, a kid with a blond Dutch boy haircut, who loved making the girls in Mrs. Tenny's homeroom scream in horror whenever he turned his eyelids inside out. He was a tough act to follow, considering he spent his five minutes of show-and-tell demonstrating how to sharpen a No. 2 Dixon Ticonderoga pencil using only his teeth.

TURMOIL

After *Music Power* came *Music Express*. This K-tel album dropped smack-dab in the middle of the 1970s, at a time when I developed a morbid fascination with current events. I watched as President Gerald Ford survived two separate attempts on his life, spaced just seventeen days apart. One of the would-be assassins, Lynette "Squeaky" Fromme, was a former member of the Manson family, who had used the Beatles' "Helter Skelter" as almost biblical inspiration for their brutal killing spree in the summer of 1969.

Any cultural turmoil that was bubbling under in the period just after Richard Nixon's resignation and the end of the Vietnam War was conspicuously missing on *Music Express*. But in spite of the optimistic pep of core songs like "Love Will Keep Us Together" and "Get Down Tonight," which was a hedonistic disco track aimed at those who like to do a little dance and make a little love, a certain degree of psychic darkness began to creep into the K-tel catalog.

Harry Chapin's "Cat's in the Cradle" depicted a father's relationship with his son, from infancy to adulthood, in the span of four verses. The dad's epiphany that his boy had basically grown up to be just like him reiterated the void left by Papa's death, as "Keeper of the Castle" had, but it also illuminated a cyclical passing of the generational torch that I could not comprehend at the time, at least not consciously.

"I'm Not in Love" by 10cc was unlike anything I had ever heard. There was no snappy drumbeat you could jump around to, and much of the sonic space was filled with what I imagined a choir of cherubs would sound like. On top of that, repeated listens pushed me to see a piece of myself in the lyrics. Just like the song's antihero, I was overcompensating to prove I was fine, trying to convince myself I wasn't feeling the way I was feeling. The state of denial in the song felt uncomfortably like my own, as I put on the best game face I could summon to mask my ongoing grief.

SCHADENFREUDE

Toward the end of the school year in June, my teacher set aside an hour for the class to make Father's Day cards. Mrs. English was an acne-scarred woman sporting '60s-inspired bangs and loose curls that turned upward at her shoulders. She spoke out of the side of her mouth in an accent that was vaguely Midwestern. She said something like "OK, class. Today we're gonna make cards for Father's Day." Then, in the face of an unenthusiastic response, she added, "Don't look at me all cockeyed!" She loved to say the word "cockeyed," and we all loved hearing her say it, for obvious, immature reasons.

After the double entendre giggles petered out, the paralysis of my heavy heart allowed me to do little more than stare down at my blank piece of construction paper, in which strands of embedded wood pulp struck my eye as cancer cells under a microscope. Anne

Brunt, a girl with braided pigtails sitting next to me, asked why I wasn't doing anything.

"My dad's dead," I said in a dry tone, aggressive in its neutrality.

"Ask a silly question ..." she trailed off, before moving to an unoccupied desk in the next row.

Having driven her away, I felt a strange little jolt of power. I was beginning to find comfort in making people feel *un*comfortable, and I was starting to see dark humor in the suffering of others.

Two of the songs on *Music Express* played right into my malevolent leanings. As an umbrella term for any song that ends in fatal catastrophe, "death rock" was not a new phenomenon. Scads of songs that don't end well have crashed the pop charts dating back to the '60s—"Leader of the Pack," "Ebony Eyes," "Dead Man's Curve," and "Last Kiss" by Wayne Cochran, which was later made famous again by Pearl Jam. I never heard any of these songs until I was much older, but here was K-tel in 1975 to school me on tragedy.

"Run Joey Run" is possibly the most melodramatic song ever recorded. In addition to singer David Geddes in the voice of the title character, the song also features the vocal hysterics of a teenage girl named Julie, whose gun-toting father apparently has it in for Joey, with whom, it's implied, she's *done it*. Julie eventually ends up taking the bullet intended for Joey and barely chokes out her last line about the two of them getting married as she nears her final evacuation, surrounded by the voices of a funereal choir, setting up the song's ultimate face-tingling chorus. I'm sure I wasn't alone at the time in thinking this song was completely over-the-top awful, but in a way that I absolutely *loved*. It was, perhaps, my first example of something so utterly bad, it's great.

The second song, "Rocky" by Austin Roberts, was about a couple who fall in love, get married, and have a child, only to be torn apart by the mother's untimely death from a terminal illness when the kid is still very young. Age differences and gender reversals aside, one might have thought this song would be my empathetic jam, but not so. My ears were turning cynical. The song trucks along in major-key bliss through two and a half saccharine verses until the bombshell drops: Rocky's wife doesn't have long to live!

I remember laughing out loud at these songs. They're the kinds of musical moments that make a listener embarrassed for themselves and everyone involved.

I'm sure in some ways my mockery was also a coping mechanism. I was bitter. At least Rocky had a line in a song to prepare *him* for what was about to happen. I felt no sympathy. I was hurting, and I wanted others to hurt, too, even if they were just figments of some songwriter's imagination. A wall had sprung up around my heart without me even realizing it. It didn't bode well for the near future. The ugliness inside me was bound to manifest itself. See you all in hell.

SCRATCH 'N' SNIFF

have this thing about songs with laughter in them. Not like the audience laughter in "Sgt. Pepper's Lonely Hearts Club Band"— that's more of a device to pull you into a simulated live show. I'm talking about songs in which someone lets out what sounds like an impromptu chuckle, some "just can't help myself" flush of giddy joy in the midst of a timeless pop moment. It's a thin line for me in deciding whether I find it endearing or infuriating. Joni Mitchell's laugh at the end of "Big Yellow Taxi"? Charming as all hell. Whitney Houston in "I Wanna Dance with Somebody (Who Loves Me)"? Eh, not so much. I just picture someone's drunk aunt at a wedding reception trying too hard to "get the party started." You can hear Sting laugh in the intro of "Roxanne," apparently as the result of sitting on the keys of a piano in the recording studio. It's the most sardonic laugh at a chord inadvertently played by one's buttocks I've ever heard. *I* even contributed to this odd song category on a 2008 track called "Message of Love," by my band IKE. I let out a genuine cackle at the end of the lead vocal take after hearing our guitarist Brett Talley from across the room do a spot-on impression of the "Yeaaaaahhhhhh" that Counting Crows front man Adam Duritz ad-libs at the end of "Rain King."

It's probably a safe bet to say that my awareness of this phenomenon of laughter in pop music began with a song that was out around the time I was nine or ten: "Moonlight Feels Right" by Starbuck. They were what you'd call a one-hit wonder, never really topping the success of their debut single, but like so many songs from this period of my childhood, "Moonlight Feels Right" transports me every time I hear it, in large part because of the laugh that singer Bruce Blackman delivers as the lead-in to each chorus. It's a wry little snicker, more of a "heh-heh" than a "ha-ha" or a "tee-hee." It's the laughter equivalent of a nod and wink, steering the listener to take the song's "moon" references as far into the gutter as they'll go.

I'm almost certain "Moonlight Feels Right" was playing on the radio when the sleepover at Matt Tower's house took its first unexpected turn, as I encountered his blinding white butt cheeks beaming over the horizon of the wooden frame at the top of his twin bunks. I shrieked at the sight, which both mortified and confused me. He laughed so hard, he farted. Lesson learned: always think twice when someone with no prior interest in astronomy says, "Hey, come here. There's a great view of the moon." How did he even know what "mooning" was? I saw in Matt a worldliness I could only aspire to.

Matt was both good and bad for me. I desperately needed a friend, and for a while, he was exactly that, inviting me over after school or on weekends, when we'd make prank phone calls to a local prayer hotline after seeing the number scroll across the bottom of the TV screen on a public access Christian program. Those types of calls came to an end when he flew too close to the sun and dialed "0" to ask the operator to look up the number for John Jacob Jingleheimer

Schmidt, prompting an immediate call back from the phone company and a demand to speak with his mother.

Matt possessed the self-confidence I lacked, having no problem talking to older, sixth-grade girls, no hesitation in taking a dare to try buying cigarettes at 7-Eleven, and no sense of shame in baring his ass in service of a joke. Plus, the kid was resilient. The previous year he'd fought for his laundry bag of Halloween candy as two kids from the apartments pinned him up against one of the three jalopies sitting in disrepair in front of the Basaris' house. A third kid came up to me and shouted in my face with the vigor of a Pentecostal preacher: "Gimme your candy; gimme *all* your candy!" My trick-or-treat bag survived, but Matt was left with nothing but road rash on his elbows and a black bandanna, which was all that remained of his pirate costume. I offered him half my candy but he refused, asking only to borrow my bag so he could go out and begin again.

Sometime during that same autumn, I watched him pick himself right back up after a sucker punch to the left eye left him tasting concrete on my front stoop. Matt absorbed the right cross, delivered compliments of a skeevy neighborhood kid from Red Mill Apartments, like it wasn't the first or last time he would be confronted with such a situation. It's hard for me to picture Matt dwelling on any of this for very long, while I, on the other hand, have never been able to forget the thinly veiled threat from the mouth of the bully's crony shouting at me from just beyond the driveway: "Stay outta this, Jap!"

The part about Matt that wasn't so good for me was that he was willing to go where the weirdest, meanest parts of my now-addled brain would lead. Together, we kept count of the number of schoolyard fights lost by Wesley Poole, a troubled midyear transfer student to the fifth grade, whom we made no attempt to befriend and, in fact, often provoked into altercations with kids we knew had short tempers.

By the time Mike Dienno gave him another bloody lip on the walking path I took every day as a latchkey kid, with a couple dozen onlookers getting off on the spectacle and me holding "Mikey D's" books, we were pretty sure Wesley was 0–50.

Matt also got on board with my disturbed idea to create a "scratch 'n' sniff" book, which we talked of sharing with our unsuspecting classmates, the joke being that the "scratch" area on each page would consist of a healthy schmear of dog shit. To make the "prototype," we scoured backyards up and down my block looking for stool samples with just the right consistency. Laughing to the point of tears, we picked up cigar-shaped turds with paper towels, then, holding our breath with distended cheeks worthy of a Dizzy Gillespie trumpet solo, we spread the canine cream cheese onto the pages of free notepads, which Mom received from pharmaceutical companies hawking medications for psychotic disorders. Ironic that the promotional swag for drugs like Thorazine and Serentil became the canvases for our demented abstracts, each brown smudge representing a skid mark in the drawers of one of the kids whom I imagined were in a club of misfits, the Barfy Hell Bunch, presided over by their leader in loserdom, Wesley Poole. So deep was my need to feel better about myself that I created an entire imaginary organization over which I could feel superior, and I was willing to handle animal feces to do it. Strangely, after a few days, the scratch 'n' sniff book no longer smelled at all. But my soul reeked.

Back in the bottom bunk, with my eyes still recovering from the lunar vision I would never be able to unsee, "The Things We Do for Love" by 10cc came on WAMS, and I started improvising a parody of the song, transforming it into "The Things We Do for Barf." It contained these lines:

You better get a knife and a fork
'Cuz I'm gonna york
And it feels like a part of me is ralphin'

My lyrical flow quickly went off the tracks when I realized there were no viable rhymes for the word "ralphin'." You have to think a couple of steps ahead in these improv situations, but I guess I couldn't resist the fact that the name of my sister's boyfriend was also a euphemism for the act of vomiting.

It was not my best work by a long shot, but Matt laughed anyway, and it's indicative of why he probably kept me around. I made my own entertainment, and he liked how I could come up with things on the spot, impressed that I "just made that up." The more irreverent and dirtier the words, the louder the laughs. In our young minds, song parodies and generally making fun were our satirical middle finger to the "old fogies" who ran our school, all of them too blind and set in their ways to even realize we were mocking everything they threw in our path.

We chuckled constantly at our ancient hawk-faced music teacher, Mrs. Fuller, as she clacked two wooden claves together, making us repeat "ta ta tee tee ta" ad nauseam. Then there was the gym teacher, Mr. Gee, opening each class with a workout record called "Chicken Fat," with the inescapable refrain "Go, you chicken fat, go." We hated him for that sinister hook he planted in our heads. What I couldn't realize at the time was that Mrs. Fuller was the first person to teach me what a rhythmic motif was, and at the very least, Mr. Gee, forcing the entire class to chicken-strut around the gym like Mick Jagger, was unknowingly training me for my future as a front man.

> MY LYRICAL FLOW QUICKLY WENT OFF THE TRACKS WHEN I REALIZED THERE WERE NO VIABLE RHYMES FOR THE WORD "RALPHIN'."

With few other outlets for creativity at this point in my life—scratch 'n' sniff books and my failed attempt at learning the violin notwithstanding—writing dirty lyrics to the songs on the radio was my way of doing something musical, if you could call it that. We were content to just keep listening to the transistor radio in Matt's room and making up whatever weird or obscene new words came to mind. We had already amassed quite a few of these parodies over the past several months, the vast majority based on the following core topics:

Fucking (which we knew nothing about)

Barfing (which we knew a little about)

The umbrella category Farting/Pissing/Shitting (which we knew *all* about)

We also had an inordinate number of songs about "getting ruptured," maybe because we had both seen *The Bad News Bears* that year and were more affected than we realized by the scene in which an outfielder takes a fly ball to the nuts. I chronicled all these parody lyrics in a flip-top spiral notebook that I usually kept in the piano bench at home.

After the litany of parodies and dirty jokes died down, Matt and I fell into a relaxed silence in our respective bunks. There was nothing awkward about it; it was the silence of two friends who were comfortable enough not to feel obligated to speak just for the sake of making sound. For a brief moment, it felt like I had a brother. It hadn't been long since Matt's actual brother, now in high school, moved out to take over his big sister's room after she'd left for college. One sign of his presence and influence remained, specifically Heart's *Dreamboat Annie*, a record depicting Ann and Nancy Wilson back to back and seemingly naked, revealing nothing but giving boys like us the chance to imagine what lay just beyond the bottom of that album cover. It seemed like a touching memento left behind to quietly honor their time as roommates.

Matt's mother tapped on the door and poked her head into his bedroom. She was sporting the wedge haircut that had swept through suburbia in the months after Dorothy Hamill struck Olympic gold.

"Phone for you downstairs, sweetheart," she said with a Tiparillo rasp, her "come 'ere" hand gesture indicating that the call was for me.

I had no idea why anyone would be trying to get ahold of me here, but I left the room, half expecting to take a crank call that Matt had somehow orchestrated and fully expecting to return momentarily. Once in the kitchen, I put the receiver to my ear and heard Tae Kyung's voice on the other end. The convivial tone I was used to from her was conspicuously absent.

"John, you need to come home. Mom wants to talk to you."

For as long as I could remember, my sister had never called me anything but Johnny. Now she was addressing me as "John"? This made me feel uneasy.

I started bunching the long coiled phone cord in my clammy palm. My own voice was landing somewhere between begging and bargaining. I told her that Mom promised I could spend the night. I asked if she could just tell me what was the matter over the phone.

My sister paused and, I suppose, decided that the answers to these questions were not hers to give.

"Mom needs to talk to you now." She hung up without saying goodbye.

JIG = UP

From Matt's place on Cordele Road, it was probably a two-minute walk back around the block to my house, but whenever I got nervous the pace of my stride accelerated like flipping the RPM switch on a turntable all the way up to 78. I was home in what felt like thirty seconds.

When I arrived, Tae Kyung and Tae Hyun were standing in the doorway, and one of them tilted her head toward the staircase, indicating that our mother was waiting for me in her room. Mom's hair, now more salt than pepper, was in curlers as she sat at the foot of her bed, the same bed where she once made me sleep on a towel covered in raw onions to combat my 103-degree fever, the same bed I had dampened with tears the night I learned about Papa. Although the room had since been rearranged, perhaps in the interest of *feng shui*, the bed was a towering centerpiece, no matter what direction it faced. As I stood before her, she maintained her silence for the moment and waited for me to spot the smoking gun. There on her silk comforter was the flip-top spiral notepad on whose pages I had scrawled all manner of obscenity and scatological perversion in the iambic meters of the popular songs of the mid-'70s. As soon as she was positive I had locked eyes on it, she picked it up, flipped it open, and began reading the first page out loud:

Table of CUNTents:
"Undercover Anus"
"Hot Pork"
"Barfy Hell Delight"
"Naked To The Limit"
"Drop The Soap"
"Don't Give Up On My Penis"
"After The Fuckin'"
"Blowing Me, Blowing You"

I have never really been one to pray, but in this instance, I mentally knelt to genuflect, in the hope that a higher power would make her stop. But she had only just begun. The words, once my funny and clever friends, grabbed me by the scruff of the neck and threw me under my own bus. In silence, I wished Mom would just spank me and get it over with, but who was I kidding? Did I really think a seasoned psychiatrist was going to give me that easy out over a psychological whipping I would remember for life? Page after torturous page, she read all of it, line by line, back to me. It swirled like a vortex of vulgarity.

Undercover anus, midnight diarrhea! Turd rockets in flight! Barfy Hell delight! Don't give up on my penis—it'll still go through! Drop the soap—Don't drop the soap baby! Drop the soap—don't bend yourself over!

Each individual dramatic reading was followed by the sound of its corresponding page ripping from the spiral binding and then being handed over to me. From the very start of this ritualistic punishment, which went on for an hour or more, I understood the implied expectation that I would receive the piece of paper, silently renounce its contents, and dispose of it in the trash, all while maintaining a contrite expression that communicated, in no uncertain terms, "I am a complete disgrace."

Mom's wastebasket was filling up with crumpled balls of paper when she got to "Torn Between Two Fuckers," my corruption of a song called "Torn Between Two Lovers," which I anticipated would be particularly uncomfortable to hear out loud since the parody lyrics retained the original's female point of view. Naturally, Mom took this opportunity to turn the tables and handed the book over to me:

There's been another man that I've needed and I've fucked
But that doesn't mean I'll fuck you less
And he knows he can undress me
And he knows I'm on the pill
There's just this empty hole in front of me
That only he can fill

The final affront that took Mom over the edge was a rewrite of "Calling Dr. Love" by Kiss. My version was titled "Calling Dr. Fuck." Of course it was.

They call me Dr. Fuck
Excuse me while I take a pee
(Calling Dr. Fuck!)
I'm here to have some sex with ye
(Calling Dr. Fuuuuuuuuuck!)

"Have some sex with *YEEEEEEEE*?!" Mom bellowed, her voice cracking on the word "ye." I wondered for a split second if her rage was amplified by my out-of-context use of Old English. In the end, it really didn't matter. My jig was up.

POMPALAISE

learned something important about myself in grade school. If someone liked me enough to be my friend or even a friendly acquaintance, it usually had something to do with my vocabulary. Of the many things I could have absorbed about the human condition and the horrors of combat from watching *M*A*S*H* on TV every week, it was the ability to use "latrine" in a sentence that impressed Bob Baylis, my co-worker during a short-lived stint at the Medill school store. I was already peppering my speech with the word "critical" by the time I started second grade, having overheard Mom inject it into a phone conversation, interrupting the otherwise indecipherable Korean she was speaking. I always wondered if she was describing Papa's condition as he lay dying.

In spite of some frequent detours into profanity, the drive to develop my linguistic chops was real, and it went beyond just entertaining my friends with synonyms for "toilet." The sometimes-awkward exchanges in our house, where English was a second language for my sisters and the third language for Mom, made it feel all the more important that I develop a rapport with America's native tongue. I saw the English language as my best weapon against those who would try to demean me or paint me as an outsider. If I could know it and speak it better than my detractors, how could they possibly make the argument that I didn't belong? I eschewed the dribs and drabs of Korean I picked up in our assimilationist household and put my grammatical focus where it would serve me best.

I also made up a lot of my own words, as I suspect many kids do. When I was seven or eight, I began referring to myself as "Jin Va," my secret code pronunciation of "John Faye." When I was ten, I coined the phrase "peel the barf," which, broadly defined, means to make a stupid or laughable mistake. This odd combination of words had its roots in my misinterpretation of a line in "Smoke from a Distant Fire," one of the many songs of my childhood whose lyrics I just heard differently. Consider it my "there's a bathroom on the right."

How might one use "peel the barf" correctly? Here's an example: I attended my first New Year's Eve party when I was around ten years old. My sister Tae Kyung allowed me to play DJ, setting me up with a turntable, a stack of records, and a chair in the hall closet at her friend Phil's apartment. Around 11:56 pm he knocked on the door and told me to cut the music and began counting down while looking at his watch.

10-9-8-7-6-5-4-3-2-1 … Happy New Year!

Multiple people then pointed out that his timepiece was about four minutes fast.

One could then say that "he really peeled the barf on that one." Or further simplified: "Yeah, he peeled it."

Most of the other words and expressions in my parallel lexicon also came with their own little backstory. The one that eclipsed all others in my personal Urban Dictionary was "pompalaise." The word sounds vaguely French, so it made sense that the term had its genesis in Canada, where I took the first, and last, ski trip of my life. Tae Kyung and Ralph were on winter break in January of 1977 and took me with them up to Mont Sutton in Quebec. I remember the thrill of staying up late and leaving Delaware in the middle of the night so we could avoid daytime traffic and arrive just as the slopes were opening up. Proficient skiers, the two of them had been to the resort the year before.

I stayed awake in near delirium for most of the drive, imagining myself on the ski lift, feeling the cold northern air on my face as I ascended amid breathtaking aerial views, my rented skis dangling on my feet, the slopes below dotted with skiers zigzagging downhill, leaving ephemeral clouds of powder in their wake.

To get to the top of a beginner's hill, I soon found out, you didn't ride on a chair lift; you had to take the T-bar. A T-bar is what's known as a surface lift—your skis never leave the ground. Basically, it's an upside-down *T* hanging from a cable going around on a motorized loop. When it's your turn to go, you need to grab onto the center of the bar with one hand, hold your ski poles in the opposite hand, then, in perfect sync with another person taking the same lift, balance your ass cheeks across the horizontal bar and hold that position while it pulls you and your lift mate up the hill.

By midafternoon I must have fallen off this thing about twenty-eight times, sometimes immediately, sometimes about a third of the way up, always before making it to the top of the "beginner's bump," slipping and sliding back downhill for a few brief seconds before skulking to the end of the line to do it all again. My instructor, Luc, had all but given up on me, instead focusing most of his attention on Jenny, a girl who was roughly my age and the prettiest girl I had seen in all my ten years.

The best part of that whole morning was watching her and thinking about what it would be like to talk to her. Even in a fairly crowded field of novice skiers, she was impossible to miss in her candy-apple-red down jacket. She had big brown eyes and a slight overbite. Her crimped chestnut-colored hair flared out from her knit cap like an Oriental fan hanging down to her shoulder blades. My immediate crush took the edge off the embarrassing sequence of T-bar disasters, but only until Jenny locked eyes with me in utter scorn after my incompetence resulted in both of us falling off the lift.

Eventually, my sister came around to find me demoralized. I was absolutely ready to leave and never come back when she offered to take me with her to ride on the chair lift, perhaps forgetting that the chair lift only took you to trails meant for people who knew what they were doing. When we got up to the top, I took one look at the steep incline in front of me and I panicked. *Uh-uhh. No way.* I would never make it down alive. Tae Kyung was probably thinking the same thing, because she decided right away that we needed another plan of action, one that would hopefully avert the "agony of defeat" crushing of both my body and spirit.

> MY IMMEDIATE CRUSH TOOK THE EDGE OFF THE EMBARRASSING SEQUENCE OF T-BAR DISASTERS, BUT ONLY UNTIL JENNY LOCKED EYES WITH ME IN UTTER SCORN AFTER MY INCOMPETENCE RESULTED IN BOTH OF US FALLING OFF THE LIFT.

She suggested we take a less daunting, if also less traveled, path. It was marked "intermediate" and would still be challenging for me, but it was no black diamond death run. No other people were heading in this direction. Perhaps sensing my continued trepidation, my sister went straight for my motivational jugular and told me there would be food waiting for me at the bottom, inside the Pompalaise, a cozy, inviting restaurant where she had enjoyed coq au vin and French onion soup during her last visit. At this point, it was hard for me even to focus, so I only got the gist of what she was saying, but cocoa sounded spectacular to me, so I was ready. Let's do this!

What Tae Kyung failed to realize—or maybe just disregarded, in the absence of any other options—was that our chosen trail, on this day anyway, was off-piste, meaning, in a practical sense, that a kid like me, who had yet to complete a full run down a beginner's hill, should not be anywhere near it. The snow was not packed. We were skiing through glades, full of trees to crash into, where the untreated snow was close to four inches deep and nearly impossible to navigate. I fell on my ass roughly every twenty feet. My sister didn't fare too much better but managed to help pick me up from time to time. It took the better part of an hour to get to the bottom of a hill that would probably have taken someone who could actually ski about forty-five seconds, had the trail been passable in the first place. I was sobbing, with frostbite now kicking in on most of my face, snot practically freezing to my upper lip. Eventually, we did stagger to the bottom, and only one thought was keeping me from completely losing my shit: warmth and food in the comforts of the Pompalaise. We walked up to the entrance, and my sister motioned for me to do the honors. I pulled on the handle of the large wooden double doors, but it did not open. Why wouldn't the door open? I needed the door to open. The door was locked. The restaurant was closed.

From that point forward, the word "pompalaise" came to mean any time you went somewhere but found it to be closed. This was but a literal meaning. Before long it came to encompass any situation that involved a sense of rejection, an act of general mockery, or things just not going your way.

Hey, did that girl ever thank you for letting her copy your homework?

Not really; she just told me I should study harder next time because we only got a 78. Oh, damn, pompalaise!

As the final curtain dropped on the fifth grade, so, too, disappeared the handful of friendships I had with kids my own age. Whether Mom sensed that I needed to be around other people or was simply pimping me out as an under-the-table worker for family friends, I spent the summer of 1977 in the exclusive company of adults, breaking most of Delaware's child labor laws. If I wasn't operating a forklift and organizing large slabs of patio slate at Sam's Flagstone, I was doing time at the New Castle Farmers Market, separating moldy cherries from their technically edible counterparts, as they commingled in the murky water of a utility sink in the back of a produce stand, which was operated by Sam's brother-in-law, a Korean man named Sam Soo. After collecting the salvageable fruit and arranging it into half-pint berry baskets, I was allowed to wander the market with a small lunch per diem.

Most days, I'd while away my thirty-minute break perusing the handful of black milk crates containing beat-up, scratched vinyl records in a corner stall whose only signage was a hand-painted piece of plywood that read "Gently Used." Completely aware I was doing something I shouldn't be, I snuck peaks into a bin marked "Adults Only," which contained numerous comedy albums by Rudy Ray Moore, almost all depicting him and one or more women in a state of full-frontal nudity. The cover of *The Cockpit* quickly filed itself under "unforgettable," with Moore stretched out on a lounge chair in nothing but a pilot's cap, his hands coyly shielding his nipples, and a model airplane placed strategically over his crotch. He was surrounded by five naked flight attendants, known at the time as stewardesses, their bare breasts completely in view.

Just behind the comedy records was a copy of what turned out to be the self-titled album by Blind Faith. Only years later would I learn they were a supergroup that included Eric Clapton, Ginger Baker, and Steve Winwood. The cover, which contained no text or context for me, featured a naked girl barely older than I was.

Ironically, aeronautics also figured into this album art, which depicts the girl holding a gold-plated, not-so-subtly-phallic airplane as she stands au naturel against a backdrop of grass and sky. Her face and hairstyle bore a close enough resemblance to ski-trip Jenny's as to make the image a source of impure thoughts for the next couple of years and an indelible reminder that I was the boy on the outside, pulling in vain on the locked door of the Pompalaise.

LETTER TO AN 8 × 10, PART 3

It was that warm sound of the solid oak stereo in your dining room that got me through the lonely autumn and the beginning of winter at the end of 1977. The dust burning off the old vacuum tubes inside the console smelled like comfort as old reliable K-tel was there for me one last time. *Right On* was a compilation of "20 original hits" with an album cover depicting a pretty blond girl wearing a blue button-down tied off in a knot just above her exposed midriff. Her thumbs-up to the camera would best be described as "Fonzarellian."

"All by Myself" by Eric Carmen became a wistful backdrop for my melancholy. You were seriously considering a job transfer to the VA hospital in Waco, and I waited in limbo for your decision, drifting through the sixth grade at Wilmer E. Shue Middle School. How different would both our lives have been as Texans, living in a city that would later become synonymous with David Koresh and the Branch Davidians? Maybe I would have joined his band and been shot up by the ATF.

I felt disconnected from my few old friends and couldn't see the point in trying to make any new ones. I felt "wise" beyond my years in a way that made me feel utterly alone. I held on for dear life to the optimism of "The Boys Are Back in Town," praying I could just make it through to another summer in Delaware. The Thin Lizzy song became an anthem of hope in my rock 'n' roll fantasy world. I could see myself, for the first time, performing to a sold-out, Bic-lighter-waving crowd, and I began singing along in earnest in a voice still well below the volume of the speakers. I even accompanied myself on the junior-size HEAD tennis racquet you bought me, hoping I would develop an interest in your favorite spectator sport. But I was no Jimmy Connors or Björn Borg. That racquet saw far more action as my "first guitar" than it ever did on a court.

I remember dropping it like a hot potato on the hardwood floor in the dining room when you startled me back to reality, coming all the way from the den to tap me on the shoulder to replay "You'll Never Find Another Love like Mine" by Lou Rawls.

Of course I obliged. I had been waiting for this. For those three short minutes, music put you and me on the same page, and I didn't have to ball this one up and throw it away in the trash.

PART III

TEENAGE FIX

Five miles or a galaxy away
Where are you tonight?

—IKE, "PURE"

PUNK BROTHERS, INTERNATIONAL

I remember the sound of raucous laughter, my teenage voice deeper than just a year before. I channeled my best Boss Hogg from *The Dukes of Hazzard* and pondered: "Whyyyyyyy is it ... that dog has a bare ass?" Smellwood chuckled in amusement, his breath visible in the late winter air. The mange on his dog Abba's backside had taken a turn for the worse in the months since his house had become my second home. Abba and her frequent sidekick, Corporal Cupcake, were just two in a congregation of former strays that Smellwood's family didn't have the heart to turn away. They didn't have the heart to turn me away either.

Smellwood's house sat about a quarter mile back at the end of a hidden gravel drive called Fells Lane. The three-story Victorian, once occupied by his great-great-grandparents and maintained with the family's long-gone old money, now shed curled chips of lead paint and cradled the exoskeletons of bygone insects in its cobwebbed window screens. It was not unusual to have to navigate an obstacle course of buckets placed under dripping ceilings on rainy days. It was a unique intersection of privilege and deprivation where the absence of creature comforts opened up the imagination.

Smellwood and I entertained ourselves discussing a tree branch that split into a V, something that might now seem to represent a fork in the road but at the time could only register in our brains as the spreading of a pair of legs.

To an outsider, it might seem improbable that Smellwood, along with his two sisters, Wez and Molly, had gone to Tatnall since they were little kids. But it was no more improbable to me than my being there. Tatnall, or "The Tatnall School, Incorporated," as I liked to call it, charged an annual tuition higher than it would eventually cost for me to attend the University of Delaware. It seemed crazy for Mom to spend that kind of money to send me somewhere I was all but determined to hate. Then again, how much more could I hate it compared to where I'd just came from?

The change of scholastic scenery had been abrupt and bipolar when I first walked into the clean, carpeted college preparatory institution that, as far as I was concerned, had accepted me only to fulfill some unspoken "misfit" quota. Gone were the taxpayer-funded classrooms where wadded pieces of notebook paper stabilized the uneven legs of wobbly desks, still standing since the days when kids practiced "duck and cover" under them. Gone were the three-quarter-sleeve Led Zeppelin shirts and shaggy bed head of a former Shue Middle School classmate, who once huffed ozone in science class and cracked up the room by calling Jacques Cousteau "Jacques Cou-Strap."

Strange, evolved creatures were all around me now, walking upright in a way that made my public-school slouch feel all the more pronounced. The seemingly refined young men at Tatnall radiated confidence from the clean lines of their dress code haircuts, trimmed neatly above the collars of their baby-blue Oxfords, or, on days when they were feeling sassy, their piqué alligator polos, popped collar optional. I saw girls roaming the halls in four-color corduroy pants, each panel of the front and back leg a different whimsical hue of their entitlement—neon pink, lime green, navy blue, sunshine yellow.

I had one tone in my school wardrobe: earth. Brown corduroys, beige button-downs, and tan Wallabees, alternated with a pair of burgundy patent leather penny loafers, which I was defiant in keeping penniless. My vision was going from bad to worse, so the glasses that had sat at the back of my locker untouched the previous year were now a necessary evil if I wanted to see anything my teachers were writing on the blackboard.

Smellwood was actually Jonathan P. Hunt, which in its own way sounded made up, as it seemed to me to be the perfect name for a fictitious prep school student. It was a name that made more sense after I met his father, who worked in the financial sector at Dean Witter Reynolds and took him out for steak dinners at the Wilmington Country Club when he had visitation. I was never invited to join Smellwood at the WCC, but I did tag along once to Sunday brunch at his grandparents' house.

"This is Evets," Smellwood announced upon our arrival, offering no etymological explanation.

His grandfather gave him a look like "Evets? What the hell is an 'Evets'?"

"Evets" was my chosen alias in our adolescent alliance as the Punk Brothers, a raggedy send-up of the Blues Brothers. Instead of Jake and Elwood, we were Evets and Smellwood.

The name was inspired by my fascination with the antics of one of our classmates, a kid named Steve. He was a classic postpubescent buffoon, unaware that almost everything he did and said was under my constant scrutiny. He was truly gifted in the art of social faux pas.

There was the failed one-cheek sneak during silent reading period, the widening of his eyes showing that even he was shocked at how loudly it reverberated off the floor, where the entire eighth grade sat cross legged, our noses buried in books like *The Grapes of Wrath*. Then there was the time he walked up to the most well-endowed girl in our class and said out loud with a pleasantly surprised inflection in his voice: "Mmm, good boobs." And, of course, the time he pushed back with vehemence at the suggestion that he felt an attraction to one of the girls who was, as they say, prettier on the inside: "Ohhhh *nooooo*, my wang would sizzle away!"

Yeah, "Steve" spelled backward. That would make a great stage name.

At the Sunday brunch table, the adults quizzed the kids with uninterested questions, eliciting monosyllabic responses. No topic in this WASP-y back-and-forth was too bland. Then Smellwood's grandmother turned her attention to me.

"So, uh … Emmet … What part of *China* are you from?"

After a short, perplexed pause, I muttered with my mouth full of eggs: "I'm from America."

I didn't bother to correct her presumption of my being Chinese. This was a tactic I came to use a lot, whenever people would ask me *where I was from*. Regardless of their intentions, even if they were genuinely curious about my background, I always viewed this line of questioning as suspect, an attempt to paint me as the alien I already felt I was. "I'm from America" was the only sentence I spoke at brunch. I felt a sinking awareness that the more things change, the more they stay the same. Only now, I was Lee Ho Fook's mustard in a Grey Poupon world.

However uncomfortable I may have been around his relatives, I felt a real kinship with Smellwood, an awareness that both of us were walking contradictions, straddling the lines dividing multiple worlds, somewhere in between being good boys and bad seeds. We never discussed the connection of our common circumstances, being raised by hardworking mothers in fatherless households, but I can't help but believe this was part of what bound us together.

My ability to craft a good insult didn't hurt, either, the more confusing to the recipient, the better. Smellwood later recalled that it was my unorthodox recess basketball taunt, thrown at one of our douchier classmates, that drew him to me. "You are a crevice of the rear," replete with obligatory rolled *r*'s, my response to our classmate's chirping about my height and presumed nationality, laid the foundation of a life-long friendship between Smellwood and me. It also provided a little meeting place for our high and low brows to conspire.

We soon discovered a mutual love of Monty Python. I had first watched *Monty Python's Flying Circus* at the age of ten when I started to stay up late on Saturday nights with the TV to myself in the basement. While my sisters were out with their boyfriends, I was mimicking John Cleese, performing silly walks in my pajamas. Smellwood and I committed most of the dialogue from *Life of Brian* to memory.

I was notably almost shoved out of a second-story library window for referencing one of the movie's funnier scenes and calling one of our more nasally endowed classmates "Big Nose." He wasn't about to take that kind of shit from me, so he pushed my shoulders with both hands. I felt my back break through a long sheet of untempered glass and heard the big shards land on the sidewalk below. Mrs. Murphy, our school librarian, escorted the two of us to the headmaster's office, me with tiny flecks of windowpane sparkling in my hair.

As far as I was concerned, that was a victory. Smellwood and I essentially saw ourselves as descendants of the French Taunter from *Monty Python and the Holy Grail*, continually doling out the most ruthless barbs this side of telling someone their mother was a hamster and their father smelt of elderberries. If you could annoy or anger someone enough to want to hit you, then you won the psychological battle.

Winning those battles was important in a household that was in a constant struggle to make ends meet. It was rare to ever see Smellwood eat anything other than cereal and milk, so I knew better than to insinuate myself into family meals whenever Smellwood's mother, affectionately addressed as "Wump" by her kids, brought home a football-sized mound of ground beef and fried it up in a cast iron skillet, firing fragrant mists of steam and tiny droplets of grease into the air. On such a winter's day, this made the kitchen the warmest room in the house, although everyone's down jackets remained zipped.

At the opposite end of the house, maybe forty paces across creaking hardwood floors, was the parlor we had commandeered as the headquarters of Punk Brothers, International. If that sounded official, that was the goal. We were moguls overseeing our own multimedia empire, or at least what felt like one. World domination is, after all, relative to how you define your world, and that house, along with the isolated grounds that surrounded it, was a cosmos unto itself.

And Wump, bless her heart, allowed us to treat the place like our own personal MGM lot.

"The Office," as we referred to it, was a barely navigable minefield of AC/DC and Van Halen albums littering the floor, alongside cheap cassettes containing crudely recorded audio to our favorite scenes from movies like *Billy Jack*, taped off of late-night UHF screenings. Only slightly more organized were the essentials needed to run our "movie division"—taped-up moving boxes and stolen milk crates labeled "wardrobe," containing hats, drugstore sunglasses, and, purchased in bulk at our biannual high school garage sale, about four dozen hideous neckties, previously owned by our math teacher, Mr. Houck. Then there were the used television sets, also acquired at the garage sale for the sole purpose of smashing them with sledgehammers in hopes of hearing the satisfying pop of exploding vacuum tubes. In the far corner of the parlor was the hand-painted refrigerator box that would become our homage to the famous Monty Python "16-ton weight," to be dropped on unsuspecting actors from above.

Smellwood's record player sat on the floor against the wall, and the self-titled debut album by the B-52's was always close by. We had paid for it with 799 pennies at the record store at Concord Mall, after watching Kate Pierson and Cindy Wilson shriek like banshees during "Rock Lobster" and "Dance This Mess Around" on *Saturday Night Live*.

I spent many waking hours on that floor, immersed in the B-52's kitschy universe, as I reviewed the contracts that we had drawn up for classmates we had roped into our own little version of the Screen Actors Guild. Mostly under duress, these kids had signed away their adolescence to us, using their appointed stage handles, which were often their own names spelled backward or simply made up, like Fred Earl Jockstone.

Fred, whose real name was Chris Bowman, lived at the bottom of the hill, a quick slip and tumble down from Smellwood's house. He was that friend who acted as the conduit to a more adult world, or at least the realm of teenage dirtbaggery. He was the guy you went to when you wanted a skin magazine but were afraid to try to buy it yourself. I gave Fred money for copies of *Penthouse, Hustler, Swank, High Society*, all under the pretext that they were for a kid from my neighborhood, who I referred to only as "Mental Ed." Fred had to have known they were for me, but he never called me out. He just played along when I handed him a ten-dollar bill and said, "Mental Ed sends his thanks."

Before he came to Tatnall, around the time we started ninth grade, Fred was bringing girls around from Alexis I. duPont High School, "AI" for short. They smoked cigarettes, went braless in tight white tank tops, and wore Jordache jeans. They had names like Franny, "Kathy the Butt," and Debbiy spelled with an *I and* a *Y*. Debbiy became Smellwood's girlfriend and joined the cast of the movie using the stage name "Smuttiy" (also with an *I* and a *Y*), in effect becoming the Carol Cleveland of our troupe. I was more than happy to be a third wheel any time she was around. I harbored a benign crush as I watched her and Smellwood interact and felt a little betrayed when they once put an aspirin on my tongue while I slept on a couch, snoring unaware as they maneuvered the tiny pill back and forth on my tongue with the tip of a pencil until it dissolved, leaving me with both a literal and figurative bad taste in my mouth.

It was inevitable that when "Jessie's Girl" came out sometime the following year, I would silently relate to the jealousy embedded in the lyrics. The mere possession of that Rick Springfield 45 triggered an onslaught of mockery from Fred, Smellwood, and his twin cousins,

Ken and Wayne, whose own musical inclinations steered them toward regular suggestions that we "blast some Sabbath."

Although I knew I was being picked on with no mercy, their ferocious ribbing actually felt brotherly to me. I bonded with my Fells Lane foster family as we got ourselves into one teenage fix after another—a collection of situations epitomized by what I came to call the "abbondanza incident."

The exact circumstances that led to the excursion were convoluted at best, but a combination of hunger, can-do attitude, and a complete disregard for law or consequence made it sound like a pretty good idea at the time to jump into the back of a rickety wooden cart to ride off in search of pizza.

Smellwood's older sister Wez, the one who green-lighted this harebrained scheme, sat up front holding the reins attached to Honey, her Shetland pony. Ken, Wayne, Smellwood, and I were seated intimately in the back as we took off at parade-route speed, not fully aware that the Christiana Mall food court was seven miles away. It took the better part of two hours to get there, clip-clopping along in the right-hand lanes of increasingly congested roads, some of them highways with actual route numbers. As we moseyed on past the Stanton Middle School, Wayne began screaming at the top of his lungs, "Vote for Nixon," and flashing Tricky Dick victory signs in the direction of confused children on the playground, who were barely twinkles in their parents' loins when Nixon resigned years earlier.

Irritated commuters began to lean on their horns as they maneuvered around us, some rolling down their passenger-side windows to make absolutely sure we heard their obscenities.

"Get outta the fuckin' road!"

We just kept on moving, three and a half steadfast miles an hour.

"What if the cops pull us over?" I asked, turning to Smellwood for reassurance.

"We'll just tell them we're Amish," he said without concern.

Wez was impervious to the car horns and the cursing and just kept her wits about her, with her eyes on the prize. At about four thirty in the afternoon, we pulled up to the mall entrance closest to the movie theater and parked Honey in the fire lane.

"Pepperoni and extra cheese" was the directive given to Wayne as he walked into the mall with our trust and the eleven dollars we had between us. He came back about twenty minutes later with the pizza and a "mission accomplished" look on his face, oblivious to what the rest of us noticed right away had gone wrong. Horribly wrong.

What the hell had he done? Had he walked with this just-out-of-the-oven pepperoni and extra cheese pizza—our only hope for sustenance and the sole reason we'd embarked upon this journey in the first place—past Orange Julius, past Chess King, past KB Toys, past the cinema entrance, out the door, and back to the pony cart, carrying it the entire time under his left arm *like a goddamned book*?

Yes. Yes, he had.

"You idiot!" we all shouted, pretty much in unison, as Wez ripped the box from Wayne's hands and opened the lid to reveal eight soggy slices of crust, congealed clumps of cheese and pepperoni now stuck, like Velcro, to the top of the box, grease bleeding through the cardboard, staining the word "abbondanza." It was a long ride back to Fells Lane.

Almost as a form of retribution, we cajoled Ken and Wayne into signing movie contracts and accepting our draconian terms: vague assurances of payment in the form of minuscule percentages from future box office receipts; total acquiescence to all decisions handed down by "Punk Brothers Arbitrary Court" (Evets Punk presiding);

and, of course, the standard provision that they arrive on time for filming with a dozen doughnuts. This was our version of movie industry craft service for cast and crew.

The doughnut clause, as one might imagine, became a central element of the PBI boilerplate. I would later have to create an addendum to the contract assigned to "Baby Cakes," our classmate Howard Read, forbidding him from purchasing said doughnuts from Mister Donut on Kirkwood Highway because of a prior incident in which the vanilla cream in his particular dozen had been fouled with the taste of cigar ash.

All these supposedly binding agreements, along with a stack of internal memos written on pads of personalized "from the desk of" stationery ordered out of the back of *Creem* magazine, were devised to ensure the completion of *The Punks Are Alright*, the motion picture we were dedicating our lives to throughout the eighth grade.

Already in full production mode, the film was shot with the Chinon Super 8 movie camera and the stack of three-and-a-half-minute film cartridges I got for Christmas just weeks before. The script to *The Punks Are Alright* chronicled the fictional life and times of the Punk Brothers, who start out as Evets and Smellwood Egggbert—yes, with three *g*'s—growing up in Wabash, Indiana.

Our cinematic trials and tribulations were, to put it kindly, *Python-esque*. Some parts didn't even hide behind the "esque," veering into all-out Monty plagiarism, grafting entire scenes from *Life of Brian* into our strange plot about a pair of talentless brothers sowing their rock 'n' roll oats.

We did manage to write in a couple of original comedic characters, my favorite being the "evangelist drug pusher," played by our classmate Tim Guare. Tim was the one who first showed me around Tatnall when I visited the school the year before I enrolled. This kid was capable of rendering discernible melodies by making fart noises with his hands, but we lacked the foresight to capture this talent on film.

Instead, we got a semi-improvised rant, imploring his celluloid congregation to "do drugs," shouting out hard-partying epicenters like New York, LA, and Chicago—"Dancing in the Streets" style—and even name-checking the spliff-loving Coptics in Florida.

Do drugs! Do drugs! We thank you, Lord, for putting drugs on this Earth. Do drugs! Do drugs! We got uppers. We got downers. We got cheap. We got expensive. C'mon do drugs! Do drugs! DO DRUGS!

He delivered this monologue with a method actor's commitment, as convincing as a tearful, repentant Jimmy Swaggart after getting caught with a hooker. Then, when he was finished, he looked directly into the camera and whispered, "Cut." Of course, we left the entire thing in, unedited.

Frames and memories from our bygone burst of teenage creativity come back to me now in grainy Super 8 flashes: Smellwood at the wheel of a stolen car, me riding shotgun, neither of us able to squelch our laughter while feigning terror at an impending collision. Jump cut to a smoldering patch of brush presented as a vehicle fire, one of us stoking the flames with a clearly visible can of WD-40. Swipe to the hospital encounter with visually impaired knights of the Ku Klux Klan, who can't seem to distinguish between third-degree burns and actual skin pigmentation. Flash forward to the long Hitchcock-ian shot in which Fred, Ken, and Wayne lip-sync their way through the entirety of "It's a Gas," a *Mad Magazine* flexi-disc composed of generic funk grooves interrupted every eight bars with the sound of a wet belch. Their complete failure to open their mouths in sync with the sound of the burps drops the performance somewhere between *Saturday Night Fever* and a poorly dubbed kung fu movie.

The final scene of *The Punks Are Alright* depicts the Punk Brothers performing at an outdoor rock concert,[1*] playing homemade plywood guitars with multicolored balloons for strings. We were far from a real band, but we played one in our movie and even smashed our instruments at the end. The Punk Brothers' on-screen drive to form a band and make music mirrored my own still-latent real-life ambitions.

While other kids our age were bored out of their skulls, all dressed down and nowhere to go, we were making the most of our time on the edge of growing up. I was starting to believe that Blondie song I had fallen in love with since I'd watched Clem Burke count it off by smacking his drumsticks against his skull on live TV.

Dreaming *was* free. At least for the time being.

1* I was still only capable of writing parodies to existing songs, so the concert included a fat-shaming country ballad called "Cow of the County," a rewrite of the Kenny Rogers song "Coward of the County," and "Bad Breath Smells," a plea for oral hygiene set to the tune of "Good Girls Don't" by the Knack.

NOSEBLEEDS

I t was November 20-something in 1981. I had just turned fifteen, and I still had a few of the crisp twenties that I'd begged Mom to include with my birthday card that year. She had resisted this idea for ages. In her mind, cash was the most thoughtless gift a person could give, but even she saw little upside to another in a succession of unappreciated sweaters that would sit at the bottom of my dresser drawer, eventually abandoned in a Salvation Army dumpster long before they could be worn ironically at holiday parties in decades to come. Maybe the money represented a tacit admission that she didn't really know what I wanted. Or that she didn't really know me.

I had already spent some of that cash on a bevy of new records, most of which were still wrapped in cellophane because two of them— the just-released *Ghost in the Machine* by the Police and *Beauty and the Beat*, the debut album by the Go-Go's—were all but monopolizing my turntable. I freaked out when I heard the concert announcement on WMMR that both bands were coming to Philadelphia, *together* on the same night, in January. No two ways about it. I had to be there.

I had been to one live show in my life, the year before, when Mom and I stopped over in Hawaii to visit my sister on the way back from our trip to Korea. Tae Im was living in Honolulu, where her husband, Randy, an officer in the navy, was stationed. On Mom's request, Tae Im took us to see Don Ho, somehow convincing the doorman to let me in underage for the early show at the Polynesian Palace. I was thrilled because I had seen Don Ho's cameo on *The Brady Bunch* back when I was five years old, and there I was, at the very venue he mentioned after serenading Bobby and Cindy with a ukulele.

The fact that he had played two shows a night at this place since 1970 became apparent the minute he stumbled onstage, seemingly intoxicated, to play for a sparse mid-week crowd consisting primarily of septuagenarian *haoles*, white tourists from the mainland. I was enthralled by his no-fucks-given showmanship, as he invited gaggles of grannies to abandon their prime rib and mai tais and join him onstage for free kisses and a chance to win some Don Ho Tiny Bubbles, which came in a Don-shaped plastic bottle of dish soap with a bubble blower attached to a screw top head. He instructed one of these ladies to position herself behind him, place her hands inside his front pants pockets, and clap twenty times. I sat wide-eyed, sipping my virgin daiquiri while the old Caucasian ladies roared with ear-splitting laughter. My sister's face was red with embarrassment. Mom's face was expressionless.

"I'm not going with you to see the No-Go's," Smellwood scoffed, seeming to take offense that I would even suggest such blasphemy.

The two of us agreed on a handful of bands, or, more accurately, a handful of records—the jointly owned B-52's album, AC/DC's *Back in Black*, *Give the People What They Want* by the Kinks, and, begrudgingly (on my part anyway), *The Wall* by Pink Floyd, a double album that inspired *The Brawl*, the Punk Brothers' unfinished cinematic Waterloo. The shooting of our second feature film only made it through "Another Death in the Brawl, Part 2" and most, but not all, of Smellwood's title sequence, a stop-frame animation of blood dripping down the front of a brick wall, spelling out the words "The Bra."

The Go-Go's were an all-girl group whose catchy three-minute pop songs with titles like "We Got the Beat" and "Skidmarks on My Heart" were somehow an anathema to my friend.

"Come on," I pleaded. "I'll pay for your ticket. I have birthday money."

Still in resistance mode, Smellwood went on to make a number of salient points. What was my plan to gain possession of these concert tickets? I couldn't just call up Ticketron and order them over the phone. I had no credit card. I had no car, or driver's license for that matter, so how did I expect to transport my sorry ass to an authorized ticket agent and then to the concert itself? And if I wanted "the good seats," I really should have camped out in the arena parking lot so I could be near the front of the line when the box office opened up.

I hated to admit it, but he was making sense. I hadn't quite thought this through.

Even if I got the tickets, how was I going to get to this show? In what conceivable scenario was Mom going to chauffeur me up to the Spectrum, from Delaware, on a school night no less, and sit there with the car idling for three hours just so I could be in the presence of five women in miniskirts and a trio of bottle blond men singing "de do do do de da da," *even if* they were the musicians who were coming to Philadelphia to change my life?

While I genuinely loved the Police, I'd be lying if I said I wasn't a little more interested in their opening act. I knew the Go-Go's were going to be my favorite band before I ever heard a note. Earlier that fall, I was flipping through an issue of *Trouser Press* magazine when an advertisement for *Beauty and the Beat* stopped me in my tracks. The faces of five ebullient women, lined up as if they were peering over the top of an implied shower curtain, sprang from the page, like a quintet of Athenas from the head of Zeus. Each band member projected her own individual girl-next-door charm, as if to say, "We're your new favorite band—whether you like it or not."

That print ad would serve as page one of a comprehensive archive, which ultimately required four massive photo albums to accommodate the wealth of Go-Go's memorabilia I would accrue: magazine interviews, *Billboard* album charts surreptitiously removed from record store displays, album reviews, picture discs, newsletters from GGFCI ("Go-Go's Fan Club International"), and, of course, the stub to the concert ticket I was so desperate to acquire.

A satisfactory solution to my problem was not going to emerge on its own. It was something I would have to orchestrate. It was time to go over Smellwood's head and talk to Wez, who, as it so happened, *did* have a driver's license. Once she was on board, he would come around.

As I had hoped, the bond we had forged against Wayne, our common enemy in the wake of the pizza incident, made Wez more than amenable to driving to the concert in Philly, this time in a motorized vehicle. She even offered to schlep me over to Bag & Baggage to buy the tickets. Strange as it may sound, in addition to being a place to purchase high-end luggage and monogrammed briefcases, Bag & Baggage—or B&B, as it was commonly known—was also an official Ticketron outlet. With an exquisite, new-car-leather smell hanging in the air, I found myself buying my very first concert tickets, barely containing my excitement as a well-dressed man behind the counter unlocked a wooden drawer and pulled out a thin stack held together with a rubber band.

"All I have is nosebleeds," he said in a sort of "you want 'em or not" deadpan.

I didn't know what "nosebleeds" meant, so I just stared at him. After an awkward silence, the man flashed a little smile of acknowledgment, realizing I was a virgin in more ways than the obvious.

"Nosebleeds are upper deck. Four-hundred-level. Not the best seats in the house." That didn't matter one bit to me. I just needed to be in the building.

I put two folded twenty-dollar bills on the counter and held the tickets like I had just been dealt all four aces in the deck.

On the day of the concert, Smellwood and I were waiting outside his house with our friend James Lang from school. James had made a few appearances in our movies and was the only other genuine Go-Go's fan I knew. Wez was late coming back from somewhere, and I was beginning to worry we would miss the start of the show. Then I heard the distant but unmistakable sound of tires on gravel. When she pulled up to the house, two boys got out of the car with her.

"This is Ray and his cousin Terrence. They're coming with us," Wez announced.

I was nonplussed. I mean, who *were* these people? It turned out she had just met them, picked them up at the mall, two random kids from Kiamensi. She must have really liked Ray. He was clearly the older of the two, dirty-blond hair, about Wez's age. He seemed cool enough when he acknowledged us with a quick nod and a "What's up." His cousin seemed a lot younger, and he was way shorter than I was, 4'10" if he was an inch. Terrence broke the ice in a high-pitched prepubescent voice:

"So. What are we drinkin' this evening?"

Smellwood and I looked at each other. This kid was, like, eleven years old at the most.

He continued: "I'm just gonna sit back and drink my Jack."

He reached into his pocket and pulled out a 50 mL bottle of Jack Daniel's, the size they give you on an airplane. He downed about half of it and let out a very satisfied "ahhhh" before putting the bottle away. He didn't offer a drop to anyone else, which spared me an awkward "No, thank you," which, in my mind, would definitely have led to *"What are you, some kind of pussy?"* and gone downhill from there.

By the time we drove past the Philadelphia airport, the six of us crammed into a '75 Astre Safari Wagon, Terrence was the drunkest fifth grader I had ever seen. Wez had the radio tuned in to WMMR's "Police concert preview," which was just a solid block of the band's radio hits, one after the other. Toward the end of "Every Little Thing She Does Is Magic," in the part where Sting chants "Ee-yo-oh, ee-yo-oh," Terrence was screaming from his spot in the rear cargo area: "Ee-asssshole, ee-asssshole, aaasssssss-hole, aaassssssss-hole, aaaaaaas-ssss-hole." I can't hear that song now without thinking of Terrence.

Once we got to the Spectrum, Smellwood and I got nervous, both of us having ignored the part on the ticket that said, "No cameras or recorders," and neither of us realizing until it was too late that we were about to receive a pat-down from a burly security guard. While I was able to sneak by with a Panasonic microcassette recorder stuffed into a mitten in my coat pocket, Smellwood had, on his person, a 35mm camera, several rolls of film, and a large telephoto lens taped to his back underneath his jacket. It had to have looked so obvious.

"What's this?" the security guy asked.

"It's a lens," Smellwood replied, pretty sure at this point that he was cooked.

"It's not a bottle?"

"No, it's a lens."

The guard waved him through. It was a miracle. We were *in*!

Terrence and Ray had gone off in search of scalped tickets, and we never did run into them again. I like to think maybe Wez decided to ditch them for the ride home, which, even in their absence, would turn out to be its own strange misadventure, as we drove in the wrong direction up Broad Street, reaching the Badlands of North Philly behind a car we just assumed was going our way, based only on its Delaware plates and a Black Sabbath bumper sticker.

Inside the arena, it was a sensory overload of exuberant voices and never-ending streams of people. From my seat near the roof of the Spectrum, I watched

I NOW KNEW WHAT EIGHTEEN THOUSAND PEOPLE SOUNDED LIKE CHEERING, CLAPPING, SINGING ALONG. IT WAS A BEAUTIFUL REVERIE. I HAD A BIRD'S-EYE VIEW OF WHERE I WANTED TO BE. I FELT LIGHT HEADED, TRANSFORMED, INHALING THE RAREFIED AIR UP IN THE NOSEBLEEDS.

the Go-Go's bound onto the stage, distant figures with teased hair and toothy smiles that beamed all the way up to the rafters. They played all eleven songs from *Beauty and the Beat* and a few I didn't know, including a new one called "Vacation." My Panasonic, recording from inside my pocket, picked up little more than garbled white noise and James Lang screaming the words to "Our Lips Are Sealed" and "This Town."

After the Go-Go's, the Police appeared to the sound of their own recording of "Voices Inside My Head." "Message in a Bottle," played at warp speed, set a hyperkinetic tone for the whole set. I don't think I actually sat in my ten-dollar seat once throughout the entire night. I now knew what eighteen thousand people sounded like cheering, clapping, singing along. It was a beautiful reverie. I had a bird's-eye view of where I wanted to be. I felt light headed, transformed, inhaling the rarefied air up in the nosebleeds.

SUBURBAN LIZARDS

"**D**ude, you're playing it wrong. It goes to C, not A," Mike Neiger said to Phil, not quite comprehending how any bass player worth their salt could mess up the intro to "I Will Follow," the U2 song that Neiger and I had obsessed over since the dawn of MTV. All eyes were on Phil, a stringy-haired blond kid with doughy arms drooping from a studded denim vest, which had the largest Judas Priest iron-on available from Spencer's Gifts grafted onto the back. I knew the audition was close to over when he cocked the pointy headstock of his black Ibanez 4-string into the air—a total phallic power move—to prevent Neiger from continuing to pound his thumb into the fretboard of the instrument to demonstrate the correct bass line.

"It's E to C, *then* E to A," Neiger reiterated.

With a quizzical expression, which then morphed into a dark shade of sheer disdain, Phil finally blurted out what he had been holding back for the last twenty minutes: "Pssssh. You don't need to *know no notes* to play rock 'n' roll!"

However many times this statement eventually proved to be true, Phil's proclamation irked the shit out of Neiger, the guitar player and lead singer in the not-quite-a-band we'd dubbed the Suburban Lizards. Based almost entirely on our mutual admiration for the most recent album by Men at Work, Neiger and I decided that the two of us had a sufficient area of intersection in our musical Venn diagram to form a creative alliance. The chance to transition from the rock band I had fantasized I was in with the Punk Brothers to playing real songs with real instruments compelled me to whitewash certain recollections from freshman year, when Neiger chanted "John Faye, Genghis Kahn of the USA!" on a few occasions when he passed me in the hall. Besides, Genghis Khan was a pretty powerful dude.

It was apparent to everyone in the room that Phil would not be the person to bring the much-needed bottom end to our incomplete lineup in time for the Tatnall Halloween dance, which was little more than a month away. Somebody—possibly our aptly named lead guitarist Danny Leeds—took a cue from the Judas Priest iron-on and started playing a song that Phil appeared to know from memory: "You've Got Another Thing Comin'." For the uninitiated, "You've Got Another Thing Comin'" is an early-'80s hard rock staple that most metal fans would grant the designation "classic Priest." The bass part begins on an F# and, with negligible deviation, stands its ground for what feels like 99 percent of the song. Phil may have had no use for As or Cs or Es, but the kid could rock that second fret on the big string like nobody's business. At the time, I didn't know what any of those notes were called either. I still judged him, though. Ignorance was not supposed to be a badge of honor.

I joined in on my drum kit partway through the song, playing as ham-fisted and apelike as I could. The sarcasm oozed off every exaggerated snare hit and the washy clang of my open hi-hats. Some unjustified sense of musical superiority left me completely unwilling to appreciate the song's fist-pumping allure. Over time I came to enjoy the steadfast commitment to harmonic tension of that unflinching F#, but in this moment, amid a maelstrom of distortion and cymbal bashing, Neiger and I exchanged glances of concern that begged the question, "Who the hell are we going to get to play bass?"

That distinction would go to Dave Racca, or "Mr. Racca," as we called him in algebra class. The newest member of the Tatnall faculty, Mr. Racca was so fresh out of grad school that he was barely a decade older than the rest of us. I don't know what possessed him, but he agreed to learn as many of our songs as possible for the upcoming October shindig at school, at which Neiger somehow talked the powers that be into letting us play. It would be the first public performance for all of us—except for Mr. Racca, who was a sage veteran in our eyes, having already played live in actual bars with his own band in college. Neiger even took to calling him "God Racca."

We spent all afternoon on the last Sunday in September in the cramped band room we had fashioned in a sealed-off portion of Neiger's basement. With the hollow wood-panel door providing a mostly symbolic sound barrier between us and the rest of the house, we flailed away at will, bringing Mr. Racca up to speed on the U2 song, along with "Twist and Shout" by the Beatles, "Cortez the Killer" by Neil Young, and my favorite cover, "So Lonely" by the Police.

Their drummer, Stewart Copeland, played a TAMA kit, too, and was pretty much the only reason I even wanted that brand of drums for myself. I did everything I could to emulate him, however poorly, mimicking his rapid-fire cross-stick patterns and his distinctive accents on the bell of the ride cymbal. I even tried using traditional grip, which Copeland used, along with drummers who played jazz or played in military marching bands. I kept up this facade of musical sophistication until one particularly miscalculated thwack on the snare drum blackened my knuckles and put an end to that affectation.

The silver TAMA Imperialstar, which I assured Mom would make future birthday and Christmas gifts unnecessary for the remainder of my natural life, formed an ostentatious fortress around me, with its oversized bass drum and two floor toms. Jesus Christ, who needs *two* floor toms? To supplement what was already more than necessary, in the tight space just above the hi-hat and just below the crash cymbal, was a trio of spanking-new, poorly tuned rototoms. If you don't know them by name, you probably know them by how they sound. Rototoms are higher-pitched drums that made their primary cultural mark in the Pink Floyd song "Time" and were a cheaper facsimile of the octobans that Stewart Copeland played on quintessential Police songs like "Driven to Tears."

For his part, Neiger was ecstatic because now we had no excuse not to play "Tom Sawyer," the Rush song that was practically required learning for every teenage rock band in the '80s. I looked ridiculous consistently flubbing Neil Peart's iconic never-ending drum fills, while Neiger outshined me with the guitar solo he had studied like it was a sacred text. It's a song I never once got completely right, but it's still my go-to in the forgiving world of rock 'n' roll air-drumming, where everyone with an imaginary pair of Regal Tip 5As is a virtuoso. Fueled by the failure to properly learn my rudiments, my opinion of Rush was no secret within our group, and I loved annoying Neiger by quoting a review that said something like "Lead singer Geddy Lee's voice is about as appealing as a smoke alarm at 3:00 am."

With only a few minutes left before the dinnertime "noise curfew," we plowed through our Halloween set and began showing Mr. Racca the changes to "Giving at the Office," an original song with overt references to sexual misconduct in the workplace. Neiger and Danny played chord inversions that they had no doubt picked up from repeated listenings of *2112* or some other Rush record I had no patience for, while I pounded out a Ringo-inspired beat that was lifted from "Ticket to Ride." We didn't get much further before Neiger's mother knocked on the door and said, "Time's up!" I felt like I heard a dash of glee in her voice that may or may not have been real, as I was prone to resenting any infringement on our rehearsal time, all too willing to ignore the fact that I was in someone else's house.

I guess it would have been pretty predictable how I reacted to the unsolicited advice shouted from the living room upstairs as we were wiping our brows with the bottoms of our soggy T-shirts: "You should write something like 'Total Eclipse of the Heart.' *That's* a great song!" This comment went straight to our creative jugular. If you listened carefully, you could hear the internal bleeding commence inside our necks.

Neiger rolled his eyes, indicating to the rest of us that he was used to such feedback. As for me, I was a dedicated detractor of that Bonnie Tyler song *and* of Jim Steinman, the guy who wrote it.

Steinman was also the songwriting architect behind Meat Loaf's *Bat Out of Hell* album, which I detested even more. I would say outwardly that the source of my hatred toward Mr. Steinman and Mr. Loaf was my intense aversion to their unapologetic grandiosity, but it was more likely rooted in the fact that I was cocksure that I would *never* see "paradise by the dashboard light." I might *possibly* see some full '70s bush by the flickering fluorescent light while sneaking peeks at the two crumpled porno mags we had stashed inside the drop ceiling just a few feet above floor tom number one, but that was a far cry from paradise.

With my future as a teenage incel cemented in my mind, we forged our earliest musical collaborations on a hairpin learning curve, doing everything by trial and error. "Bag Lady" was an attempt at a minor-key character sketch of a homeless woman in Chicago. The two verses and the refrain, "Bag Lady, goodbye," were culled from about three dozen examples of my first non-parody song lyrics, which were collected in a binder from the 5&10 with the title *BORBO-RYGMI* printed in dot matrix caps on the cover. "Borborygmi," a word I gleaned from a George Carlin record, is the technical and onomatopoeic term for the gurgling sounds created by the movement of intestinal gas. While I can only suspect that I thought this was a clever way of saying I was writing from my gut, the lyrics pontificated on subjects I knew little or nothing about.

I was a sixteen-year-old kid who had never gone to bed hungry, had never been to the Windy City, had never actually seen a street person. Yet there I was, thinking I could tackle the plight of the homeless with gravitas, all because I had been through some other shit that I was not yet able or willing to write about *and* because I thought my part-time job as a paper-hat-wearing Taco Bell grunt had somehow provided me with a worldview.[2*]

That day of the first practice with Mr. Racca, Neiger started powering down amplifiers and airing out the room. The opened door seemed to pop like a champagne cork, dispersing the musk of rock from three teenage boys, along with a hint of a grown man's after-

---

[2*] Aside from the Eastern European accent my manager used on drive-through customers to entertain himself ("Velcome to Taco Bell!"), about the only practical knowledge I gleaned from my twelve-hour-a-week run to the border that summer was a curious piece of classified information about what we referred to as "the drippings." The residual taco grease, the color of the red-orange flame on the classic Les Paul I had so often visually conjured in my tennis racquet, was drained by the bucket on a daily basis from steaming mounds of low-grade ground beef. I would pour the liquid fat over top of layers that had already solidified in a fifty-five-gallon drum next to the dumpsters out back. I asked my manager, "What do they do with this stuff?" He gestured with his eyes in the direction of two teenage girls staring into compact mirrors, meticulously reapplying bright red lipstick after having put away a couple of Burrito Supremes. "Avon, motherfucker," he said.

shave. I heard the *Action News* theme song coming from the speaker of a glowing television set on the other side of the basement. Neiger's grandmother was seated on one end of the couch. Although there was plenty of room for me to sit, I stood back where she couldn't see me.

I had gotten into a little spat with her a few weeks before, when I opined that Wayne Newton's performance on the Jerry Lewis Telethon was one of the worst things I had ever heard. He was doing a cover version of "Elvira" by the Oak Ridge Boys and butchering what I felt was the coolest part of the song, the break in which bass vocalist Richard Sterban sings, "Giddy up oom poppa oom poppa mow mow." She snapped at me, as if criticizing Wayne Newton was a sacrilegious act: "*You* couldn't do it any better," she countered. Puffing out the broad chest that Papa had passed down to me, I summoned the lowest frequencies I could muster and sang the line back at her. She *knew* I nailed it but acknowledged nothing, refusing to give me the satisfaction.

The lead story on the six-o'clock news that night was that the station's weatherman, Jim O'Brien, had died in a skydiving accident earlier that afternoon. My heart raced and my breathing grew short as I watched his misty-eyed colleagues mourn in real time. Jim O'Brien was a beloved personality in the part of the world where I grew up, but why was I taking it so hard? Even as Papa's death was fading into the far reaches of my psyche, I could still be snapped right back to 1973, feeling tectonic shifts all around me upon hearing of the unexpected passing of anyone I had the slightest connection to, even if it was the local TV weatherman.

I felt the same way about my classmate from school, Marc, who had taken his own life, at seventeen, in March of that year. I often thought of the Steve Martin jokes he'd told on the bus ride for our seventh-grade field trip to Colonial Williamsburg, and the photo

I'd snapped on that same trip as he was striking the King Tut pose he wouldn't live to see the Bangles repopularize with "Walk Like an Egyptian." I even thought about his snacking habits, which I found fascinating because he often ate raw green peppers from a plastic baggie. I smiled when recalling his complete sense of impropriety, which compelled him to fart into the microphone I had hooked up to the Super 8 projector to reinforce the vocals from the final concert scene of *The Punks Are Alright* at the screening we held at Smellwood's house. I wanted to remember him in detail, in much the same way I wanted to remember what I could of Papa, in part because I wished so badly that someone, anyone, would remember me and the quirks of mine that they found curious or charming after I was gone.

On the night of the Halloween dance, the four of us—"John Iguana," "Mike Chameleon," "Dan Gecko," and Mr. Racca, who refused to take a reptilian pseudonym—congregated at the side of the stage. Neiger was a ghoulish front man in powdery whiteface, fingerless gloves, and a tattered black cape. In lieu of a full-on costume, I'd donned a headband fashioned from the cutoff sleeve of a leopard print T-shirt. It was, to me, both functional and fashionable, designed to keep the sweat out of my eyes and make my hair stand up like a cluster of asparagus.

My vantage point from high atop the wobbly wooden riser brought with it a sense of confidence I had never known. During a brief soundcheck, all four of my limbs thumped and flailed, semi-independently, to create the loudest sound I'd ever heard. All the guitars combined, with amps turned up as loud as they would go, could not match the thunder coming off those drums. As I swiveled on my throne, waiting to start the show, I felt a genuine connection with the world. The sea of people gathering in front of the stage was about to experience a real rock 'n' roll band.

An enthusiastic DJ with a pronounced lisp introduced us from his booth on the opposite side of the gymnasium: "Pleathe welcome … the Thuburban Lithardth!" We were off and running. Neiger launched into "I Will Follow." I followed, pounding on the mounted toms before settling into the song's New Wave–y groove. Mr. Racca hit all the notes that metalhead Phil had flubbed. We nailed the dead-stop ending as tight as U2 themselves, or at least it felt that way, and the audience erupted with the same over-the-top enthusiasm that I now know high school kids are capable of conjuring in almost any situation, whether they're making a few classmates and their math teacher feel like rock stars or jumping up and down on the side of the road, shaking signs for a carwash fundraiser to lure passing motorists.

Taking the hysteria at face value, I clicked my sticks to count off "Twist and Shout," barely allowing for a second of dead air. We tore through the song, and I marveled at the positive vibes I felt radiating from the audience. *They love us!* I thought, as they all sang along off-key with the "ahhhhs" in the song's closing crescendo. The response grew even more frenzied, and I'm fairly certain was the opening salvo on my long road to hearing loss. If that show had ended after six minutes, we all would have gone home feeling like John, Paul, George, and Ringo, holding on tight to memories of our classmates screaming for us at ear-splitting volume.

The show did not end there.

One lesson I've had to learn many times over is that the rock 'n' roll gods with one hand giveth, and with the other, they taketh away. It was as if they needed us to taste both the sweet and the sour, and faster than Neiger could say, "We wrote this one," the jury of our peers dispersed as if the cops had just arrived to break up a house party, leaving the unfamiliar chord progression of our first original song to fall like a tree in the forest. Did we even make a sound? By the time the song ended, to the golf-clap applause of three adult chaperones and the lisping DJ, we were facing a complete reversal of fortune. Mr. Racca surely knew from experience that this is just what happens in situations like this, and Danny was so laid back that he didn't much care who was listening. He was just having fun playing his Fender Telecaster.

Neiger and I took it personally as we watched our expectations crumble under the weight of reality. We had built this up as *our* big night. Each musical nuance and clever turn of phrase we had so meticulously crafted would be acknowledged and appreciated. Everyone else seemed to understand implicitly that we were the basement band that had been thrown a bone by the administration. We were the free entertainment, providing a sonic backdrop while the other kids socialized and ate Pop Rocks, some washing them down with Coca-Cola to debunk the myth that this is what killed Mikey from the Life cereal commercials.

He likes it! Hey, Mikey!

I signaled to Mikey Neiger to approach the drum kit. "We're sucking," I whispered emphatically.

"Thanks for the encouragement," he whispered emphatically back.

I'm not sure why we whispered; we were really in no danger of being overheard.

There was no one within forty feet of us. I've come to see this moment as pivotal. It would have been so easy just to give up. To his credit, Neiger turned back around to face an empty gymnasium, and some sense of resolve in all of us kicked in as we threw ourselves back into the set, and I set off on an enduring quest to return to the bliss of those first six minutes.

NO APPLAUSE

su·pine
/'soo,pīn/
adjective
—lying flat on one's back
—failing to act or protest as a result of moral weakness or indolence

Before I hit puberty, my taste in music was defined by K-tel International, a hand-me-down collection of bubblegum 45s, and a few albums by sensitive singer-songwriters dressed in faded denim. *After* my balls dropped, I began making musical choices driven by what medical professionals refer to as "a raging boner." Let's be honest: Was my purchase of *Head Games* by Foreigner driven by its men's room album cover scene depicting a miniskirt-clad girl, her ass perched on the edge of a urinal as she scrubs graffiti off the wall with a swath of toilet paper? Or did I think "Dirty White Boy" was *just that good?*

I bought *Candy-O* by the Cars and the Knack's debut album, *Get the Knack*, on the same day in 1979, as I stood on the precipice of becoming a teenager. Listening almost exclusively through headphones in a supine position on the floor, I often stared at the Cars' album cover—a painting of a fiery redhead in high heels lying on the hood of a Ferrari—while I played the Knack album with its not-so-subtle references to dirty minds, getting it up, and face sitting.

I came for "My Sharona" and "Good Girls Don't," but I stayed for a song called "Siamese Twins (The Monkey and Me)." While the Knack was more than adept at conveying the hormonal urgency of teenhood, this song delivered a different kind of titillation, the thrill of saying exactly what's on your mind, telling the world how you *really* feel. The lyrics are from the point of view of a conjoined twin who wants to off his brother, wishing upon stars for the demise of his other half. I saw a clear correlation to the Korean Irish duality within me, the strange bedfellows grafted together, the yin wanting to overthrow the yang. At the time, I exalted my Irish side. I wanted to feel and be seen as more "white" because I felt like my Korean blood had given me nothing but grief. I wanted so badly to remake who I was, cast myself in a different light.

In the subterranean world of my high school years, the portal to that reinvention was punk rock. Around the same time that Mike Neiger and I were in the basement at his parents' house, writing the songs that went over like a fart in church at the Suburban Lizards debacle, I was spending just as much time getting an education in anarchy at Keith Green's house, downstairs in his finished basement, which was carpeted in a welcoming wall-to-wall plaid.

Keith was the Methodist son of a Baptist father and a Jewish mother, which, in my estimation, made him as close to "mixed" as one was going to find in Bridleshire, his upper-middle-class neighborhood in Hockessin, Delaware. There was a cartoon on Keith's refrigerator door that his dad had drawn. The caption read: "Everyone is someone else's weirdo." That was some fortune-cookie-level profundity as far as I was concerned.

I first began hanging around at Keith's back in the ninth grade, when the Punk Brothers filmed a scene at his house. His sister shouted, "Mom thinks you're having an orgy!" from the second-floor landing as we struggled to capture some dialogue between Smellwood and Smuttiy in the dimly lit attic. It was a reflection on the generosity of Keith's parents that they even permitted his continued association with me, as the first time I brought him up for filming at Fell's Lane, an errant BB gun pellet to the gut landed him in the hospital.

I spent as much time as I could at Green's, trying to find any excuse to bang on the Blue Sparkle Andy K drum kit that I eventually bought for forty dollars. I never missed an opportunity to suggest taking the twelve steps down to the rec room for an impromptu session of noisemaking. I bashed those drums during a brief stint in a punk trio called Special Olympics, the brainchild of our band leader Steve Hentkowski, whose brother had dated Keith's sister. Keith and I played what you might call *subservient* roles as the group's rhythm section, my drums and his bass providing the chaotic foundation for Steve's hyperdistorted guitar stylings. Hentkowski was a couple of years our senior, old enough to have formed some strong opinions, which I often found hilarious. I was more than happy to engage in the merciless thrashing behind his forty-five-second diatribes against rednecks, Santa Claus, meter maids, and Girl Scouts, whom he referred to collectively as "the green horde." Perhaps for the best, Special Olympics never ventured above ground from the world below. The world wasn't ready, and neither were we.

Keith had other things on his plate and on his mind. Grades were important to him. He was a wiz at all things math and science, and he was book smart and tech savvy at a time when it was a big deal that our school had just purchased its first student computer. The single desktop was housed in a study room adjacent to the library, and the few other kids who could navigate the computer beyond the on-off button used it primarily to program its voice utility to repeat "Mrs. Murphy sucks" in a robotic monotone.

I, on the other hand, was passing Mrs. Chady's chemistry class by the skin of my teeth, or more accurately, by the skin of my left arm, which could store a surprising number of abbreviations from the periodic table of elements if I used a Pilot Razor Point pen. The only notable hint of scientific interest within me was my decision to store an uncooked yam on the rear deck of my Mustang, to document its petrification and transition to a shriveled, caramelized lump over the course of several months.

That experiment ended abruptly when Steve Palmer, who had appeared in *The Punks Are Alright* under the stage name John Passwater, declared one afternoon that enough was enough and shoved me aside as I was unlocking my car, reaching his lanky arm into the back and confiscating the yam. He held it high above his head and out of my reach, hoisting it in the air like the Olympic torch, as he jogged in faux-slow-motion across the blacktop and tossed it onto the roof of the school.

I had a far better time of it with my English classes. I found strange comfort in relatable outcasts, misanthropes, and otherwise bizarre humans every time I turned a page in books like *Cat's Cradle* by Kurt Vonnegut Jr. I reveled in oddball characters like Lyman Enders Knowles, the elevator operator in chapter 28, who grabs his own ass and shouts "Yes, yes!" every time he makes a point. I recognized complicated little pieces of myself in *Everything That Rises Must Converge*, *A Raisin in the Sun*, and *The Catcher in the Rye*.

American lit was held in a remote hallway, far from most of the other scholastic activity, and it felt like a refuge. I arrived early one day to enjoy the seclusion in Mrs. Gallagher's room for a few minutes after lunch, sitting at my usual desk in the back row. I was a few seats from Stacey, a girl who sometimes rode the same bus as I did. We were the only two people in the room, just keeping to ourselves, when Ricky White walked in and took a seat in the row in front of us. Ricky was what you might call "high school famous," as he had allegedly once hot-wired someone's car in the student parking lot and took it for a joyride in the middle of the day. It was widely noted that this was the only time such a thing had occurred in the fifty-plus years since the school's inception.

Ricky peeled down the cellophane wrapper on a Sunbeam honeybun, then turned toward the back wall and proceeded to go downtown on it in the single most erotic display of food consumption I had ever seen. Or heard. He licked the frosting with the tip of his tongue and smacked his lips with every bite, before pausing with a bolus of chewed-up dough in his mouth.

"You know," he said as he swallowed, "I could go for a nice big fat juicy *cunt* right about now. Whatdya say, Stacey? *Man*, I would split you in two."

He let that hang in the air for a second and then turned back around, saying nothing more, almost as if he was already over this fleeting little thought that he felt the need to share. I was speechless.

Stacey was speechless. Ricky went back to his honeybun. In a way, I could imagine how Stacey might have felt. Things had been said to me in my life that called for a response but left me impotent in my silence. I should have said something, called out the disrespect. But another part of me felt a misguided envy, not for what he said but how he said it. He was able to just say what was on his mind—didn't care how offensive or out of line it was. I couldn't do that. All I could manage to do was sit there, expressionless and incapacitated, supine in the face of what had just transpired.

That kind of passivity made me a master of the poker face. I played my angst close to the vest, my internal workings invisible to the casual observer. But I needed an outlet for the pressures I carried with me, the expectations, external or self-imposed, the shortcomings, real or perceived. I was looking for something or someone to give voice to what I struggled to articulate. Thank God for Henry Rollins.

Sometime in 1984, on an MTV alternative music show called *The Cutting Edge*, Henry Rollins, the lead singer of Black Flag, appeared in close-up wearing a dark sleeveless T-shirt and delivering a spoken-word piece called "Family Man." Here was this intense, long-haired punk with the thickest neck I had ever seen on a human being, speaking directly into the camera with a stare that could give Charles Manson chills.

His description of crucifying a tainted "Saint Dad," a man who takes no chances, a man concerned with being first on the block to put up his Christmas lights, was so blunt, so twisted, so strangely exhilarating, it gave me goose bumps. To a kid who kept it all inside, especially my feelings about being fatherless and my anger over being denied a proper goodbye, "Family Man" had a free-flowing honesty I desperately wanted for myself.

While I had already formed some pretty vacant associations around what I thought punk rock was, I wanted more of the kind of over-the-top vitriol that I got from that one spoken-word clip. Within days of seeing Henry Rollins on MTV, Keith and I were lying on the floor in his basement staring up at the ceiling while we immersed ourselves in Black Flag, the Meatmen, MDC (which stood for Millions of Dead Cops), and *Not So Quiet on the Western Front*, a forty-seven-song double album compilation of early '80s hardcore, brimming with rapid-fire blasts of apocalyptic noise. We laughed after a momentary lapse into confusion when we first put on *World Full of Hate* by the Fartz (with a *z*). The music sounded really slow for a hardcore record. It wasn't until I read the fine print on the label that I discovered that although it was a twelve-inch album, it was mastered to be played at 45 rpm. Once the switch got flipped, this stuff was faster than fast, and I loved it. I *needed* it.

The track titles alone made these newly acquired records essential listening: "Salt on a Slug," "Mr. Tapeworm," "Orgy of One," "John Wayne Was a Nazi," "Corporate Death Burger." I laughed my ass off listening to "Reagum," a song about Ronald Reagan picking his nose and eating it. Then there was "The Oven Is My Friend," a psychedelic anomaly by Church Police about a guy who puts his tongue on the element inside a 480-degree oven. As one might well imagine, this music provided hours of adolescent entertainment, but the one needle in this nihilistic musical haystack that summed up everything I wanted to take away from punk rock was a spoken audience interaction on a track by Naked Lady Wrestlers:

> *You know, I heard a little bit of applause. NO applause! Save it for some band who needs it. Save it for some band who's wondering whether or not people like 'em … Because we know*

*we present the QUALITY music and we don't give a shit WHO
the fuck likes it … doesn't like it …
It's just that … All of you people are going to hear the music
that I DEEM NECESSARY … for the next … oh, however
long I fuckin' feel like it!*

Keith ran cross-country at Tatnall. He was captain of the team
and won MVP our senior year. Coincidentally, this was the same
season the football team won just a single game out of the ten they
played. That team was coached by our gym teacher of many years, a
high-strung man who may as well have been the inspiration for Mr.
Buzzcut on *Beavis and Butthead*. I remember him taunting a wiry-
haired Jewish kid during a sadistic game of dodgeball back when we
were in eighth grade:

"Sloan! Your hair looks like a Brillo!"

When Keith stood at the podium during the sports awards
assembly to accept his personal and team accolades, he tore a page
from the punk rock playbook and addressed the 1–9 elephant in the
room.

"You know … I heard a little bit of applause. NO applause! Save
it for the team who needs it."

The coach cornered him after the ceremony.

"Think you're pretty funny, doncha?" Pffft. *DUH.*

The punk album that we listened to the most, in the twilight of
our innocence, was *Fresh Fruit for Rotting Vegetables* by Dead Kennedys.
I really grew to love the song "When Ya Get Drafted," which became
my daily morning pick-me-up once I received the government-issued
postcard, sent to every seventeen-year-old boy in America, instructing
me to register with selective service before I turned eighteen.

It's quick, it's easy, and it's the law.

Keith and I went down to the Newark post office together and gave the US government all the information it needed to send us off to die for our country. We celebrated with a couple of "draft" root beers before heading back down to the basement to bash on our instruments and blow out our eardrums, as we stood on the verge of our new lives as college students and—ready or not—young men.

THE MONEY NOTE

NO EXCUSE

I had every reason to feel good. I was finally out there playing music. For our freshly christened band—No Excuse—in the fall of 1984, *out there* meant anywhere in New Castle County that would have us. Initially, at least, the only place that said yes was the Barn Door. Often referred to as the "Darn Bore" by detractors and true believers alike, this tiny club on Tatnall Street in Wilmington served as a rite of passage for pretty much every fledgling act for whom the First State was ground zero.

Intimate to a fault, the stage was nothing more than an elevated landing occupied by day with two or three tables for a business lunch crowd, the crowd that subsidized the bar's nocturnal transformation into a proving ground for young rock bands playing their first bar gigs.

Mike Neiger, Keith Green, and our new lead guitarist, Mike Simpson, were almost literally rubbing elbows onstage. Audience members had to walk *through* the band to get to the bathroom. This happened several times during our first show. Neiger had to repeatedly lift the neck of his Ibanez electric midsong, like a gate at a toll booth, to let the full-bladdered or intensely nauseated pass under the single, interrogation-style lightbulb that illuminated the bathroom hallway. My hi-hat stand was shoved aside by more than a couple of stumbling drunks, whose collective olfactory backdraft wafted onstage with each entrance and exit.

At the end of the night, we waited to receive the pittance that I would be embarrassed to even mention out loud to Mom. She would surely retell her stories about my uncle, who had such a great voice that he could have been a legitimate opera singer. *Even he*, with all his natural ability, knew the economic pitfalls of trying to make a career in music. His passion was reduced to a hobby, and he became a government bureaucrat. I had heard him sing in Korea when I was there and was struck by his 80-proof rendition of "O Sole Mio." It was the bittersweet sound of an inebriated man whose dreams of becoming the Korean Enrico Caruso had been vanquished.

Sobering thoughts to be sure, but I didn't dwell on them. The first time you get paid for doing something you love is pretty great, regardless of the amount. I was excited when Art Callahan called the band over to collect the cash that was rolled up and getting soggy in the palm of his hand.

Practically revered in the musical bubble we were looking to infiltrate, Art had a reputation as a Hilly Kristal–type figure, a club owner fighting the good fight at a venue considered by many to be Delaware's own incarnation of CBGB. A heavy-set teddy bear in an unassuming polo shirt and glasses, practically immovable from his perch atop a painted-green milk can at the end of the bar, Art had seen enough bands pop their first-gig cherries at his club to feel quite comfortable speaking his mind, and, so, he did.

"Listen, fellas. You seem like nice kids, you brought in a decent crowd, but I have to say this: Don't you ever play 'Help!' in my bar again unless you intend to go for the high notes."

Landing somewhere between practical advice and a physical threat, the comment stung because I knew exactly what he was talking about. I felt it the instant it happened. With the probable exception of Mom, every person in that bar knew what that Beatles classic was supposed to sound like. The backing vocals propel the word "help" with ascending insistence, each repetition higher than the last, culminating in a final urgent plea, sung in a soaring falsetto that I had imitated countless times before in my bedroom. It was my job to hit that high note, the note that everyone was expecting, the *money note*.

During the performance, I sang the parts exactly as they were written all the way up to the point when my voice felt like it might crack in my upper register, and in that moment, instead of going for it, I caved and shifted a full octave lower, as if Barry White had suddenly taken control of my vocal cords. It was an egregious musical anticlimax.

For days after the show, mental replays of my *vocal interruptus* left an unwelcome stain on the afterglow of having completed my public debut with No Excuse. Art Callahan left me feeling as if I had defiled something sacred. I wouldn't return to the Barn Door for more than a decade, partly out of embarrassment, but I was grateful he'd said what he said. He was right. If I really wasn't prepared to go for the high notes, literally and metaphorically, why even bother? Almost overnight, it wasn't enough for me to just be out there playing music. I needed to be great, or die trying.

ONE TRUE LINE

As a late teen trying to figure out how to make a life for myself in rock 'n' roll, I had a long, long way to go in every regard, especially with songwriting. I was relying on my bandmates in No Excuse to transcribe and make musical sense of my ideas, most of which persisted in skirting around the edges of what was really going on inside me. I was busy trying to be clever like Elvis Costello, whose "angry young man" persona I very much related to. What I didn't quite get back then was that he wrote from both the head *and* the heart. For every witty turn of phrase, there was something deeper at stake. He *knew* this world was killing you. I was trying as hard as I could *not* to know, blurring my emotional lines at every opportunity. I was more concerned with what Elvis would call "verbal gymnastics," somehow unable to write that *one true line*. The closest I got to that lofty goal was a couplet from a song called "Obscurity," which was otherwise considered B-list material for the band.

> *I never go to parties 'cuz where would I end up*
> *In the kitchen drinking root beer from a Dixie cup*

Of course, that was based on the presumption that there would be invitations to parties in the first place, which there were not. That was fine by me. People not "getting" me or my songs afforded me the luxury of feeling misunderstood. I remember Keith sitting down with his mother, trying to explain why so many of my lyrics, with titles like "Script Tease," "Life in the Express Lane," and "Theatre Absurd"

(British spelling, of course), were not really trying to be *universal*. He went to the wall for me, defending the cryptic references, the bad puns, the *concepts* of the No Excuse canon.

Dark Side of the Moon had nothing on "Surf and Turf," our "Wipe Out"–inspired antianthem about a guy who wants to ride some waves but also suffers from a combination of laziness and aquaphobia. To avoid the ocean altogether, he just mimes a bunch of surfer-dude moves on dry land.

> *Surf and turf—Don't need a towel*
> *Surf and turf—Like fish and fowl*
> *Surf and turf—The tide's always low*
> *Surf and turf—Let's go go go!*

Somewhere in those lyrics, there's a fitting metaphor for where my head was at. I wanted all the excitement of the big waves, but I wasn't even prepared to get my feet wet. Maybe the songs knew me better than I did.

Keith's mom, who was a huge Beatles and early rock 'n' roll fan, gave him a look like, "You poor bastard," all but pitying her son for playing in a band that required an instruction manual to appreciate. It was like watching my friend trying to explain why my private joke was funny. I don't know if I felt worse for him or for me.

OUT FRONT

As No Excuse played more shows in late 1984 and into 1985, I began to notice something about my voice, a payoff for all those teenage hours spent with my tennis racquet in front of the stereo speakers in my bedroom. Belting out songs with big choruses like "Surrender" by Cheap Trick and "Death or Glory" by the Clash, while faking guitar chords I had yet to master, helped build up an instrument I didn't fully realize I had. Gradually, and then suddenly—to coin a phrase—I could project. I could get your attention even if you were all the way up the block. Even while pounding on the drums, my harmonies began to have more presence than Mike Neiger's main melodies.

When I took the lead vocal on "Gone to Canada," a topical song about draft dodging, my voice opened up as if a pair of invisible hands that had been wrapped around my neck my whole life had suddenly fallen away. My confidence as a singer was beginning to line up with the posed bravado in the photograph of twelve-year-old me that I kept on my desk. Rocking out in a homemade paper crown and a phony mustache cut from the elastic band of a brown sock, this was a snapshot of aspiration, a boy dreaming big dreams, hamming it up with an unplayable Stella acoustic, whose two rusty strings would make anyone who laid their hands on them a candidate for a tetanus shot.

Neiger saw the writing on the wall and relinquished his vocal duties to me. I was now the lead singer, but I was still the drummer, and I was clearly not Phil Collins, or Don Henley, or Levon Helm. These were singing drummers who made it look easy. I was just a kid who was trying to multitask, and I made it look like the hard work it was. For so long, I had been afraid of being seen but not heard. Now, I was being heard but barely seen.

THE DEAD HORSE

Maybe it was a blessing in disguise that audience members would only see me in a series of obstructed glimpses, sweating profusely behind the kit, as I struggled to play and sing at the same time. I spent the majority of every performance in perpetual "turn your head and cough" position to reach the microphone attached to the end of a short gooseneck next to the hi-hat.

It was clear that someone had to pick up the visual slack. Mike and Mike had written such involved guitar parts for themselves that they rarely looked up from their fretboards. It ended up being Keith stepping into the spotlight to provide an unlikely one-man stage show. At a predetermined moment during the set, I would break into a tribal tom-tom beat, at which point Keith would take off his bass to perform "the Swale." The Swale was a dance he conceived in dishonor of the horse that had recently won two-thirds of the Triple Crown before keeling over and dying a premature death a week after taking the Belmont Stakes. The moves to the Swale were a cocktail of steps lifted from '60s fad dances like the Swim and served with a twist of simulated electrocution thrown in for good measure.

When the band opened for a midnight screening of *The Rocky Horror Picture Show* at the State Theater in Newark, Keith debuted the Swale and was aggressively pelted with the toast that audience members usually reserved for hurling at the screen during the movie. As it turned out, this was a sign of their intense affection, and we got our first taste of a following from this crowd of artsy misfits.

The dance portion of our stage show, however, was short lived and came to an unceremonious end after a club gig at Three Cheers in the Newark Mini Mall. Keith decided to Swale for the second time in one night, after we had already played our opening set. He convulsed maniacally to the headlining band's cover of "I'm a Believer" by the Monkees. Directly thereafter, Keith disappeared into the bathroom for over an hour to throw up the two Popeye's chicken breasts he had consumed at our pre-gig meal earlier that day. He emerged from the men's room only after the bar was closed, looking like he had suffered war atrocities.

Not long after the Swale incident, Keith announced his retirement from rock 'n' roll at the age of nineteen to focus on his electrical engineering degree at Delaware. My own priorities were coming into sharper focus too, and that meant more changes for the band. It was time to become a true front man, time to go for *all* the money notes.

PART IV

SALAD DAYS

Where do you go to stunt your fear
You say anywhere but here
But I think you should know by now

—THE CAULFIELDS, "RICKSHAW"

BEAT CLINIC: JUST THE FACTOIDS

In late 1985, after Keith Green gave his notice to No Excuse, we changed the name of the band to the Beat Clinic. Mike Neiger switched from guitar to bass to make room for his old elementary school buddy Chris Ryan to play rhythm. Chris's jangly twelve-string Rickenbacker acted as the chocolate in the peanut butter of Mike Simpson's jazz and metal stylings, landing the Beat Clinic at the sonic intersection of "Heaven Knows I'm Miserable Now," "Hot for Teacher," and "Mr. Tambourine Man."

I often introduced Chris onstage as Chris "I Shit You Not" Ryan, a reference to his preferred method of answering the question "Are you shitting me?"

Scott Kohlmorgen, a native New Yorker with the handsome good looks of Robert Duvall, answered our ad for a drummer and joined the Beat Clinic in early 1986, replacing me behind the kit.

Scott had an engineering degree from Drexel University in Philadelphia, where he had played drums in a cover band called ETC, which I would only pronounce in Yul Brynner's accent from *The King and I*:

Et-ceterah, et-ceterah, et-ceterah.

A few years older than the rest of us, Scott had a big-boy job, working for Morton Thiokol, the company responsible for the faulty O-rings that caused the space shuttle *Challenger* disaster that January. Doing what any bandmate worth their salt would do with that information, Chris taped a phony, unsent note to the wall behind Scott's drums in our practice space:

Boss, don't launch the space shuttle. It's going to blow up.
Love, Scott.

The Beat Clinic played the University of Delaware Spring Fling in May of the year Scott arrived, opening for Southside Johnny and the Jukes. They had temporarily dumped the "Asbury" from their name. Our set got written up in the student newspaper, *The Review*. They printed a midsolo close-up of Mike Simpson, who was the only one among us really walking the walk of a rock 'n' roller. Looking cool in his porkpie hat and floral-print smoking jacket with black velvet lapels, Mike was fully entrenched in his persona as "The Fly," a nickname derived from a ubiquitous pair of insect-eyed aviator shades that seemed to remain on his face whether the sun was out or not.

Mike Neiger left the band abruptly sometime toward the end of that year. The musical kinship that began in high school with him writing "D to Am" over my shitty lyrics about a Chicago bag lady had faded. I was resentful and hurt that he called Chris and not me when he quit. I kept a xeroxed picture of his face over the bullseye on my dart board in Mom's basement as a reminder that he left me without saying goodbye. I guess I still had abandonment issues.

Scott called up Tom Marks, the bass player from ETC, to fill in for the shows we had on the books when Neiger left. Tom was this tall blond virtuoso with a wavy '80s mullet and wayfarer sunglasses.

Onstage, he went by "T. Marks," sort of like T. Rex. His chemistry with Scott gave the Beat Clinic its first real rhythm section, and he ended up staying for a year and a half.

Newark's music scene was happening. People went out every night of the week. Regional cover bands like the Nerds and Y-Not were the most popular, but there was a lot happening on the original side of the tracks. There was punk, power pop, reggae, funk, and just plain unclassifiable weirdness, all of which could be found on Pumpkinhead's compilation tapes.

"Pumpkinhead" was Jerry Lehane III, a stocky, soft-spoken, ubiquitous figure with the uncanny ability to be everywhere at once—hawking cassettes of his band the Moaners while regaling anyone who would listen with stories of how he had created the logo for *Star Trek: Deep Space Nine*, his design inspired by the shape of an air vent in the men's room at a Roy Rogers fast food restaurant. He also claimed to have ghostwritten hit songs, like "I'm Not Your Man" by Newark-legends-gone-national Tommy Conwell and the Young Rumblers. Jerry would explain his rendition was originally "I'm Nacho Man," written at the Deer Park, the historic venue at the end of Main Street whose Wednesday nacho nights attracted everyone from students to professors to motorcycle gangs.

Whenever we played the Deer Park, we always worked with a soundman named Jim, who sported shitkicker cowboy boots and an impressive afro that, depending on how recently he had run a pick through it, drew comparisons to the MC5 or the Black Panthers. Mostly, he reminded me of Bob Ross, the guy who painted "happy little trees" on PBS.

Jim began the setup at every show with a signature rallying cry:

Let's get wired!

Thus would commence the positioning of massive PA speakers and a meticulous threading of a mammoth hundred-foot audio snake through the rafters of the venue, a signal to all in the vicinity that it was going to get loud.

The manager at the Deer Park was a dick. He was always giving us shit about arriving too early or too late, never failing to warn us about the volume. One night, Jim went missing from behind the soundboard. Unbeknownst to us, he had already been gone for several minutes by the time we began playing a cover of "The Boxer" by Simon and Garfunkel.

If you listen to the original record, there isn't much drumming on it except in the chorus when a massive snare drum drenched in reverb goes off like a cannon. The setlist I had given to Jim had a large asterisk by "The Boxer" with specific instructions: "Massive 'verb on snare during *lie-la-lie* part."

It was dark in the room, so none of us realized that two songs earlier there had been a confrontation and that Jim had walked out of the bar to have a full-on mental breakdown, so when it came time for the big snare drum hit, instead of a climactic explosion, it was more like the sound of a band being crushed by the giant foot from *Monty Python's Flying Circus*.

Lie-La-Lie … *pfffft!*

Everyone in the crowd just burst out laughing. We cut the set short to look for Jim and found him on the front steps of the club, his face buried in his hands.

"It's just not fun anymore," he sobbed in his distinctive baritone. He was right. Newark wasn't that fun anymore.

We started playing shows in Philadelphia with the help of a guy who became our first manager, an architect aptly named Bill House. Bill got us our first gig at JC Dobbs on South Street. It was a huge deal to me to play down the block from Zipperhead and Tower Records, the destinations of my high school pilgrimages to the big city. We opened for one of the most popular bands in town, the Daves, whose lead singer, Bekka Eaton, inspired me to incorporate theatrical elements into our stage show. There was the oversized American Express card pulled from my back pocket during our song "Don't You Know Who I Am," and the detached receiver from a red telephone, held up to my ear during the guitar solo in "Wrong # 4 Me," a long-standing original with a titular numeric nod to Prince.

I debuted these props during a big show at the Grand Opera House in Wilmington. We were opening for Emo Philips, a comedian with deadpan delivery and a pageboy hairdo, not unlike the straight-bang bowl cuts I endured as a little kid. The setting at the Grand was what I imagined it was like for the Beatles playing Royal Albert Hall, when John Lennon told the people in the cheap seats to clap their hands and the rest to rattle their jewelry. I convinced myself that the best way to cut through the hoity-toity bullshit was to dance around onstage with what became my most infamous prop: a toilet seat draped around my neck.

In the spring of 1987, we entered a national battle of the bands—the Energizer Rock 'n' Roll Challenge, sponsored by the battery company that would a year later adopt a bass-drum-pounding pink bunny as its marketing mascot. In '87, their spokesperson was a frightening bleached-blond Australian named Jacko, who hawked their 9-volts by yelling "Oy" into the camera.

The master of ceremonies for the contest was a then-unknown comedian named Sinbad. Before we went onstage, he asked me how we wanted to be introduced, and I recited a variation of something I had heard on *Late Night with David Letterman*:

"And now a band that hates the itching but loves the scratching: the Beat Clinic."

It came out of Sinbad's mouth as, "And now the band that loves the itchin' and the scratchin': the Beat Club!"

This was actually funnier than any of his jokes.

We made it all the way to the finals and finished in second place, losing out to a band from Boston called the Rhythm Method. "Rhythm Method Beats Clinic" was the imaginary headline that rolled around in my head for days after this agonizing defeat.

If nothing else, our strong finish in the Energizer contest provided Bill House with the ammo to get us into more clubs in Philadelphia. We played shows at the Khyber Pass in Old City, the North Star Bar by the art museum, the Trocadero in Chinatown.

Bill always referred to clubs as "rooms." When trying to sell us on taking a show at the Barbary in Fishtown, he said something like, "It only takes fifty people to fill the room ... The fact that they called *me* shows that they care about what they put in their room ... I'm telling you, it's a great room. And it's decorated with pirate's booty and doubloons!"

We also played at the Empire Rock Club in Northeast Philadelphia, which was a haven for metal bands like Cinderella and Heaven's Edge. The place had a unique smell, different from the clubs in Center City—a mélange of stage fog, hair spray, and body parts too long cooped up in spandex.

Bill House eventually got us in the door at the Chestnut Cabaret, another major coup. The Chestnut was part of a three-venue circuit owned and operated by Steve Mountain, who managed the Hooters. Our first show was with the Indigo Girls before anyone knew who they were. After seeing us, Amy Ray wanted to trade records, but we didn't have one at the time, so she just gave me a free copy of their first independent EP.

Our second show at the Chestnut was an opening slot for dance-pop diva Taylor Dayne just as "Tell It to My Heart" was moving up the charts. Ms. Dayne entered the club wearing designer sunglasses and holding a double dog leash with two toy poodles attached. The crowd was full of *Dancin' on Air* rejects who couldn't have cared less about us, but a huge muscle-bound man wearing a ninja headband and full black body suit was completely into our set and did an entire free-form ballet alone on the dance floor. It was like watching Mikhail Baryshnikov trapped in the body of Mr. T.

Taylor Dayne ended up going on almost two hours late because the venue failed to provide the correct wine requested in her contract, and instead of just telling them, she made them go item by item through the rider until the oversight was discovered and corrected.

T. Marks left the band in 1988, having endured one too many ninety-minute drives to Newark from his home in Lancaster. Discouraging auditions for bass players ensued, which yielded telling remarks from the candidate pool:

Nah, I don't play any root notes, that's boring for me.
Sorry about that, man, but these strings are, like, really old. Tell you what, though. Put new ones on her and she'll sing all night!

I would have taken the kid who said "You don't need to know no notes to play rock 'n' roll" over these idiots any day.

After a temporary stint with "Potassium" Rich Stevens, yet another member of ETC, Chris Ryan took it upon himself to leave a desperate, if serendipitous, message at the home of bass player Sam Musumeci. It just so happened to be the very night Sam had walked out of his own band's rehearsal, where his lead singer lay incapacitated while strung out on heroin.

Sam became the Beat Clinic's fifth and final bass player, making his inauspicious debut at M.R. Doc's in Hockessin, where we endured the wrath of an angry collective of Philadelphia Flyers fans for blocking their view of the hockey game on the wide-screen TV behind us. Out of pure instinct for survival, we ended the show with a cover of "Wild Thing" by the Troggs, a song we had never played before, but one that tamed the animus in the bar. I jumped around like a maniac, shoving the mic at hostile faces to sing along—the same faces that had made cartoonish Asian noises under their breath just audible enough for me to hear throughout the show.

After we were done, Sam's father, an old-school Sicilian who had dealt with prejudice against Italians and had fought off advances from the Philadelphia mafia to use his store as a mob front, approached the stage.

"Sam, introduce me to the contortionist."

He shook my hand, appearing impressed with my performance, and just maybe with the fact that I had faced down my detractors.

TOWNIE

This town just goes around, around, around

—THE CAULFIELDS, "AWAKE ON WEDNESDAY"

Although a twenty-one-and-over venue, the Stone Balloon had a reputation for letting in pretty much anyone who presented even the most blatantly falsified identification. The first time Lisa ever came to see me play there, she used an ID belonging to a girl named Nina Luden, whose only physical resemblance to Lisa Beth Holderman was that she also had blond hair. The doormen at the Balloon knew. They had to have known. They just needed to see *something*.

Primarily a haven for cover bands that provided the background hook-up music for close to a thousand inebriated students on Thursday "mug nights," the Stone Balloon was also a regular stop for national acts who were either on their way up or on their way down. Bruce Springsteen had played there in the summer of 1974, over a year before *Born to Run* would land him simultaneously on the covers of *Time* and *Newsweek*. The Beat Clinic started to play support gigs there, warming up the crowd for less-than-compatible headliners like Meat Loaf, who had been reduced to leaving the stage after every song to take a hit off the oxygen tank that was, perhaps, a standard demand in his rider by then.

Iggy Pop came to Delaware to play Newark's biggest bar in September of 1988 with a then-unknown Jane's Addiction as the opening act. The day after the Iggy Pop show, word started getting around that the opening band had been thrown out of the club for exposing themselves and pissing on the walls. On their way out of town, they got into a huge fight at the Denny's on Route 273. A subsequent issue of *Rolling Stone* contained a blurb confirming that the guitarist from Jane's Addiction, Dave Navarro, had suffered a broken nose and a pretty vicious beating in the bathroom, courtesy of some belligerent locals all jacked up on Grand Slams and PBR.

That was Newark for you, a college town and a hick town all at once. If I was struggling with my own set of contradictions, here was the perfect place for me to not quite fit in. Just like me, Newark had its own unlikely dichotomy—one part live-it-up-while-you're-young Blue Hens and one part life's-a-bitch-then-you-die blue collars— townies, as they were known. Of course, that's an oversimplification, but as the running gag of my life went, I was both student *and* townie, and didn't feel particularly comfortable in either skin.

I wasn't exactly connecting with my tribe as a musician either. My increasingly frequent performances with the Beat Clinic exposed me to a culture that might best be described as "alcohol fueled." Most everyone I encountered drank, moderately or more. Chris and Sam enjoyed a few Rolling Rocks at gigs, and we all should have seen bad moons on the rise over the wall of empty cans in Mike's bedroom long before he realized he needed to go odorless and switch to vodka.

As for me, I was disinclined to indulge, coming home from shows completely sober and alone in sweat-soaked clothes infused with the smell of cigarette smoke and no money to remove from my pockets before loading the whole saturated pile into the washing machine at Mom's house. Every penny we made went into a band recording fund, as we saved up for studio time that was off in a distant, murky ether. I wanted so badly to prove to Mom that I could make my living from playing music, but that was a waterfall I would have to chase for a good while longer. In the meantime, it felt like I was just going in circles.

Mayor William Redd was hell bent on running the cruisers out of 19711. Newark was his lawn, and he wanted the sons of bitches off it. He worked with the city council to push through one of the most serious anticruising ordinances in the country, willing to pay serious overtime for a couple of cops to sit in their patrol car and write down all the passing license plate numbers, so if they saw anybody go by more than twice between the hours of 8:00 pm and 4:00 am, they were gonna get 'em!

Of course, it hardly worked. Every Friday and Saturday night, Newark was gridlocked with multitudes of the supposedly young, wild, and free inching along Main Street in their Chevy Nova teen-mobiles—windows down, stereos cranked, beer cans open, looking for any kind of trouble there was to be had.

The two-mile loop began just past the McDonald's at the far east end of town, stretched the entire length of Main down to the turnaround by the Deer Park and the railroad tracks, then headed back the other direction on Delaware Avenue, until it all ended up at the same place it began. It seemed a pretty apt metaphor for Newark: everybody on the same road to nowhere.

When you come of age in the same zip code where you lived as a little kid, it shines a whole different light on your hometown. Any idyllic notions I might have been holding on to about Newark in the years since Papa died were limited to the landmarks from my childhood that were still standing: Blue Hen Lanes, Bing's Bakery, Woolworths, and St. John's R. C. Church, from which I narrowly escaped Catholicism with only a baptismal waterboarding. A lifetime of stale communion wafers and handsy priests now seemed like a small price to pay, if only Papa were there to see me through to adulthood.

In my mind, I was wise beyond my years. By the time I was seven, I knew what death was. By the time I reached grade school, I knew what racism was. At an age younger than most, I knew what an orgasm was.

But when it came to true matters of the heart, the feeling of actually loving someone and being loved back, I was the very essence of the word "townie"—provincial, closed off, anything but worldly.

Lisa and I met in her dorm room on the same floor where I had resided during my first two years at Delaware. Keith Green and I were visiting our friend Jay Martin, who was still living in Cannon Hall. We hadn't seen each other much since Keith and I moved across campus to live in Sharp Hall, just off Main Street. I wanted to take a look at the mural that was painted in the basement lounge when we were sophomores. Each one of our floor mates was depicted as cartoonish sea creatures, me wearing a leopard-print fez that I specifically requested to commemorate my stage attire at my first public performance in eleventh grade. Billy Wiggins, who went by "L. Bill" Wiggins as an ironic nod to L. Ron Hubbard, was shown holding an Elvis Costello record in his fin. The two of us were simpatico, having spent many an hour in that lounge pining over girls who wouldn't give us the time of day, unaware that both his future wife and my future ex-wife would later be residents on that very floor.

When Jay, Keith, and I wandered by Lisa's open door in room 007, I recognized her right away.

"Holy shit, *Scandinavian Chick*," I whispered internally.

L. Bill had given Lisa this designation after previously scoping her out in the dining hall. Practically every female we took note of received a title and was henceforth referred to as some kind of "chick." Most of these monikers were purely observational. There was "Mod Chick," "Haughty Chick," and "Oompa Loompa Chick," whose overzealous use of self-tanning products gave her face the look of sunbaked adobe.

Males were not exempt from our strange nomenclature. You had "Smarmy Guy," "Brooklyn Guy," "Cardigan Man," and a fellow so nondescript and devoid of personality that we dubbed him "Guy with No Name."

This was all a projection of our own insecurity, our immature need to feel some sense of control or superiority over those we had classified. What a comfort to spot "Pathos Guy" walking to class, or even better, "Pathos Man," a completely different person, whose bad posture and perpetual outpouring of anxiousness were just a little worse than my own. I'm not so sure that was actually even true once I was in the presence of "Scandinavian Chick."

Lisa and her friends were in the midst of an impromptu "'70s party" and invited Jay to come in to introduce Keith and me. I don't quite recall what it was about the gathering that made it so '70s; everything was pretty 1986 as far as I could see. I got a big kick out of the *St. Elmo's Fire* movie poster on the wall, depicting Rob Lowe in all his Brat Pack glory, looking tough with his dangling earring and a saxophone cradled under his arm.

As with just about any social situation in which I found myself at the time, I didn't say very much at first. Then one of the girls, I suppose in the spirit of "'70s-ness," began singing "Sunshine Day," a song I knew right away was from *The Brady Bunch*. The sugary melody rang in my ears like a Pavlovian bell, and before long, my rabbit-hole knowledge of Brady trivia was rewarded with the searchlight smile and witchy giggle that stole my heart.

I was smitten, sitting there cross legged on Lisa's throw rug in my thrift-store suit jacket and skinny tie. I couldn't even bring myself to look directly into her stunning blue eyes; it was like staring at the sun. Not that falling in love would be *that* simple. I mean, it would be for *me*, but her situation was a bit more complicated.

THE SUGARY MELODY RANG IN MY EARS LIKE A PAVLOVIAN BELL, AND BEFORE LONG, MY RABBIT-HOLE KNOWLEDGE OF BRADY TRIVIA WAS REWARDED WITH THE SEARCHLIGHT SMILE AND WITCHY GIGGLE THAT STOLE MY HEART.

"Looks like Felicia's going *solo*," her next-door neighbor, Sandy, blurted out with a puckish inflection, perhaps a benign signal to the room that Lisa was unattached.

"Felicia" was Lisa's nickname among her hall mates, rooted in the similarity of her kicky blond bob to that of Kristina Malandro's character on *General Hospital*, another show from which I retained a mental bank vault of useless information. But I guess none of it was truly useless if it made Lisa smile.

It all clicked that the '70s party was to take her mind off the fact that she was now on the rebound, having just broken up with her boyfriend, a guy named Rob, who appeared to be nearly twice her height in the picture still taped to the wall by her bed. They had been together for almost a year, not an insignificant amount of time for a couple of nineteen-year-olds.

I had never even been on a proper date. I certainly did not count the time a year earlier when Keith and L. Bill offered up a "dream date" with me as a joke prize during Billy's radio show on WXDR, the university station. Neither one of them thought that someone would actually phone in, but you could never underestimate the power of sheer boredom in Newark.

There was nothing boring about Lisa. I knew immediately that there was something worth nurturing, some Cinderella spark between us. I played the long game, and we cultivated a real friendship over the span of weeks, sharing midnight laughs watching black-and-white Charlie Chan movies in the basement lounge, neither one of us making a move. I didn't want to be the rebound guy; I wanted to be her man.

Like so many breakups, hers did not fully take right away. I was despondent on the night she told me she and Rob were going to give it another try. I left Cannon Hall with a lump in my throat and a knot in my stomach. I made it about halfway home before I let out a howl of despair and heaved my backpack as far as I could throw it, making my way across campus in a blur of tears.

My friendship with Lisa survived her second go-round with Rob, and I survived the night he showed up at my dorm, agitated and dressed in black, supposedly looking for me. Luckily, I was out at a local rock show a couple of blocks away. L. Bill and Keith reported seeing him as he prowled the hallway, sweating profusely in a menacing ski cap. Our code name for him became "Night Stalker," in reference to a serial killer who had murdered over a dozen people in California, several of them Asian, including a man literally named Peter Pan. Lisa told me the next time I saw her that she was officially done with Rob.

I didn't quite know what to do with that information. Should I declare to her what was already obvious? That I was in love with her?

Should I give her space? What was I to her now? Still just a friend? A shoulder to cry on? I had so many questions.

"Do you want to go on spring break with me?" I asked impulsively, offering up a week in Mom's timeshare condo in Myrtle Beach, with no idea if Mom would even entertain such a thought.

To my amazement, Lisa said yes. It was the closest I would ever come to a proper proposal. We knew neither of our mothers would greenlight this idea if it was just the two of us going by ourselves, so I convinced Keith, L. Bill, and his roommate Biff to come with.

It was spring in name only, as Lisa and her mom pulled up by the tennis courts in the Cannon Hall parking lot to find the rest of us bundled up in our down jackets ready for the blustery wind at our backs to propel us on the first real road trip of our young lives, a precursor to the many tours in my future and a litmus test for the deepening affection I felt for Lisa. Her duffle bag was stuffed to the gills, and she was concerned it might not fit into the trunk of Keith's parents' Honda Accord.

"Oh, don't worry about it," I said. "It's malleable."

I had no idea in that moment that my use of the word "malleable" instantly transformed me into son-in-law material in the eyes of Lisa's mother.

The spring break that launched our love, took my virginity, and added ten pounds onto both of us became the template for the happiest times of our relationship. I fawned over her, made her personalized fortune cookies, removing the factory-installed Confucian platitudes with a pair of tweezers and replacing them with my own handwritten romantic notes. Most days, we embodied the romcom notion of the perfect couple our friends kept telling us we were.

Perhaps prophetically, the only times I felt a twinge of tension in the dynamic between Lisa and me was when our more insular world of private jokes and microwave lava cakes collided with the world I was creating with the Beat Clinic. Lisa loved music, and we loved a lot of it in common, especially songs we had grown up listening to on the radio. But something I did not understand at the time was how hard it might be for Lisa to navigate dating the lead singer of a band, even a quartet of local boys with a following you could hold hostage in a standard-sized bank vault.

The adrenaline surges that I felt while writhing around under hot lights and barking my lyrics into dented microphones often took hours to subside after a performance. My aftershow moods could range from obnoxiously gregarious to flat-out distant to the point of dissolving into myself.

Justifiably, Lisa found me insufferable in these situations. I just couldn't manage to walk off-stage and slip comfortably back into my otherwise easy rapport with her. After something I said or didn't say left her in tears at the Buggy Tavern, Wilmington's closest facsimile to a biker bar, her appearances at shows became somewhat less frequent and usually came with a side of obligation.

Luckily, our pros outweighed our cons for a long while, and by 1989 Lisa had graduated and was working a desk job back home in New Jersey, living with her parents, saving money, and trying to work with me to plot our next move together. We both wanted the idea of "us" to succeed, even as we struggled to figure out how to make that happen while living ninety miles apart.

Although we would find our way back to each other, live under the same roof, adopt cats, and eventually get married and have kids, something from that period of separation remained embedded in our relationship at every point forward, in the same way that Newark itself, and the townie I still am, felt embedded in me.

MARCH OF DIMES

Earl was always trying to get a rise out of Gus. "Hey, Gus. When did you *go gay?*"

"Fuck you, Earl," Gus replied, rolling his eyes, seeming to know better than to engage any further.

The dog days of summer were upon Newark, and Gus, who worked at the sandwich shop next door, had taken to wearing his dark Italian mane in a ponytail, giving the back of his neck a little relief from the heat and Earl a little ammunition for some homophobic ribbing. Earl was a boisterous, rotund young Black man, an avid *Gauntlet* enthusiast, and the only other delivery driver working the day shift with me at Pizza Pie, a sibling-owned operation located in the 896 Shoppes out on South College Avenue.

With pizza, sandwiches, a bakery, and a liquor store offering the allure of all four food groups, our little strip mall was a one-stop shop for workers at the Chrysler auto plant, which was less than a mile down the road. These men, who spent their days assembling Plymouth Acclaims and Dodge Spirits, provided a healthy percentage of the lunchtime business at Pizza Pie.

I had three managers at The Pie. Chris was the one who'd hired me back in the spring. It may have been one of his final executive decisions before getting out while the getting was good, giving the place another six months, tops, as he moved on to a better job. I don't know how much satisfaction he took in being right, but I do know that my day managers, Derek and Pat, weren't just fiddling while Rome burned. If anything, they were striking the matches, and before long, I was helping them fan the flames.

Even though they were younger than I was, these guys seemed like older brothers to me, the kind who were more than happy to be bad influences. They started in the pizza business as teenagers, drank beer underage at the Monsters of Rock tour, drove cars with T-tops, and gave very few fucks, if any.[3*]

The job paid minimum wage: $3.35 an hour. School was still out, and business was generally slow. Chris had neglected to mention during my interview back in April just *how* slow it might get on the day shift by August, instead touting a potential wage of more like eleven dollars an hour "once you add in all the tips." He told me I could make even more if I moved up to the night shift, but I

[3*] The story of legend that best exemplifies who Pat and Derek were as pizza guys before I arrived involves an asshole from Robscott Manor, an adjacent neighborhood whose street names I never did manage to commit to memory. Completely ignoring the posted sign out back that read "No Dumping," this guy rode up in his pickup with several bags of trash and tossed them right into Pizza Pie's dumpster, in complete view of Pat and Derek, who were shooting the shit on a smoke break. Derek yelled out, "Hey, you can't dump that here!" receiving, in return, a lowered driver's side window, a raised middle finger, and the sound of squealing truck tires as the guy peeled out of the parking lot. My future managers were not the types to simply accept this kind of transgression. Derek was willing to bet money that something in those bags would give the perpetrator away, and sure enough, among the likely contents of chicken bones and decaying banana peels in the very first bag they ripped open, there was a discarded bill with the guy's name and address printed right on it. Within minutes, the two of them pulled up in front of the guy's house in Pat's car, and with the T-tops removed, hoisted every last Hefty Cinch Sak back out onto the guy's lawn, giving him the finger as they drove off leaving him with his own personal landfill and the knowledge that The Pie was not to be trifled with.

wasn't about to jeopardize my availability to the Beat Clinic. With the expenses of simply *existing* as a band piling up, I needed to be able to play any gig on any given night of the week. So I continued to make peace with my poverty.

It wasn't long before I realized that I wasn't cut out for the delivery racket.

Gratuities—for me, anyway—were hard to come by. In the absence of GPS or the most basic sense of direction, I felt my nerves begin to fray as I searched for faded or hidden house numbers on the streets of cookie-cutter neighborhoods, ultimately returning to the store none the richer after handing off a now-cold pizza to an irritated third-shifter who was in no mood to say, "Keep the change."

With Earl citing seniority to snag most of the deliveries anyway, I began spending more of my time helping out in the store. Kimmy, the cute counter girl who worked the register when I first started the job, had gone AWOL. No one had seen the owner Ray in weeks, either, and the last documented sighting of his brother Mike was on the day the ice machine went on the fritz.

The ice man cometh, dude. All over her face! Hahahaha!

These were pretty much the only words he ever spoke to me, as he sauntered past, like a real-world version of Shaggy from *Scooby Doo*, carrying two ten-pound bags of ice in each hand.

The noon lunch rush was Pizza Pie's fiscal saving grace, and it was on me to serve what seemed like the entire Chrysler assembly line on their lunch break, doling out slices and fountain drinks while Derek and Pat teamed up to meet the demand, assembling pies for the oven, their faces dripping with sweat, flour dusting their forearms.

I pinned my financial hopes on a panhandler's paper cup sitting on the counter near the cash register with about nineteen cents in starter coins keeping it from blowing away. The Chrysler cohort was already lit up after visiting the liquor store a couple of doors down. They formed a daunting and impatient line all the way back to the March of Dimes charity gumball machine that propped open the front door at Pizza Pie. I stood behind the counter in my oversized jersey and red baseball cap, my bangs pressed to the top of my eyebrows.

A thin-lipped, mullet-sporting UAW member approached. He had already dispensed with his brown paper bag from the liquor store, dangling the four remaining beers in his six-pack by the plastic rings.

"Ahhhhh, soooooo. Gimme two *peppeloni srices*," he enunciated, reversing his *r*'s and *l*'s to the great amusement of his co-workers.

I could feel the blood moving through my carotid. Every internal impulse told me to react, call him white trash, throw hot pizza in his face, something. But I didn't. It wasn't like it was the first time in my life that I had dealt with this sort of thing, but now it was coming at me from the mouth of a grown adult with bad breath and summer teeth, and a virtual mob of like-minded cronies seemingly there to reinforce my silence.

I hated these motherfuckers. I didn't even want to think about the fact that they were making ten times more money than I was, getting drunk in the middle of the day and giving me shit. If I'd had the nerve, I would have taken the Louisville Slugger we kept under the counter in case of emergency and bashed his head in. Instead, I just took his money and took another one for the team—the team on which I was the only member. Choking down my anger felt like swallowing lava back into a volcano that was all but ready to erupt.

It was clear I needed to be taken off the register, so Pat gently tapped me on the shoulder and quietly suggested I go to the back room to make the sauce.

The sauce *recipe*, if you could call it that, was a brief list of ingredients and portions taped to the lid of a white twenty-gallon plastic garbage can, its interior stained orange and pink from the countless batches that had come before. It was a fairly simple concoction, and the process required just a few basic steps: dump in about ten institutional-size cans of off-brand tomato sauce, throw in a few fistfuls of salt, pepper, sugar, and oregano, and stir.

"Stir" was where things got a little dicey. The kitchen was not equipped with any sort of mixing utensil—no whisk—so the ingredients had to be blended "the Pizza Pie way," the method that Pat taught me my very first week on the job. Pulling my sleeve up toward my shoulder, I plunged the entire length of my right arm, all the way up to the pit, into the garbage can, moving my limb like an oar through the thick red pool of pureed tomatoes and spices, agitating the mixture until the clusters of salt, pepper, sugar, and oregano, along with whatever hairs or exfoliations came off me, were evenly distributed throughout the several gallons of our signature sauce. Once everything was blended up to standard, the final step was to take the thumb and forefinger of my left hand and slide them from shoulder to nail against my skin, like I was removing a giant condom, to ensure every last drop of sauce made it into the bucket.

After I hosed off my arm in the utility sink, I returned to the front to find the place emptied out. Pat rested sideways in the back booth like he was reclined in a bathtub. The heat made everything feel sluggish. The smell of raw onions and sweaty cheese hung in the air as I laughed about my attempt to browbeat an elderly woman out of the ten cents she claimed was her rightful discount for a fountain soda—"Just gimme the dime, grandma!" Pat contemplated the state of the dedicated tin of oily fish that sat uncovered in the small fridge under the counter, waiting for the one guy in Newark who ordered anchovies on his pizza.

From the corner of my eye, Derek appeared to rise up from behind the counter.

He looked bound and determined, like he was standing at a critical crossroads. He walked around front to reveal his hands gripped around the handle of the baseball bat I had imagined I'd use to kill the guys from Chrysler. In what seemed like slow motion, he raised the wooden club over his head and began to run full steam toward the front door.

"Nooooooooooooooooooooo!" I screamed in total silence.

Derek let out an audible bellow that sounded almost inhuman as he swung the bat, landing a direct, explosive hit on the March of Dimes charity gumball machine, sending broken glass and multicolored gumballs skittering across the floor and out onto the sidewalk. With a few more quick swings, the top of the dispenser was completely destroyed, allowing access to the hundreds of dimes accumulated in the base of the machine. For the moment, no one spoke. Derek beamed, like a proud hunter providing for his family, as Pat and I ran over to view the carnage. Within seconds, any passerby would have seen three grown men kneeling on the floor, stashing handfuls of ill-gotten coins into bank deposit bags.

In a way, this was the predictable conclusion of my time at Pizza Pie, except I wasn't just taking a dime from a disgruntled customer. I was stealing from an organization whose original mission was to combat polio, the disease that my very own sister had suffered from. That said, sixty dollars divided three ways was nothing to sneeze at.

Derek and Pat could cut years off their lives with the quantity of smokes they could buy from our in-store cigarette machine, which required only eleven dimes for an entire pack.

While we were in the back booth counting coins and laughing hysterically over our score, Gus appeared in the doorway, walking into the crime scene, surveying the situation with a devilish grin on his face.

"Fuck. Now we have to cut *you* in?" was the subtext of our collective sigh. OK. Sixty dollars divided *four* ways was nothing to sneeze at.

"Just gimme the dime, grandma" × 150.

I marched out of Pizza Pie to head off to another unpaid Beat Clinic gig, bits of broken glass and crushed gumball stuck in the soles of my shoes, and all those dimes in my front pockets just burning a hole.

INDEPENDENCE DAYS

When John F. Kennedy spoke before 120,000 German citizens in 1963 to declare his solidarity with West Germany, twenty-two months after the construction of the Berlin Wall, his statement *Ich bin ein Berliner* was intended to mean "I am a Berliner," as in "I am one of you." However, some armchair translators at the time claimed that JFK had actually said "I am a jelly doughnut," a *Berliner* also being a traditional jam-filled pastry enjoyed throughout the Fatherland.

Had the *Berliner* been available at Theo's Family Restaurant in Dewey Beach, Tom Moore, the Beat Clinic's occasional sound engineer, would certainly have ordered one. Late-night breakfast was practically a necessity whenever we performed down the street at the Bottle & Cork, especially on the days we played the club's afternoon "jam session" in addition to three sets at night. The need to replenish carbs was never more evident than when Tom turned on his ginger charm to request one of seemingly every conceivable gluten option on the menu, including but not limited to a bagel with cream cheese, raisin toast, an English muffin, a buttermilk biscuit, and a short stack of pancakes.

Thanks to our manager, Vikki Walls, a former housewife and secretary turned rock 'n' roll facilitator, we had become summertime fixtures at the Cork, where we peppered our substantial catalog of upbeat originals with unexpected covers like "Spinning Wheel" by Blood, Sweat & Tears. In the year-plus since taking us on as a priority client, Vikki had been a managerial wunderkind. She had secured funding for us to record our first CD. She landed us a slot in New York at the annual conference for the *College Music Journal—CMJ—* where we watched the Red Hot Chili Peppers run amok through a banquet room wearing nothing but socks on their cocks, destroying the promotional booths of several college radio stations. On top of that, Vikki had booked us enough paying gigs to finance a complete line of Beat Clinic T-shirts, the most esoteric depicting the unauthorized likeness of Wilford Brimley and my favorite line from his many commercials for Quaker Oats:

You want something warm inside o' you?

Things were actually starting to happen, and the band began walking the thin line between confident and cocky. In the midst of a discussion about our upcoming trip to Berlin, Tom Moore rattled off a sentence in German that perhaps proved *he* should have been one of Kennedy's speech writers.

Ach sehen sie sich meine große hosen forelle.

Roughly translated, this means "Check out my large trouser trout." Of all the useful sentences we could have committed to memory before hopping an international flight to Deutschland as one of the American bands slated to play the Berlin Independence

Days Music Conference in the fall of 1990, this nugget of locker room humor was what the members of the Beat Clinic chose to retain.

As we cruised thirty-five thousand feet above the Atlantic, optimism burned bright within me. I had not been out of the country since I was thirteen, and now I was en route to my first show on international soil. The Beat Clinic was going global.

Symbolically, the Berlin Wall had fallen about a year before our flight. The physical demolition of the wall was still ongoing, but reunification between the German Democratic Republic and the Federal Republic of Germany was now a done deal.

After more than ten hours in the air, we landed at the airport named after Otto Lilienthal, the German engineer whose work had influenced Wilbur and Orville Wright in the early days of aviation. With guitars and suitcases in hand, Sam, Chris, Mike, Scott, and I walked the concourse in search of the English-speaking chaperone we were assured would be waiting to escort us to our hotel.

We scanned the line of relatives and chauffeurs holding up placards with the names of family members and VIPs, but as the minutes dragged on with no sign of a sign that said "Beat Clinic" on it, it was clear we were on our own—strangers in a strange land with no grasp of the language other than how to say "check out my large trouser trout." As our frustration and sense of entitlement became audible, we must have come off like typical Ugly Americans. And like all Ugly Americans, we found a way to deflect the blame for our own shortsightedness onto someone else—in this case, Vikki.

"She *promised* somebody would meet us at the airport," more than one of us complained, like the spoiled brats we were revealing ourselves to be.

No one brought up the fact that we had done the absolute bare minimum in preparation to navigate four days in a foreign country.

There wasn't so much as a phrase book or a dictionary between us. I had picked up only one other random German translation from my friend Julian, a British kid I met in high school. I could only seem to recite it in the menacing Teutonic accent he took such pleasure in aping:

Ich lebe für mich!

"I live for me." It was a fitting sentiment for a group of twenty-somethings with their lederhosen in a bunch over having been stood up at the airport. We eventually decided we had waited long enough for our German Godot and went in search of a taxi large enough for all five of us and our literal and figurative baggage.

Chris, who had become the band's de facto tour manager, showed our driver a handwritten note with an address on *Wilhelmstrasse*. After about twenty minutes fraught with wrong turns and frustrated grunts, it became apparent that our cabbie was not used to taking people to East Berlin. That was the part of the city that people were dying to get *out of*, not into. At one point, he just threw his arms into the air and shouted, "Fick!" providing a potent addition to our scant German vocabulary. Realizing that "fick" meant "fuck," the rest of us laughed and shouted it back at him.

Fick! Fick! FICK!!

Frazzled and rather worse for wear, we finally made it to the hotel, which was really more like a youth hostel and, by our logic, the perfect place to harbor hostility. The mental scorecards were out, ready at the slightest provocation to put another black mark in the Vikki column.

She had worked tirelessly to bring us to this moment in our career, networking at South by Southwest in Austin and forging connections with promoters like Jim Clevo from Cleveland and the

German publishers who'd booked us in Berlin, but her aggressiveness with the fundraiser thrown to offset our travel expenses had left us feeling ambivalent. Our friends in other bands did not appreciate the pressure of personal phone calls strongly encouraging them to attend the show at the Coyote Cafe or flat-out fork over some money. A rising tide might lift all boats, or maybe it might just drown everything in its wake.

Our East Berlin hotel was uninspiring, if not totally unfamiliar. In some ways, it felt like a college dorm: shared bathrooms, twin beds with wafer-thin lumpy mattresses, dim lighting. Opened drapes did little to reinvigorate dated wallpaper and served only to reveal an austere panorama outside. The one interesting thing to look at was *das Fernsehturm*—the Berlin Television tower—a structure similar to the Space Needle in Seattle.

A RISING TIDE MIGHT LIFT ALL BOATS, OR MAYBE IT MIGHT JUST DROWN EVERYTHING IN ITS WAKE.

A few of us ventured into the streets in search of sustenance. If there were any restaurants to be found, they were well-kept state secrets. There was virtually no evidence of human activity, nowhere to spend the deutsche marks we were hoping to exchange for something to eat. The sounds of car horns, or jackhammers, or police sirens that might compose the noise pollution in any other city felt distant and muted in the east. Maybe everyone was at Big Sexy Land. The giant sidewalk poster advertising this West Berlin strip club was like a garish neon sign beckoning the moth toward the capitalist flame. And there we were: on the wrong side of Berlin with nothing in our bellies and nothing to entertain us while we waited our turn to rock in a newly free world. We blamed Vikki for that too.

We traveled on foot to the Brandenburg Gate, an eighteenth-century monument that had stood in disrepair and in desperate need of a power-wash for nearly three decades just behind the Berlin Wall. Throughout its long and storied history, the gate had symbolized both division and unity, tyranny and freedom, war and peace. Military processions celebrating the victories of Napoleon and Adolf Hitler had passed through the five walkways between the gate's Doric columns. It had served as the backdrop for Ronald Reagan's "tear down this wall" speech in 1987. It had been bombed, defaced, neglected; and yet, there it stood.

Pariser Platz, the public square beneath our shoes, had once been part of the wall's "death strip," a heavily patrolled gauntlet of trip wires, attack dogs, and guard towers, ostensibly there to keep intruders from entering, but East Berliners knew all too well it was really there to keep *them* from leaving. Now, it was lined with street vendors, like any other tourist trap. We descended like a pack of ravenous wolves on a young man in a tie-dye T-shirt selling bratwursts from a cart. We inhaled two or three each and listened as he confided his ultimate wish: to go on spring break in Daytona Beach, Florida. Sun, sand, girls, NASCAR—this was how he wanted to spend his wiener money and newfound freedom. And who could blame him? Everybody wanted a piece of the American dream. I was no different.

I'm sure I would have returned for more brats and lofty aspirations the next day, had it not been for a stroke of good fortune. Exploring the other floors of our hotel/hostel, Chris and I stumbled into a small meeting room with the remnants of a breakfast that no one had bothered to clean up. The heft of the linen tablecloths and ceramic dishes was out of sync with our own flimsy accommodations. I got the distinct feeling we were not supposed to be in there. We were the hoi polloi interloping in first class.

First class in this part of town added up to a punch bowl of hard-boiled eggs, along with some crusty white bread and a pitcher of milk that had sat out long enough to reach room temperature, but I was not feeling picky, and I ate my fill.

Chris thought better of consuming one of the eggs with a hairline crack in the shell, instead opting to hurl it out an open window and watch it smash against the building across the street. He had a pretty good arm. This act of insolence in the face of what were first-world problems in a second-world city was utterly satisfying, for both perpetrator and spectator.

Scott, the only one of us with a room all to himself, had apparently spent the morning jerry-rigging an outlet with a voltage converter so he could plug in his hair dryer. Chris and I encountered Scott in the hall just as a hotel detective walked up to interrogate him about his suspicious tampering. It was almost as if the rumors that everyone in East Germany was under surveillance were true.

Mr. Kolhmorgen. May I have word with you?

It was about as close to a brush with the secret police as one could hope to avoid. Scott, looking a little shocked he had been found out, apologized profusely and claimed ignorance of the fine-print regulations against messing with electrical sockets. He managed to wiggle his way out of the situation with just a reprimand and stern instructions to return the outlet to its original state. He would just have to towel dry for the remainder of the trip. I slinked off, relieved I didn't get busted for eating the hard-boiled eggs. Chris went back to his room and took a leak on the sidewalk from two stories up.

By the night of the show on our last day in Germany, we were just hungry, tired, and feral enough to believe we were about to blow the roof off our designated venue, a bar located on the second floor above a bookstore. We arrived early to inspect the back line of drums and amplifiers that Vikki had assured us would be provided. Chris asked the sound man, who spoke some English, if he knew when it was coming. He said it would be getting there "soon," but in a way that left it up to interpretation as to whether he really believed that or was just placating us.

The wires of communication were crossed in translation. The band from Italy on directly before us lugged their battered gear onto the stage and began a spirited performance, while we stood there in our paisley shirts and black vests, with no drum kit, no bass amp, no guitar amps, and only thirty-five minutes until the show we had flown over four thousand miles to play. Not even the Thermofax hard copy of the European publishing deal we had been offered earlier that day could pull our collective mood back from the brink.

Sensing our desperation, the Italian band offered to let us use their equipment. We plugged in and bashed away, as the Beat Clinic banner I had stuffed in my luggage hung askew, duct-taped in haste to the back wall. The healthy crowd was polite, well behaved in a way that felt like they were waiting for permission to let loose. Or maybe we just weren't that compelling. Of course, before ever admitting that, we would blame the lack of food, or lack of sleep, or the weird Warsaw Pact electricity. Anything or anyone but ourselves. Easier still, we could just blame Vikki.

The show did end on an up note, thanks to the double shot of high-energy covers by the Ramones and R.E.M. that served as our *heil mary*. The audience pogoed and sang along to "I Wanna Be Sedated" and "It's the End of the World as We Know It (and I Feel Fine)," allowing us to leave the stage with a modicum of dignity, to determine later if it was all worth it. The jury was out.

With no desire to spend our last few hours in Germany at the hotel stewing in our own mixed feelings, we made the unanimous decision that it was time to make the pilgrimage to Big Sexy Land. We boarded the S-Bahn with nothing but the vague knowledge that we needed to head west. We couldn't even manage to get that right. As the train sped eastward, it took a while for anyone to notice the surroundings were looking more desolate, not at all metropolitan.

We had been too busy trying to figure out how to pay our fares and wondering why we were the only passengers on what could have ended up being a midnight train to Poland. When we finally realized we were going the wrong way, farther than ever from Western civilization, we sprinted off that train at the next stop, certain we had narrowly escaped spending the rest of our lives in an East German gulag. We managed to get to the other side of the tracks and hop a westbound train, again without paying.

"Free transportation!" Mike said. "The last great bastion of communism."

We never did make it to Big Sexy Land, instead exiting the S-Bahn somewhere on the cusp between East and West Berlin. We found ourselves in an open plaza directly in front of a cold and eerie edifice. The five of us stood in silent awe of its imposing architecture, rife with ornate stone figures that stood like grotesque gargoyles in the low-lying fog. It may have been the Reichstag, or any number of historic German buildings that had seen the full spectrum of human potential for both good and evil. We were standing freely on ground that had once been controlled by both Nazis and Soviet communists. Berlin was a city coming to grips with its dualities—the plenty to the west, the scarcity to the east, the determination of its present, the horrors of its past. All these things would inform its future.

Back in the States, the Beat Clinic struggled to reconcile our own past, present, and future. Unable to simply appreciate the Berlin experience for what it was—a once-in-a-lifetime opportunity to play for an audience deserving of the freedom and connection we all sought in rock 'n' roll—we could only view it in terms of our own self-interest. In our minds, the trip had been much ado about nothing. The publishing deal didn't pan out, the showcase created no interest, and too many details surrounding our comfort had slipped through the cracks.

Instead of considering the fact that maybe we just weren't "next-level" quite yet, we had to make somebody the scapegoat. We concluded that it was time to declare our independence from Vikki. We called the meeting—made her drive the hour to Wilmington from Dover—and sat there beating around the bush, afraid to drop the hammer, until Sam offered a cold sayonara.

"You see, here's the door ... we're on one side of it ... and you're on the other."

Vikki looked wounded but took the hint. She stood up and closed the door with finality as she walked out, leaving the Beat Clinic to contemplate what we had just done, behind a wall of our own making.

DRIVEWAY MOMENT

had been driving Mom's Audi 5000 for several years by then, after she replaced it around her sixtieth birthday with another Audi, a Coupe GT, maintaining brand loyalty in spite of a *60 Minutes* exposé lambasting the automaker for the 5000's alleged problem with "sudden unintended acceleration." A reason for a massive recall if ever there was one, this issue apparently sent the car lurching toward innocent garage doors and unsuspecting children.

Had she been a man, I might have accused Mom of buying the Coupe GT as the result of a midlife crisis, but in Korean culture, turning sixty is a big deal. *Hwangap*, as it's known, represents the end of a sixty-year cycle on the lunar calendar, which Mom kept track of in addition to the traditional Gregorian calendar. It was a bit of a shock to see her behind the wheel of a five-cylinder two-door with a sunroof and a massive spoiler on the back. It pissed her off that her insurance rate went up because she had unwittingly bought herself what State Farm defined as a "sports car."

One might have thought I was racking up the miles, driving to and from out-of-town gigs, to Baltimore or Dewey Beach or Harrisburg. This was not at all the case. It had been a year since Chris Ryan left the Beat Clinic—not all too long after we had parted ways with Vikki Walls—and Mike Simpson, Sam Musumeci, Scott Kohlmorgen, and I recast ourselves as the Caulfields. As a nod to Holden Caulfield, the main character in *The Catcher in the Rye*, our new moniker wasn't just a name change—it represented a sea change. I was the new rhythm guitarist in the band, now having to play, in real time, the chords to all the new songs I had written. I was finally taking creative charge and getting ever closer to writing what was really in my heart.

Musically speaking, I was growing up.

The problem was, as good as I felt the band was becoming, it was hard to get the word out about the Caulfields in the pre-internet early '90s. In large part, it felt like the people who knew us were missing the Beat Clinic, the band that played tragicomic unrequited lust songs like "Three Little Words," the words in question being not "I love you" but "let's be friends." They missed the band with the lead singer whose uncanny Michael Stipe impression on covers of "Losing My Religion" and "The One I Love" made people out on the street think for a split second that R.E.M. might be playing a secret show at a bar called Knuckleheads.

I insisted that the Caulfields rely on our own material, maybe because I was really only comfortable playing the guitar parts for songs I wrote myself, but it was also a conscious decision to dispense with the crutches. We no longer had three hours' worth of music reinforced with covers, but just one forty-five-minute set of untested originals, now influenced as much by the sound and angst of the grunge era as we had previously been by the song craft of the '60s. This turned out to be a tough sell in our old familiar haunts.

The brand-spanking-new banner that I'd ordered with such optimism was rolled up and gathering dust at the bottom of the stairs in Mom's basement. Very few people would ever see "The Caulfields" emblazoned in black on white vinyl in a book-smart typewriter font, seeking that elusive nexus between rock 'n' roll and high school summer reading.

With the exception of an ill-conceived tenure at another pizza job, this time at Domino's, where I drove in a state of perpetual anxiety, running red lights to deliver some guy's large sausage and mushroom before the "thirty-minutes-or-less" guarantee kicked in, the Audi 5000 wasn't really going anywhere to speak of. Nor was I. Life began to feel like little more than a montage of the moments between leaving the engine running at the curb and sprinting up a driveway to a door in the hope I had made it in time.

I saw an ad in the paper describing "short-term positions" available from Diamond State Telephone, the local Bell Atlantic carrier. They needed drivers to distribute the new phone book, which was hot off the presses. The last thing I wanted or needed was another low-wage delivery job, but I knew it was only temporary, and on the upside there was hardly any interview process. All I needed was a driver's license, proof of insurance, and room in the trunk.

The guy in charge pointed to a folding table cluttered with an untidy heap of what he referred to as "manifests," computer-generated clusters of loose paper stuffed into clear plastic sleeves. These were the lists of addresses whose inhabitants were waiting to let their fingers do the walking once I showed up with their new Yellow Pages. Any given manifest covered dozens of houses across multiple neighborhoods. To go through the entire document would require numerous trips back to phone book HQ, which was basically a Sunday school room at a church up on Polly Drummond Hill Road.

After picking my poison completely at random, I pulled the Audi around back and began packing the precious cargo into the trunk. It only held about twenty-five or thirty phone books, a number that didn't seem like it would make much of a dent. I piled more in the back seat and on the back shelf, obliterating any visibility of traffic in the rearview mirror. I stacked about eight more onto the front seat and a few on the floor for good measure. Pulling out of the parking lot, I had no clue where I was going. I grabbed the top page out of the packet and glanced at the first address. Without an atlas or a time machine to jump ahead into the age of Google Maps, I was completely lost. The car bottomed out every time I hit a bump, literally scraping asphalt under the weight of my failing adulthood.

I didn't know what to do. I turned into my old neighborhood and drove toward Mom's house, almost wishing for a little sudden unintended acceleration into a telephone pole or something else that would stop the momentum of my trajectory. I made a clumsy left into the driveway and slammed on the brakes. Dwarfed by a mountain of phone books, I turned on the radio to drown out the sound of a grown man falling apart. At the top of the dial, I tuned in an alternative rock station from Philadelphia. The signal was cut

THE CAR BOTTOMED OUT EVERY TIME I HIT A BUMP, LITERALLY SCRAPING ASPHALT UNDER THE WEIGHT OF MY FAILING ADULTHOOD.

with intermittent static, but the lines in the song that needed to reach me came through loud and clear.

The song was called "Creep," and as I bawled my eyes out, I knew for certain that I didn't belong here either. A loud *tap tap tap* on the passenger side window startled me and I turned the radio off. It was Mom. I'll never forget that look in her eyes. There was a hint of distaste that our unwritten rule of stoic nonreaction to disappointment had been broken, but there was mostly sadness, the sadness of witnessing her only son crying in a way she hadn't seen since she broke the news that his father wouldn't be coming home.

ESTATE TALES

DOOHICKEY

Probably sensing the air of desperation in my voice as I recounted the Bell Atlantic debacle and how I had sobbed uncontrollably, blasting the car radio in Mom's driveway before schlepping the whole payload of phone books back to where they came from, my friend Vince had an idea.

Vince had graduated from Tatnall a couple of years behind me and was close with our mutual schoolmate Peter Flint. Peter's parents were looking to hire an assistant for their two groundskeepers at "Flintstead," their aptly named property out in Centerville.

"They *named* their house?" I asked, somewhat triggered.

"Well, it's not *just* a house," Vince began to explain.

Assistant groundskeeper. Hmm. That sounded horrible. Vince reminded me to take it for what it was—a stopgap measure. I couldn't ask Mom for money because I knew she would give it to me. I had to keep making my own way.

As soon as I drove out to Flintstead to meet with Peter's dad, Peter Sr., whom I had previously known only as a substitute math teacher at Tatnall, it all began to make sense. He didn't have to teach math. He didn't *have* to do anything. These people weren't rich, or even filthy rich. They were *wealthy*. Wealthy like the du Ponts, Delaware's first family of chemicals, who they were actually related to. Flintstead was so large it had a two-lane road dividing the property in half. There was a pretty nice house on the left-hand side just when I turned into the driveway, but this was not *the* house; this was the guest house where young Peter lived an early-twenties bachelor life. To get to *the* house, I had to follow a narrow lane back far beyond any visibility from the road. No wonder they needed two groundskeepers. *Of course* the place had a name. It was like Southfork on *Dallas*.

My first day on the job, I met with the head groundskeeper, Chip. He was a friendly, no-nonsense guy, talkative, a bit of a mountain man with a black mustache/beard combo, and a serious farmer's tan from what looked like a lot of years denying his arms the benefit of sunscreen.

Chip explained that I'd be doing a little bit of everything on the estate. Some days I would work with him, and some days I would be with Russ, the other groundskeeper. On my first day, however, I would be completing my inaugural task at Flintstead by myself.

"I gotta head out for a while to help my wife," Chip said.

"Oh, is everything OK?" I asked.

"Yeah, just a pain in the butt. Ladies room at her job keeps overflowin'. I told her, 'Ya need to put a sign in there: NO DOO-HICKEYS IN THE TOILET!'"

"Doohickeys?"

"Yeah, you know, doohickeys," Chip said before lowering his voice to a whisper, "for, uh, *lady problems*."

I nodded, barely concealing my inner promise to myself to remember this moment for life.

"Anyways, good to have you on board," Chip said. "Glad to have the help."

I discovered pretty quickly why he was so glad. It seems I arrived just in time to take care of some unfinished business. He led me over to an empty wooden chicken coop caged in rusty wire mesh that had seen far better days. Chip handed me a shovel and an N95 mask from the back of his truck.

"Listen, I know it ain't pleasant, but I'm gonna need you to clean this out."

Mortified, I took a closer look.

"What's all that white stuff?" I asked.

"That's chicken poop," Chip replied.

"Is it supposed to be *white*?" I asked.

"Well …" He paused. "It's been there a while. Technically, Russ was supposed to do this a couple years ago."

I put the mask over my nose and mouth, entered the coop, and stood atop layer upon layer of petrified chicken waste, several inches deep in some spots.

Strangely amused by my new nadir, I said out loud, "I am literally shoveling shit for money," as I watched Chip drive off in a cloud of dust to solve the doohickey problem.

SALT LICK IN THE WOUND

"Catch any worms yet?"

"Excuse me?" I said.

"Catch any worms yet?"

"I'm sorry, I don't understand."

"The early bird catches the worm."

"Ohhhhh, right. Um, no. No worms yet," I said, smiling my awkward smile.

Thus began my 7:00 am exchange with Mrs. Flint—the elder Mrs. Flint, I should say. She was a tall, matriarchal-looking woman with a full gray head of hair. Pushing ninety, I presumed, she was already awake and fully dressed at the ungodly hour when I stepped inside her house to begin the day working with Flintstead's senior groundskeeper, Russ.

"Everything all right in here?" Russ chirped as he ambled into the room, where I had waited without a buffer for the last twenty minutes. "New kid isn't bothering you, is he? Heh-heh."

Russ was much older than Chip, probably in his early seventies. His legs appeared rail-thin in his bootcut jeans. He wore wire-rimmed glasses and an old-school engineer's cap. I got the impression he had been there a long, long time. While I knew by this point that Chip was the lynchpin at Flintstead, working with Russ felt like an apprentice-ship with a master, a master of doing the absolute bare minimum. It was seriously impressive, the way he could dance around the simplest of tasks, expanding them into beautifully choreographed ballets of subtly time-consuming false starts, tangential conversations, and lengthy cigarette breaks. He only smoked one-hundreds.

Russ led me down to the basement in Mrs. Flint's house, ostensibly to paint an old wooden chair.

"Ah, let's see," he sighed, prying open a can of kelly-green paint with a putty knife. "Hmm. I might try to get the tint on that a little lighter. What do you think?"

"Uh, it looks … green," I said, not really having an opinion.

"Yeah, it changes once it's on the wood," he said, smoothing out his silver mustache with his thumb and forefinger. "I think I got some swatches in here somewhere."

He began rummaging through what looked like random piles of junk. Every couple of minutes, while *not* locating the book of paint swatches, he found something that piqued his interest and began a discussion about it. At one point he unearthed a small canister of buckshot pellets.

"You hunt?" he asked.

"Um, no," I replied.

"We let the hunters in for part of the year just to keep the deer population from going crazy," Russ explained.

"Oh, is it hunting season?" I asked.

"Good question. Not sure about that. I'd have to check the by-laws."

"The by-laws?"

"Oh, yeah, there's a whole book of 'em back here."

It felt like I was following Russ through a maze as we made our way to another section of the basement, where he located the book up on the shelf above a cluttered workbench. It was true. Flintstead had its own by-laws. I didn't really know what by-laws were, but I gathered they were devised to run the property like the virtual sovereign nation it was. Russ laid the book out in front of him and read aloud from a paragraph of by-legalese on the subject of wildlife abatement. The wording sounded official.

While he read aloud, Russ's eyelids drooped into a faint expression of disappointment as he appeared to conclude that taking me out into the woods to shoot a deer in order to avoid painting the chair was not an option.

"Break time!" he shouted, glancing at his watch and turning away from the still open book of by-laws.

We had killed a full hour without a drop of paint touching a brush. We walked outside and stood under a tree near the garage. Russ lit a cigarette as a small pointy-eared brown dog ran up, panting and hopping up on him, looking for a treat.

"Where's your piece o' salt?" Russ taunted the canine, as he went into the garage and reached into a large bag of rock salt.

After fishing around for a second, he pulled out a sizable chunk and offered it to the dog, his arm outstretched, demanding a show of obedience as a condition of receiving the shittiest treat in the history of man's best friend.

"Sit, Boo Boo, sit!" Russ exclaimed.

The dog could not contain its excitement and kept panting and frothing at the mouth, unable to calm down.

"C'mon, Boo Boo, sit," Russ continued. "You don't have a problem."

Well, yeah, he *did*. He was being ordered to beg for salt. This went on for some time. Russ kept calling the dog Boo Boo, which I'm certain was not its actual name. I knew what he was trying to do. He was making a reference, a dated one at that point, to the phrase "Sit, Ubu, sit" spoken by producer Gary David Goldberg after the closing credits on *Family Ties*, a network sitcom that had been off the air since 1989. I became increasingly annoyed, like I would if I heard somebody say "nucular" over and over again. I pictured myself grabbing Russ by the throat and shaking the life out of him as I screamed, *It's Ubu, you idiot, Ubu! Not Boo Boo, UBU!!!*

I felt like I was losing my mind, as I snapped back to reality only to watch a confused animal roll a hard-won clump of sodium chloride around on its tongue, waiting in vain to register the slightest note of pleasure, before finally letting the piece of salt drop from its mouth and walking away.

"Well, beggars can't be choosy," Russ proclaimed, shrugging his shoulders before lighting another cigarette.

VIDI, VICI, VENI

I was not unfamiliar with the great American hallmark of masculine domesticity. I had done my time, spending the Sunday afternoons of my youth gassing up the ancient push mower that had lived on Mom's back porch since the mid-'70s. It was one of those warhorses that required no fewer than ten vigorous yanks on the starter rope to get it running. There was always a winded pause after six or seven pulls to save my rotator cuff and keep the carburetor from flooding. Once it turned over, though, that thing spat out a hail of clippings that could sting the ankles of anyone standing in the line of fire.

I took it in stride when Chip put me on grass duty one morning. I really couldn't call it "mowing the lawn." That term suggests a structured, finite activity. You start in the front yard, you cut in straight rows, you move on to the backyard, maybe try the checkerboard design, but either way, you're done in about an hour. Grass duty at Flintstead wasn't like that. I could ride atop the flaming red Gravely tractor inching along in the same direction for hundreds of yards without having to turn around to go back the other way. The acreage felt infinite, like I could never possibly cover it in its entirety before the grass began to grow back.

It was the kind of summer day that was hot at 9:00 am and only getting hotter as it progressed. Other than a pair of clear safety goggles, there was nothing to shield me from direct sunlight, no shade, not a cloud in the sky. I had no ear protection, and the unforgiving drone of the engine and the spinning blades beneath the deck of the mower throbbed in my eardrums and vibrated through my entire being. I barely looked where I was mowing, instead focusing my eyes on the block-letter Gravely logo staring back at me from the engine cover, mocking the oblivion into which my life was heading on a sputtering lawn tractor. I muttered the words "Frankly, Mr. Gravely" to the vague tune of "Frankly, Mr. Shankly" by the Smiths.

Frankly, Mr. Gravely, you're a fucking cunt.

I repeated that over and over, like a mantra, like a twisted compulsion. There's a line in "Frankly, Mr. Shankly" where Morrissey sings about wanting to go down in musical history. Riding atop that lawn mower, this impossible dream felt about as distant as anything could ever feel. A sense of doom crept in on me, like the door of opportunity was closing before my eyes.

I began to consciously talk to myself, just to hear the sound of something other than "Frankly, Mr. Gravely, you're a fucking cunt" in my head. This brought me no closer to any sense of comfort, only closer to confronting my painful truth.

This is what chasing your dreams looks like. Shoveling chicken shit. Cutting other people's grass. You've really made it, John. You're, like, bigger than Jesus now.

I always liked that variation on the quote attributed to John Lennon about the Beatles being more popular than the son of God, but it never felt like a line in a song until that moment. I stopped the Gravely in its tracks, disengaged the blades, and turned off the engine as the words just poured out.

I'm bigger than Jesus now
And I love her

I'm bigger than Jesus now
Up above her
I'm stage diving off the church of the holier than thou
Oh, I'm bigger than Jesus now

This was the chorus to what became "Devil's Diary," the song that led to the Caulfields' record contract, the song that cracked playlists at modern rock radio stations all over the US and Canada, that made the pop singles chart in Australia, that landed me a publishing deal with Warner Chappell, that paid for the deposit on the house where my kids would grow up.

Moments after my lyrical epiphany, I drove the Gravely to the edge of a small orchard of peach trees and parked again. The fragrance of the ripe low-hanging fruit filled my lungs. I channeled the voice of Russ and audibly murmured, "Break time!" I chose a perfect peach from the closest branch and devoured it on the spot. Streams of nectar dripped from the corners of my mouth and merged at my chin, where syrupy patches of peach fuzz took up residence.

THE CATHOLIC IN ME KNEW I WAS GOING TO HELL. THE ATHEIST IN ME KNEW I WAS ALREADY THERE.

I leaned back in the mower seat with my wheat-colored work boots propped up on the steering wheel. Clasping my sticky fingers behind my neck like I was lounging in a hammock *just thinking up deviltry*, I took pleasure at this oasis in the middle of my existential desert. The juice of the peach, reconstituted with my sweat, stirred my most primal urges.

The Catholic in me knew I was going to hell. The atheist in me knew I was already there. The devil may care, but then again, maybe not. Eventually, as the voyeuristic sun put a sting on my afterglow, I started the Gravely back up and lowered the blade deck, mowing over the evidence of my indulgence before heading back to clock out for the day, singing all the while: *I'm bigger than Jesus now.*

I would spend two more seasons working at Flintstead before a confluence of events allowed me to quit my final low-wage job before beginning my professional music career in earnest. I gave the Flints a proper two weeks' notice, during which Chip addressed me only as "Hollywood" and Russ continued to address the dog as "Boo Boo."

THE END OF THE SALAD DAYS

Although the term had loftier origins in Shakespeare's *Antony and Cleopatra*, "salad days" was a phrase I learned through repeated viewings of the Coen brothers movie *Raising Arizona*. The main character, played by Nicolas Cage, uses the term to refer to happy, innocent times, and I often repeated his monologues verbatim during extended instrumentals at Beat Clinic shows.

Our love for each other was stronger than ever, but I preminisced [*sic*] no return of the salad days.

This is pretty much how I felt about Lisa around the time of our engagement, the same year I would see the Caulfields' musical fortunes finally take a turn for the better. Lisa and I had been a couple for close to seven years, and while it wasn't exactly a "shit or get off the pot" ultimatum, she made it clear that it was time for us to take the logical next step in our relationship, a move that I cosigned with half my heart. I was on a path to signing a major record contract, something I had dreamed of my entire life, and that's where most of my attention went.

I still held on to Tae Hyun's initial reaction to Lisa, upon seeing the wallet-size high school photo of her that I carried around with me when we first became joined at the hip.

"Oh my God, John, she's beautiful. She's a keeper," Tae Hyun said, as she marveled at Lisa's feathered blond hair and shiny teeth that were almost blinding in spite of the fact that she was a smoker for most of her senior year until she quit cold turkey during a serious bout with the flu.

"All you two ever do is eat and laugh," Lisa's sister Kari said to us after it became clear we had established a bit of a pattern. What else did we need? For a time, it seemed like midnight snacks and NBC's Must See TV were the keys to our love surviving into old age. This was the reverie of our world on the cusp of our adulthood beginning in earnest. We had shared our first apartment together in Newark while Lisa started her master's degree. I worked yet another pizza job at Domino's while the Caulfields toiled away.

Although we had no yard for our cats, we drew emotional parallels between ourselves and the characters in that Crosby, Stills & Nash song "Our House." Everything was easy. Sort of. Until it wasn't.

When one of our three cats—Virgil—died in our second apartment in Wilmington, we mourned as if we had lost a child, both of us walking around under a cloud of gloom for well over a month, traumatized by the cat's sudden heart attack that even my panicked attempt at mouth-to-mouth resuscitation couldn't forestall. With our domestic innocence abruptly ended, we ate our feelings and turned to weekly episodes of *Seinfeld* and *Frasier* for comfort. A certain monotony crept into our existence as partners, punctuated by real-world problems like overdrawn checking accounts or smashed car windows. We each bought The Club, a then-popular steering wheel lock, which we thought would somehow protect us from such indignities. This was what it was to be grown up, I supposed.

I don't even remember proposing to Lisa. I just recall a dryly rational, adult discussion in which she stated that it was time. Seven years was enough of a test run. We went to the jewelers together and picked out rings—a no-frills gold band for me, a two-piece engagement-and-wedding-ring combo for her. It felt like ordering very expensive fast food.

We were about nine months from our October 1994 wedding date when Tae Hyun called. I knew things had not been good between her and Tae Kyung. There had been a blowup over the Christmas holiday out in California, where they both lived about twenty minutes from each other. Tae Kyung and her family were late arriving for a dinner that Tae Hyun had taken all day to prepare, and things deteriorated into an argument that resulted in Tae Kyung's departure before anyone had a chance to sit down to eat.

Everything I knew about the incident was secondhand information, but it seemed all too reminiscent of the early-'80s Christmas at Mom's house when Tae Hyun exited before dinner in a similar fashion.

By the time I had hair in my armpits, I was the only one of Mom's children still living at home. Tae Im and Tae Kyung had moved out west, and while Tae Hyun would be making the trip down from her home in Massachusetts, she would be splitting her time between our family and that of her husband, Greg. The food was on the table and ice cold by the time Tae Hyun and Greg arrived over an hour late, having made a late departure from Greg's parents' house in Lancaster. I had never heard Mom yell like that. Even through the floorboards in my bedroom, where I slinked off to hide from the fighting, the mix of English and Korean epithets was crystal clear and jarring. Tae Hyun left the house in tears, and eventually Mom and I sat down and ate cold turkey and stuffing in silence.

It seemed so strange how the shoe was now on the other foot and it was Tae Hyun triggered by a tardy arrival. Apparently, the fallout with Tae Kyung, combined with Mom and Tae Im's disinclination to take Tae Hyun's side in the ensuing couple of weeks, prompted her phone call to me.

She told me that she would not be coming to the wedding, that her daughters—my nieces—would not be my ring bearers, that she was cutting all ties with Mom, with Tae Kyung, with Tae Im—and, although she didn't say it, I knew she was cutting ties with me. I was stupefied. I couldn't believe I was being dumped. I'd had nothing to do with the petty bullshit that surrounded that Christmas dinner or the ghosts of Christmas dinners past. Now I was losing another important person from my already-fragile support system.

Up to that point, I had spent more quality time with Tae Hyun than with anyone else in my family. The summer I spent at her house when I was fifteen provided me a cache of visceral memories and life lessons.

She'd recognized I needed an outlet for my teenage angst, enlisting me to help remodel her downstairs bathroom, an experience that taught me that the pen was not *always* mightier than the sword—or in this case, the sledgehammer—as I harnessed years of pent-up aggression to reduce the dilapidated tiles and drywall to a mildewy pile of rubble.

I learned never to light a gas grill with one's face too close to the burners, as I ran with my hair on fire off the pier in the backyard and dove headfirst into the lake behind Tae Hyun's house.

I learned that tragedy could strike in an instant, in the most unexpected places, as I watched news footage of a hotel walkway collapse at a Hyatt Regency in Kansas City.

I had my moments of peace and reflection, too, rowing Greg's canoe out into the water as the sunshine found its way onto my shoulders.

"This man seems troubled" was Tae Hyun's deadpan quip after we both heard "Who Can It Be Now" by Men at Work for the first time on the radio that summer. The song's hyperneurotic lyrics, sung from the point of view of a guy hiding out behind the locked door of his apartment, were funny and all too relatable to me.

Whether or not she liked the bands I liked, I always felt like she actually listened and took an interest in what interested me. More than anything else, this is what made me feel close to her.

Her frank opinions about the music I listened to made it possible for me to trust her when soliciting her thoughts on my own songs. Or when she told me that Lisa was a keeper. As fate would have it, I wouldn't be able to hold on to either of them. My salad days were truly a thing of the past.

PART V

THE A&M YEARS

All I wanna do
Is make your rock 'n' roll dreams come true

—IKE, "ROCK N ROLL DREAMS"

FOR RUDY

I t was the largest wake I had ever attended. Not that I had much to compare it to.

A long and winding line stretched out to the parking lot at St. Anthony's, as hundreds of people, from sobbing Italian relatives to long-haired musical *paisans*, waited to pay their respects on a cold late-January day. Once inside, many chose not to remove their dark sunglasses, as if to shield their eyes from the infinite reflections of grief that surrounded them. The receiving line was a gauntlet of game-faced family members—siblings and their spouses, and a mother who tried but could not speak through her pain.

Then there was Ritchie, holding it all together by a thread. Ritchie Rubini was already a legend in Delaware, having proved himself as one of the most explosive, creative drummers to sit behind a kit in any of our three counties. I had first seen him as the driving rhythmic force in Honour Society, a moody, textured rock trio led by an eccentric blond front man who, in my estimation, was way too good looking to be as talented as he was. I got to know Ritchie a little bit when the

Caulfields warmed up small but enthusiastic crowds for the band he played in with his departed brother.

Ritchie was the last person standing between Rudy and me. I walked over to the casket, wanting so badly to commune with the rest of the mourners and let my pent-up emotion become part of the whole, but all I could say was, "I'm sorry, Rudy." I was caught up in my own personal version of half-Catholic guilt.

It had been quite the improbable series of events from the late fall of 1993 up until this heartbreaking moment as I stood over Rudy's body. After more than a year of struggling to get the already-limited number of original-music fans in the tri-state area to fully embrace the Caulfields, I had come to believe we were out of time and would fall apart for good in a month or two if no ray of hope shone in our direction. That ray somehow appeared in the form of a series of gigs opening for Matt Sevier, a Delaware guy who was now ruling the roost in Philadelphia. The Beat Clinic had done shows with his old band, the Motion. His most memorable show flyer included the tagline, "It ain't the Meat, it's the Motion."

Since acquiring management and setting his sights on Philly, Matt's independent album *Faultlines*, which Rudy produced, became the biggest local independent record in years, thanks in large part to serious airplay for the single "Marry Katherine" on the burgeoning triple-A radio station WXPN. Ritchie played drums in Matt's backing band and was effusive in his welcome when we arrived at TJ Rafters to open a show they were videotaping for Prism, a local premium cable channel.

After our forty-minute set, Matt's manager, Doron Segal, waved me over to the bar. Doron had come up in the business as a teenage entrepreneur, scalping tickets to Grateful Dead shows, earning the nickname "Ticketron Doo-ron." Jovial and informal, wearing a T-shirt and baseball cap, he didn't put out the same standoffish vibe that some of the other managers in the city did. He was approachable and wasn't afraid to come off like a fan.

He gushed over our performance and my songs to the point where I began to feel uncomfortable, like I was getting smoke blown up my ass. Then he stopped midsentence as if struck with an epiphany:

"You got a tape? I know a guy who would really dig what you're doing."

He was talking about Rudy. I told him about my prior history with the Rubinis.

Doron indicated that if Rudy produced some proper studio recordings for the Caulfields, he might possibly be able to help us achieve some of the success that Matt was currently enjoying.

The next day, I drove the mile and a half from my apartment in Trolley Square to the house on the 1900 block of Elm Street, where Rudy and Ritchie grew up, in the heart of Wilmington's Little Italy. Rudy answered the door with a welcoming smile and open arms, and quickly reached for the cassette of four-track recordings in my hand. He wasted no time firing up the stereo and popping in the tape, which contained lo-fi demo versions of some of the Caulfields' core songs— "Devil's Diary," "Awake on Wednesday," "Rickshaw," "Fragile." I was antsy, just standing with my hands in my front pockets, as Rudy tapped his foot and nodded, looking more convinced of something with each passing second. Watching him listen to me, I couldn't help but think of the song "Excitable Boy" by Warren Zevon, because by the time the first chorus of "Devil's Diary" was over, he went from exuberant to damn near maniacal.

"DUDE! 'Bigger than Jesus'?! Are you kidding me? That's a fucking hit, man!"

By the end of the last song, I could barely escape back to my car between Rudy's jubilant expletives and words of praise. I must admit it was exciting to have that kind of positive feedback, especially at a time when it felt like no one else was listening. Less than twenty-four hours later, my phone rang. I picked up and barely got out the word "hello" before I heard Rudy singing on the other end, "I'm bigger than Jesus now!" It was so loud that the phone distorted. Rudy called me every day for a solid week, almost as if he felt he needed to be more ardent than the other producers he perhaps assumed were beating down my door. Did he not realize he was the only one?

"Listen. John. Would it be OK with you if I sent this to a friend of mine at A&M Records?"

I couldn't help but let out a "yeah, right" smirk before I said, "Sure, no problem," absolutely positive that he was bullshitting me. Who the hell would he know at a record company, especially one like A&M? So much of the music that I'd listened to growing up was released on this label, dating all the way back to my sister's Carpenters and Cat Stevens albums to Captain & Tennille, Rita Coolidge, Peter Frampton, and Pablo Cruise 45s I acquired as a preteen to albums by artists I loved in high school—the Police, Joe Jackson, Squeeze.

"My friend Mark works there," Rudy said. "He's been doing A&R for Janet and Sting, but he's looking to start signing his own bands."

Janet? As in Janet *Jackson*? And Sting? As in *Sting*?

"No way. How do you know this guy?" I pressed.

"He grew up in the house right behind here," Rudy said.

Mark Mazzetti had, in fact, lived a stone's throw from the Rubinis. The backs of their homes shared a common alleyway. Mark had big show-biz dreams growing up and followed his bliss to a job at A&M, first working records in the Philadelphia radio market, then eventually moving out to Hollywood, into a house where Axl Rose once lived.

The white grand piano that probably survived countless renditions of "November Rain" came with the place. Although Mark was overseeing projects for Sting and Janet Jackson, he had not himself signed anyone to the label yet and was primed for that next step, ready to nurture an unproven act and lead them to the platinum promised land.

My internal defense mechanisms demanded I remain unmoved. I had been through this process enough times before to know not to get my hopes up. Previous representatives like Vikki Walls and entertainment attorney John Luneau had sent Beat Clinic CDs to every major and independent label there was. A&R guys always had the same response: No. "But keep sending more songs," they would say, never completely slamming the door. I was sure this would be just another case of music-industry blue balls.

Within days, however, the phone rang. "Are you sitting down, dude?"

I wasn't. I preferred to stand.

"Mark listened to the songs. He LOVES them. Fucking LOVES them. He's flying home for the holidays next week. He wants to come to a gig. Let me know your schedule—anything in Wilmington, Philly; I'll even drag him up to New York."

My heart sank. We had nothing on the books in December. Nothing in Delaware. Nothing in Philadelphia. Nothing in New Jersey. And definitely nothing in New York. I had long since lost my taste for playing eight weeks of phone tag to get a Wednesday night at Kenny's Castaways.

"Wait, you're saying you have *no* shows coming up?" Rudy barked.

"Nothing until January," I said.

"Dude, I have a vice president of A&R from A&M Records coming to your hometown to see you perform. You don't have a fucking show? You CREATE a fucking show! I don't care how you do it!"

I'm not sure if Rudy realized what a brilliant idea he had just blurted out, but there it was. We would create our own showcase. Doron, who had the savvy to officially offer to manage us as soon as he learned Rudy was shopping the tape, reserved a room at the "Opera House," which I referred to in a 1994 interview as "a real junky rehearsal space off Route 76." This was where we played the "show" that got us the offer that would change everything.

A few days before Christmas, Rudy and Doron ushered Mark Mazzetti into the rehearsal room at the Opera House, and with the three of them standing against the back wall as our only audience, we launched into a short set consisting of six songs, all of which would eventually appear on our first album. That was all it took.

"I'm sold!" Mazzetti said after we were finished. "I'm going to sign you."

It was unbelievable. It wasn't real. Of course, I was thrilled, but I couldn't bring myself to accept it. Surely, some unforeseen shoe was waiting to drop.

Mazzetti flew back to LA the first week in January, leaving us with his handshake promise and instructions to hire an entertainment lawyer who should call A&M's legal department a few weeks into the new year once the company was up and running again after the holidays.

Our first show of 1994 was the kind of engagement that would keep any band about to sign a record contract from getting too full of themselves. With a few inches of snow already on the ground and more in the forecast, we arrived at Rex's in West Chester, Pennsylvania, which was just as I remembered from when it was known as Joe's Sportsman's Lounge back in the '80s.

The last time I touched a microphone in that building, two bikers incited a full-on barroom brawl, culminating in a trash can full of glass beer bottles flying across the dance floor. By rights, we should have called the whole thing off, but I was still punishing myself over the time when, years earlier, I had feigned illness to bag out of a gig at a Delco dive bar called Cheecho's. I was certain that the unruly crowd of locals, already Bud-drunk by our 7:00 pm load-in, was going to eat me alive.

For most of our set at Rex's, the band was close to outnumbering the audience, which included the bartender, the sound guy, and a handful of people who lived within walking distance of the club. Rudy hadn't showed up as he had promised, but none of us thought any less of him. It was a disaster outside. I figured he'd done the sensible thing and just stayed home, but shortly after we got offstage, the door swung open, and Rudy walked in. He was shivering, dressed like it was springtime, with only a suit jacket to protect him from the elements. He had wet snow caked in his hair. His face was soaked from what looked like a combination of sleet and sweat.

"What the hell happened to you?" I asked.

"I'm so sorry man," he said. "I got lost."

He had been walking around in near whiteout conditions for close to an hour. He was parked five blocks away. All four of us offered to drive him back to his car, wondering why he hadn't worn a proper coat.

"No, man, it's cool! I'll be fine. Let's talk tomorrow, OK? Hey, get ready, you're gonna be famous!"

He walked back out into the blustery night, all smiles and optimism.

That's how I wanted to remember Rudy, going off like a firecracker, radiating joy for the music and the musicians he loved. Not lying there motionless in an open casket, eyes closed, one hand crossed tastefully over the other just above his waist. I didn't want that Rudy, silent and surrounded by crying relatives in suits and black dresses except for that one uncle who shows up to *everything* in a turtleneck.

THAT'S HOW I WANTED TO REMEMBER RUDY, GOING OFF LIKE A FIRE-CRACKER, RADIATING JOY FOR THE MUSIC AND THE MUSICIANS HE LOVED.

One look at that guy, and all I could think about was David Letterman's quip to Clint Eastwood during Johnny Carson's final week on the *Tonight Show*:

Would it have killed you to wear a tie?

I wanted the Rudy who would have found that funny, the Rudy with the infectious laugh and the shit-eating grin on his face, feigning a heart attack whenever a pretty girl walked by, like he was Redd Foxx in *Sanford and Son*.

Ay Madonn'! You see that chick? Jesus Christ, I'm sittin' on a fuckin' pack o' hotdogs here!

I don't think I ever completely understood what he meant by that. Maybe it felt like he had eight boners or something? However you wanted to interpret the hyperbolic erectile imagery, the bottom line was tears streaming down your face from laughing so hard. Those were the good kind of tears.

Instead, less than two weeks after one unlucky night in the snow, a case of walking pneumonia, and a diabetic coma, he was gone, way too soon, at thirty-six, and we were all crying the bad kind of tears.

I touched Rudy's hand and said goodbye. On my way back to my seat, Mark Mazzetti walked up to me and grabbed me by both shoulders.

"We *have* to make this record now," he whispered directly into my ear.

"I know we do," I said. "For Rudy."

BABY BAND

In the weeks after Rudy died, life in the Caulfields ramped up in a serious way. Just a few months earlier, I was hanging by a thread, miserable, throwing my back out at Flintstead, wondering where I was headed with the band. It was an all-time low. It didn't matter that I was sitting on what I considered to be the best songs I'd ever written. If it wasn't for the events that led up to and resulted from handing that hiss-laden no-fi demo tape off to Rudy, how much longer could I have gone on?

I was tired of working shitty jobs, taken solely for the purpose of leaving my nights open for gigs, and still not making enough to be able to tell Mom no when she silently slipped me a bank envelope of cash to cover groceries or my electric bill. I had been pursuing music full bore for close to a decade, and at twenty-seven I was no spring chicken anymore by music-business standards. Now, by the grace of all that went down, I was on a New Jersey Transit commuter train with my bandmates, heading up to the law offices of Grubman, Indursky & Schindler in New York City to sign a seven-album deal with A&M Records.

When you're new to all this and someone offers you a seven-album deal, you start thinking, "Wow, that's like going from 'I Want to Hold Your Hand' to 'Mean Mr. Mustard.' I'm going to have an incredible career." It all *sounds* pretty incredible until you actually read the contract—or have your New York entertainment attorney explain it to you. It turns out that the seven albums are all at the label's option, meaning *they* can drop *you* at any time for whatever reason, but you, the artist, can't leave until your seven-record obligation is up.

That doesn't sound fair, does it? And why seven albums, and not six or ten? "That's just the industry standard," our lawyer Jonathan Ehrlich said in a characteristic deadpan on more than a few occasions, as I sat on the client side of his desk on the thirty-first floor of his Manhattan office, coveting the set of yin-and-yang-decorated Chinese stress balls I had given him as a thank-you. Jonathan was a kind but imposing figure, in spite of being basically no taller than I was. His articulate, deliberate speech and glassy, no-blink stare kept one prevailing thought in the front of my mind at all times: I was glad he was on *my* side.

It was his stone-faced certitude that would later keep me from going off the deep end after turning in our first album only to realize I might have inadvertently plagiarized a Jellyfish song in the melody of "Devil's Diary." He calmly sent a well-worded letter to songwriters Andy Sturmer and Roger Manning and secured a gratis license for their song "New Mistake," along with an assurance that they didn't even think it sounded like I had lifted anything.

That same confidence allowed him to negotiate a guaranteed second album into the Caulfields' A&M contract.

"You're really lucky I landed that," he told me. "They don't do that for every baby band."

I did not care for the term "baby band," which was music-business lingo for a freshly signed, unproven act. In my mind, we had been *around*. We were already legit, bona fide, with years of experience and hundreds of shows under our collective belt. *Who the fuck* are you calling a *baby band*?

As we each navigated our copies of the inch-thick contract, obeying the "sign here" stickers that were, ironically, in the shape of little red flags, what I didn't yet understand was that the term "baby band" fit the Caulfields to a *T*. We may have *thought* we knew what we were doing as music-scene veterans from the second-smallest state in the country—and even that was an iffy presumption—but when it came to the real music business, a world of attorneys, accountants, personal managers, tour managers, booking agents, record labels, publishing companies, contracts, royalties, band agreements, etc., etc., etc.—well, let's just say I wasn't enjoying my Yul Brynner impersonation quite as much as I used to.

In this new world, the Caulfields were as green as they come. And when you're green, those who are not green treat you as fair game. For our first album, A&M agreed to an advance of $250,000. *Holy shit*, you say. My sentiment exactly. That seemed like a huge sum of money. It *was* a huge sum of money to me and to the rest of the band. And we would be allowed to keep everything that was left after we delivered the record. I felt like I was living that line in "Rosalita" when Bruce Springsteen shouts up to Rosie's window after getting a massive check from his record company.

Then reality set in, and we had to pay the commissions. When your band signs a deal of this magnitude, chances are you didn't arrive there on your own. You probably had some help and became indebted to some people along the way: your manager, for example. Our management agreement with Doron asked for a commission of 20 percent on everything we made—not after expenses, but 20 percent of the gross. Then we paid Jonathan a 10 percent commission on the contract advance. He had more than earned his keep, so we figured it was worth it. Doron's 20 percent cut felt a little deep, but it was only one of many times we would say yes to something when we were told it was merely "industry standard."

Besides, Doron did, after all, get the ball rolling with Rudy. Plus, he negotiated a deal with our new business manager, Bert Padell, known in the industry as the "accountant to the stars." After taking a ten-minute phone call with Madonna in the middle of our first meeting, Bert agreed to waive his usual 5 percent of a client's gross from our initial advance. He didn't have to do that, but from one look around his downtown Manhattan office, which was lined with gold and platinum records and rare baseball memorabilia signed by clients like Joe DiMaggio, it was pretty obvious he didn't need our measly $12.5K.

We were grateful for that gesture and just considered the money we would have paid Bert as part of the budget we would use to make the record. If someone were to hand you $12,500 today, you could make a great-sounding album and even have money left over to get it mastered or pay for digital distribution. In the midst of the alternative rock era, when business at high-end recording facilities was booming, that particular sum would buy precisely six days of studio time. When the Caulfields began laying down tracks for what would become *Whirligig*, our major-label debut album, the "baby band" from Newark would need close to three months and $140,000 to get it done.

FOUND MONEY

I t wasn't as if we didn't have options back east. We could have gone up to New York to Electric Lady or Fort Apache in Boston. We could have done the really smart thing and gone to Studio 4, right outside of Philly in Conshohocken. We could have recorded with the Butcher Brothers, who were coming off producing one of my favorite guitar albums in recent memory—*Saturation* by Urge Overkill—and we could have slept in our own beds at home, preventing thousands of dollars from hemorrhaging from our A&M advance.

But that would have made too much sense. The prevailing mentality was to spend the money that we, the Caulfields, had been fronted and would eventually have to pay back, recouping, not through gross record sales but through a thin sliver of those sales, the 12 percent royalty rate spelled out in our contract. Taking into account further deductions for promotional copies, cracked jewel cases, and whatever else could be charged back to us, it boiled down to this depressing fact: one album sold at the suggested retail price would yield a royalty hovering somewhere around a dollar and change. We would practically have to go gold just to break even.

Honestly, as far as I was concerned, it was all found money. We would cross the payback bridge when we got to it. In the summer of 1994, that bridge was the Golden Gate. Sam, Mike, Scott, and I were heading to California to make our debut album at the Plant in Sausalito.

This was all Kevin Moloney's idea. Kevin's name kept coming up in band discussions of A&M's three-page list of potential record producers. A native Irishman, he began his studio career as an assistant on U2's first album, *Boy*, and had notable success as a producer with Sinéad O'Connor's debut *The Lion and the Cobra* in 1987. I remembered seeing the MTV video for her single "Mandinka" and feeling simultaneously fascinated and scared shitless of her. Who was this woman with the shaved head? More recently, she had ripped a picture of the pope in half on live TV. If Moloney could work with *her*, he could certainly handle the Caulfields.

ONE ALBUM SOLD AT THE SUGGESTED RETAIL PRICE WOULD YIELD A ROYALTY HOVERING SOMEWHERE AROUND A DOLLAR AND CHANGE. WE WOULD PRACTICALLY HAVE TO GO GOLD JUST TO BREAK EVEN.

We were all-in on Kevin, and on his proposal that we record at the Plant, which charged $2,000 a day for a lockout in Studio B, one of its two main recording rooms. A "lockout" means no one else can book a session in your studio, even at night, after, like Elvis, you've left the building. You get to leave all your gear set up for when you come back the next day, which may not sound like a big deal, but it really makes a difference. The only issue is, in addition to paying for all the hours that you're there recording, you're also paying for all the hours that you're *not* there recording, which, in our case, included Saturdays and Sundays because Kevin wanted his weekends off.

Whatever. It's found money, right?

We booked the studio at the daily lockout rate from early June until the middle of August. Then we hired a recording engineer, Tracy Chisholm. A notable producer in his own right, Tracy had recently scored a big modern rock radio hit that I loved—"Feed the Tree" by Belly. We hadn't expected to hire a separate engineer, but Kevin made the argument that he could work a lot more efficiently in the studio if he had a right-hand man. It would be a great pairing, like George Martin and Geoff Emerick. OK, so we'll use up more of the budget to pay a second guy to set up the mics, tweak the EQ on the console, hit "record"—all stuff that the first guy is totally capable of doing, but whatever, it's found money, right?

Cash was just flying out of our recoupable account at A&M, including a pretty penny for lodging—a room at a nice hotel for Tracy; a five-bedroom band house, complete with a hot tub on the patio; and for Kevin, a private houseboat docked at the marina about a hundred paces from the studio on Bridgeway.

The Plant was impossible to miss, with its huge 2200 address stenciled in white over the slanted redwood planks on the building's exterior. The front entrance depicts a playful scene of rock 'n' roll animals—literal animals—carved directly into the wooden double doors. There's an owl playing the saxophone, a pig playing the trumpet, a bear on fiddle, a dog strumming a left-handed guitar, a drumming fox in a tuxedo, a frog crashing two cymbals together, a beaver with a squeezebox.

Right beyond that front door was a universe with the warm welcoming glow of a lava lamp illuminating a high school friend's basement. The walls of the front hallway were decorated with the yin-and-yang-shaped wooden invitations from the studio's 1972 kickoff party, which was attended by two Beatles and countless other luminaries from the halcyon days of rock royalty. The narrow corridor leading back to our new sonic playground came straight out of a carnival fun house, complete with warped walls and sloping floors that turned wheeling a road case into a psychedelic experience.

Sly Stone had basically lived in this place. Rick James recorded "Super Freak" here. Prince did his entire first album here, long before he built Paisley Park. KSAN, the San Francisco rock station that aired a profanity-laced interview with the Sex Pistols on the night before they imploded at Winterland in 1978, had done a series of live radio broadcasts here, capturing performances by artists ranging from Bob Marley to Linda Ronstadt to Link Wray. In short, I was stumbling in the footsteps of giants.

The tracking room in Studio B was a time capsule of posthippie aesthetics, painted with trippy earth-tone stripes and decorated with pillowy acoustic wall hangings shaped like paisley tear drops or sperm, depending on whom you asked. In the control room, a large tapestry covered the back wall. A guitar, supposedly left behind by Carlos Santana, appeared randomly in a different spot every day. A twenty-four-track two-inch tape machine stood next to a plethora of rack-mounted outboard gear. There was so much to see, so much to marvel at.

It wasn't until I stopped to take a good look at the sixty-four-channel console, the Neve 8086, the exact board in the exact spot where Fleetwood Mac recorded *Rumours*, the year I was nine going on ten, that I began to feel the weight of the opportunity I had been given. I was excited, to be sure, but that excitement was coupled with a feeling of responsibility not to sully what had come before me. Maybe part of it was the residual effect of all the times Mom reminded me to respect my elders. Maybe part of it had to do with Rudy. Maybe another part, albeit a tiny one, was me starting to accept the possibility that my being here was no accident, that I belonged here, and that it was time to show what I could do.

If you were to play back the master tape at the end of our first day at the Plant, there wouldn't be that much to listen to. For my own part, I spent most of it gobsmacked in complete silence. After everyone was finally done drooling over the gear and the history inside Studio B, the first several hours of the session were spent focused exclusively on the drums, not actually recording anything yet, just figuring out how they should sound. Scott must have tried out close to ten different snare drums, all with different characteristics that affected the vibe of the kit in some subtle or not-so-subtle way. He had his choice of aluminum shell, maple shell, mahogany shell, steel hoops, or wooden hoops. I think he ended up going with the vintage Ludwig that our road manager, Tony DeVitto, picked up from Black Market Music in San Francisco.

Beyond the snares, there was the rest of the set to contend with. Kevin demanded consummate precision from Scott, directing him as he tuned each drum on his brand-new DW five-piece kit, paid for with found money, of course.

"C'mon, Scotty, give us a little more bottom end on rack two."

I could listen to Kevin Moloney's voice all day every day. He spoke in a rapid-fire cadence that sounded to me like a bastard combination of Irish and British accents.

The strangest thing I'll never forget about Kevin is that he pronounced "urine" two different ways, neither of which sounded like the word "urine." In one instance he might take a sip of a skunked beer and say "Uwww, this beer tastes like *yur-een*." Then he might recount the experience a few minutes later and say, "The beer was foul; it was like drinking *yur-ein*." I never asked him about it, but the question always remained in my mind: Yur-een? Yur-ein? I mean, which is it?

"OK, Scotty, now gimme the floor."

Scott, who was himself the kind of guy who always kept a drum key handy, didn't seem to mind this level of meticulousness, at least not for the first hour. Then I could tell he was beginning to lose his patience. I would be getting annoyed, too, if I had to sit there whacking a floor tom a couple hundred times in a row while two guys on the other side of the glass fiddled with every conceivable switch, knob, button, and slider within arm's reach only to tell me to give the tuning lugs another quarter turn and start the whole process over again.

In recording vernacular, Studio B was referred to as a "dead room," meaning it was designed and soundproofed to have virtually no natural reverberation. In the '70s, this was perfect for achieving the tight, dry drum sound that you hear on Fleetwood Mac songs like "Dreams" and "Go Your Own Way." As much as I love those songs, that's not the kind of sound we were looking for. Our drums needed to jump out of the speakers. Scott's playing style, while tight and full of attention to detail, lacked a certain rock 'n' roll abandon, which was what Sam was trying to draw out of him when he walked into the tracking room to persuade Scott to go for a more aggressive, washy sound. Sam suggested that Scott ride the crash cymbal instead of playing the hi-hat on the intro to "Devil's Diary."

Scott dropped the gloves right out of the gate: "Why would I take suggestions from you? You didn't even go to college."

Sam hit back: "You fucking asshole, I did go to college! I just didn't finish."

That was their relationship in a nutshell. They were the only rhythm section I knew of with a drummer who explicitly told the bass player never to look at him onstage. Their wives were best friends, yet Scott and Sam could barely tolerate each other.

"Leave him alone, Salvatore Schillaci!" Kevin yelled as he motioned for Sam to get back in the control room. "Salvatore Schillaci" was the name of an Italian footballer playing for Inter Milan at the time. His name had become Sam's alias in recent months because no one we encountered in the music business seemed capable of correctly pronouncing "Musumeci." Even Mark Mazzetti, our own A&R person, who was himself Italian, could only get as close as "Musamakamikamaka."

Sam returned from his unsuccessful mission looking resigned to let Scott do his thing. At most any recording session, there's already pressure on the drummer. If a band is not tracking live in the studio with everybody playing at once, the drummer has to track the song by himself, playing from memory, or with the help of a very minimal scratch track. They have to nail every accent, every fill, every change in dynamics, and they have to do all this in time with a click track, a computer-generated metronome that keeps the beats-per-minute consistent throughout the song.

Anyone else playing on the recording can go back and fix mistakes they made during a take, but the drummer has to play the entire song correctly all the way through, because it's a lot harder to go back and "punch in" something they messed up. One of the assistants from the Plant told us firsthand horror stories, recounting endless hours of tape splicing and editing on Lars Ulrich's drums recorded down the hall in Studio A, where Metallica had more or less a permanent lockout.

Scott made it through some pretty solid takes for a couple of songs. They were well executed, but they still sounded a little polite, as he made quite sure not to use any of Sam's college-dropout suggestions. Tracy proposed a radical idea borrowed from Tchad Blake, who was the engineer on Suzanne Vega's album *99.9 F°*. Blake ran a lot of drum tracks on that record through a SansAmp, which was like a tube amp in an effects box, primarily used on guitar and bass to achieve a gritty, overdriven sound. The sonic result of this technique on the Suzanne Vega record was a dark twist on her usual New York coffeehouse folk pop.

After Tracy connected the SansAmp directly in line with Scott's drum tracks coming through the Neve console, Kevin sprung up off the ergonomic kneeling stool he had brought with him to the studio and grinned like the devil as Tracy refined the sound.

He kept the clean, unaffected drums intact, then blended in just enough distortion from the SansAmp to make the combination sound absolutely massive. And also kind of weird. It wasn't at all what I expected the drums on our album would sound like, but there was something about it that was different and interesting.

At the end of the day, we all sat around in the control room and shot the shit. I had my first one-on-one conversation with Tracy, who grew up near Philly, going to Flyers hockey games as a kid before moving up north to start his career in the Boston-area music scene of the late '80s. Tracy had been the engineer on *Nicely, Nicely*, the first album by Blake Babies, a Boston band fronted by Juliana Hatfield, one of my all-time favorites. I grilled him about what it was like to work on the Belly record, having been a big fan of their lead singer Tanya Donelly when she played guitar in Throwing Muses.

Through Tracy, I was one degree of separation from all these artists I adored. It was pretty intoxicating. I started to feel more of that elusive sense of connection I had been searching for. Even though I barely did anything besides listen and observe, it felt like we had all made it through our first day at the Plant together, each of us acclimating in our own way at a studio where it was easy to believe that the ghosts of great recordings past would be scrutinizing our every move.

Any such philosophizing came to an abrupt halt when I heard hysterical laughter coming from the tracking room. I ducked around the corner to find my bandmates gawking at Tony DeVitto, lying on his back on top of a small riser at the far end of Studio B. I watched as he hoisted his legs into the air and bent his knees up to his chest, bringing the back side of his army-camouflage cargo shorts into full view. He then positioned a cigarette lighter in the vicinity of his bullseye, and in what seemed like, and was in fact, a flash—a puff of blue flame—his physical release acted as metaphor for the passing of tension within us all.

"Jesus Christ, Tony!" Sam yelled from a safe distance. "We're paying two thousand bucks a day in here, and you're lighting your fuckin' farts on fire!"

I had never been part of a more gut-wrenching, tear-inducing, cathartic bout of collective laughter than the one Tony gave us that night. Now it felt like we could relax and get down to the business of making an album.

I can't think of a better way to spend found money. Can you?

ECOSYSTEM OF A VAN

Any starstruck kid with even a passing interest in mastering the air guitar can picture themselves in the thick of it: the nomadic fantasy of life in a rock 'n' roll band. You are at the center of it all, from the moment you roll up fashionably late to soundcheck, all the way to the third encore, the meet-and-greet, the after-party, the hotel lobby, and whatever happens around about 4:00 am when you have to clear the lobby. And you always wind up back at the center of your aspirational universe: the fifty-foot custom tour bus that delivers you in comfort and luxury to every stop on a road trip that never ends.

The distinction that most people fail to make in these splendorific daydreams is that being a rock *musician*, even one signed to a big contract, does not automatically make you a rock *star*. The term "rock star" has been co-opted anyway, used far more these days to refer to athletes or influencers or tattooed pastry chefs—just about anyone besides actual working musicians. And for good reason, I guess. Those other people make money.

While I did receive a couple of sizable advances just before Lisa and I tied the knot in the months just after *Whirligig* was recorded, the only time I even got close to a tour bus throughout my four years as an "A&M Recording Artist" was the third week of the Caulfields' cross-country expedition supporting our label mates Del Amitri. "The Dels" were a Scottish band whose hit single "Roll to Me" was the best—and probably only—two-minute song on the radio in 1995.

At one of the tour's more sparsely attended shows, somewhere in the depths of Florida, Del Amitri's guitarist Iain did some serious damage to a fifth of Wild Turkey, or as I came to call it, "Waaaald Tearkay." Tony DeVitto, a bad influence when it came to the brown liquors, had left a full bottle of bourbon on the head of Iain's Orange amplifier onstage. It was the perfect night to take advantage of free booze in the sort of place where the crowd was noticeably more enthusiastic *after* the show was over and the DJ started playing "Hey Man, Nice Shot" over the PA at twice the volume of the live bands.

By the end of last call, Iain was laid out on the dance floor with a bouncer hovering over him yelling expletives, decipherable only by the shape of his cartoonish mouth. Ritchie Rubini, who had replaced Scott Kohlmorgen as our drummer after *Whirligig* was recorded, just happened to be standing in the vicinity with me when the bouncer aggressively pointed at us, then pointed at Iain, then pointed at the exit sign, in an apparent signal to get him out of the club, like it was *our* responsibility. I'm sure it looked quite comical to anyone who saw the two of us, neither one over 5'6", each grabbing a shoulder of an incapacitated, walrus-mustached, mutton-chopped Scotsman well over six feet tall. Somehow we managed to assist him across the parking lot to Del Amitri's $1,000-a-day tour bus.

As we tapped on the door, one of the crew members emerged, looking mildly irked before noticing Iain practically in a heap on the asphalt below. Rolling his eyes, he gave Ritchie and me a quick nod that said, "I got this from here." We stood off to the side and watched him latch his forearms under Iain's armpits and, with brute strength, pull him into the bus before closing the door in our faces without so much as a "Smell ya later."

We didn't need no stinkin' tour bus. The Caulfields got from point *A* to point *Z* in a classic made-in-America conversion van, painted in nothing-to-see-here factory white. Just one look at this type of vehicle could launch me back to the late 1970s, into a world where all tube socks are pulled up as far as they can go and "Baker Street" by Gerry Rafferty is on the radio three times an hour. I can see my near-pubescent self riding shotgun in my future brother-in-law's white van, the one he and my sister would take on their cross-country honeymoon the following year. That thing was a straight-up *shaggin' wagon* with deep pile carpeting, a foam mattress in the back, and a toilet you could piss-but-not-shit in. I guess you can't have everything, even when you're partying like a rock star.

There was no toilet in the Caulfields' van. You had three options if you needed to pee. In a relatively low state of urgency, the most civilized choice would be to request an official detour to a rest area or a truck stop. Of course, there might not be one for a hundred miles. You could also relieve yourself on the side of the road. Everybody's had to do that in a pinch. However, if the shoulder is too narrow to safely pull over and there's nary a Petro or Flying J or Pilot to be found, your only choice is to keep it "in house." Urinating into an empty container while in a moving vehicle is never a desirable state of affairs. It's a desperation you come to through your own poor planning and negligence, but once you arrive, you've reached the point of no return.

In situations like this, the receptacle is everything. A wide-mouthed plastic jug is a best-case scenario for obvious reasons. Ritchie once used his own empty wine bottle, a trickier proposition requiring much greater concentration. By far, however, the most desperate act of vehicular micturition is to relieve oneself out of an open window. No one is safe during this nuclear option. If you tour the country long enough, you'll hear more than a few cautionary tales of drunken, contorted bodies whizzing into subzero winter gusts while singing, "you are the wind beneath my wang," only later to discover, on the side of the van, the strange phenomenon best described as "pissicles."

Let's face it, musicians are savages, and the Caulfields were no different. The carpet in our van was stained with the crumbs of ground-up Cheez-Its and other savory snacks. Thrice-worn socks and a vague musk reminiscent of a high school locker room infused a humid fog that hung in the air at all times. As unappealing as all that may sound, we had no choice but to make the van our home. It was a living room, a dining room, and a bedroom all in one. You know how they say you spend a third of your life asleep? Well, we spent at least a third of ours driving all over creation in a plain white machine of mystery, trying, but often failing, to sleep.

The captain's chairs and cutesy features of a conversion van are better suited for the weekend warrior than the traveling rock band. We barely even used the on-board VCR with its ten-inch built-in TV screen. The only VHS tape we had on board was a dub of a dub of a dub of a porn compilation presented to us as part of a "care package" from Terry, one of our A&M marketing reps. It felt as if the scenes on this tape had been hand-selected to induce what Cher Horowitz from *Clueless* would have called a "shame spiral." I still can't unsee the one close-up that prompted me to call one male performer's wrinkled scrotum a "goddamned petrified kiwi fruit."

I placed the blame for this trauma directly at Terry's feet the next time I saw him in Los Angeles and was met with utter disappointment.

"No! You didn't watch it to the end? He absolutely *litters* all over her face!"

Our first van didn't take long to fall apart. With a loaded thirteen-foot trailer hitched to the back, the Dodge was no match for regular uphill climbs over the Appalachians, even at the snail's pace of first gear. The transmission blew somewhere just outside of Virginia Beach, a seven-hour drive from that day's gig in Augusta. We were scheduled to be one of the headliners at "Butt Jam '95," a cleverly branded benefit concert to save the Butt Memorial Bridge, the namesake of Archibald Butt, a notable military figure from the late 1800s and an unfortunate drowning victim on the *Titanic*.

Channel Z, the local modern rock station playing "Devil's Diary," was the driving force behind Butt Jam, and the owner, a radio mogul known only as "Super Frank," reacted like we had fucked him with no lube when he received the news that we would have to cancel our appearance. He pointed out—in the subtlest way possible, of course—that it would be a damn shame if the station had to drop the record in light of our letting down all those listeners who had been waiting to see us in the flesh.

We got the message loud and clear, and Tony got on the horn to contact every private plane company in the Virginia Beach yellow pages. A few phone calls later, he had chartered a same-day flight to Georgia and took one for the team on his personal Amex to the tune of $5,400.

Standing on the tarmac of a small airfield, the Caulfields made the requisite "day the music died" references while the pilot wrote down how much each of us weighed and distributed us and our gear as evenly as possible throughout the plane.

The interior of the private jet was more cramped than the van for most of us, except for Sam, who commandeered the co-pilot's chair and partook of the free snacks. I sat in my tiny seat with clenched fists and closed eyes, "American Pie" playing on the jukebox in my head, as we took off into the air, weighing in at maximum tonnage.

We made it in time to play the show in Augusta and save our radio spins. After a few handshakes and T-shirt sales, we got right back on the plane and returned to Virginia and our broken-down van.

We waited in limbo for days as Doron made groveling phone calls to the record company. With another recoupable wad of money thrown our way, we found ourselves in a brand-new Ford E-250, a beast of a vehicle that felt more like a tank. This van was built for survival. It became our permanent inner sanctum and, not surprisingly, a battleground for our individual freedoms.

It didn't take much for Sam and me to get on each other's nerves. The slightest whiff from one of his Marlboro Lights would set me off, even if he was riding up front with the window cracked and I was stretched out on the highly coveted back bench.

"Do you *want* me to lose my voice, little man?" I would yell up to the front, most certainly causing my vocal cords more damage than Sam's secondhand smoke.

"Shut your dirty little mouth, ya asshole," Sam chirped back.

"You cocksucker, if I can't sing, there's no fuckin' show!"

While our language may have seemed harsh to the horrified casual observer, it was actually a comedic buffer, as the profanity and cadence of almost everything we said to each other was done in the manner of the most-played CD in the Caulfields' universe: *Shut Up, Little Man.*

For the uninitiated, *Shut Up, Little Man* is an audio vérité recording that chronicles the drunken arguments of two elderly alcoholic roommates, one gay, the other bitterly homophobic. Any insult we wanted to hurl was actually softened the more we inhabited the bellicose voices of Peter and Raymond, the central figures in *Shut*

Up, Little Man. I thanked Tracy Chisholm every day for having introduced us to the recording back when we were making *Whirligig.*

Four o' clock, it's time to get up for the morning!

Though it was a little closer to two thirty in the morning, I took great pleasure in screaming this direct *Shut Up, Little Man* quote into Sam's right ear, startling him from a sound sleep in the front passenger seat during a rest stop in Michigan. Ritchie and I had just observed a large man standing at a urinal repeatedly thwacking his penis into the air. Ritchie opined that perhaps this gentleman had just gotten out of jail and that this was his way of "presenting." Theories aside, sharing the account of this experience upon our return to the van simply could not wait.

Sam was pissed at my wake-up call, but he responded in character.

You goddamn fuckin' piece-a-shit! All you are is a piece-a-shit!

I giggled in the same mocking and sinister manner that Raymond did on the CD.

Heh heh heh heh heh!

The more abusive the attacks were between us, the more satisfying the exchange.

Interacting almost entirely in persona somehow made the miles and each other's idiosyncrasies more bearable.

There was also the music. One might think that we would give our ears a break between shows and indulge in a little peace and quiet during long treks, but you'll never get your tinnitus badge with that attitude. Two gigantic CD wallets, which held 256 compact discs each, occupied a permanent spot on the floor between the driver and co-pilot. When we weren't listening to *Shut Up, Little Man,* there was a cornucopia at our fingertips, the closest thing to Spotify you could get in the '90s. Any given drive might include a goulash of the Beatles, Stevie Wonder, Pixies, AC/DC, Sheryl Crow, Matthew Sweet, Liz Phair, the Replacements, Smashing Pumpkins, Carole King, the Posies, Teenage Fanclub, ABBA, Sugar, Ben Folds Five, Afghan Whigs, the Beach Boys, Belly, Jellyfish, Weezer, Patty Griffin, Elastica, the Cardigans, Bad Religion, Lemonheads, the Jayhawks, Marvin Gaye, XTC, and lots of Juliana Hatfield.

Whatever the selection, it was almost always played loud, for active listening, never quiet enough to be considered background noise. The general rule was that whoever was behind the wheel had first dibs on the CD that went into the player, especially if we had to leave directly after a show and drive overnight. Good luck trying to sleep with Soundgarden blasting at decibel levels OSHA would consider unsafe. On the other hand, the sheer volume coming out of the speakers might be the only thing keeping the driver awake, and by extension, the rest of us alive.

A band member might take the occasional shift to break the monotony and get to pick the house music, but the vast majority of the time, the person with their foot on the gas was Tony. He kept one eye on the road and one in the rearview mirror, surveying the peanut gallery fray, mocking all us "sick little men," and making twisted comments that almost always took me by surprise.

"Hey, buddy," Tony murmured one night while I was his navigator in the passenger seat.

He motioned his thumb toward Ritchie, who was fast asleep, sitting up straight on the second bench seat, snoring through his wide-open mouth as if he were frozen in a perpetual yawn.

"Jimmy Sickdick is A. C.," Tony said with the hushed voice of an undercover informant.

"A. C.?" I replied, trying to figure out what he meant as I turned around to look.

Tony leaned in and whispered, "Awaiting cock."

Early on in the tour, Ritchie had earned the nickname "Jimmy Sickdick," an amalgam of two separate incidents that occurred within a couple days of each other. After settling into our shared hotel room at the Quality Inn Hall of Fame in Nashville, Ritchie went to use the bathroom, whose interior design included a gigantic mirror, positioned for optimal viewing of frontal nudity. Forced to see his manhood awash in unflattering fluorescence, he emerged genuinely concerned.

"Dude, my dick is, like, all mangled and gray. I don't know, man. It looks … *sick*."

Choking back my laughter, I told him it was probably from non-use, being bunched up in his pants during the long drive.

At our tour stop in Atlanta, the two of us were scheduled to do a local TV interview at the Ten High, the venue in the basement of the Darkhorse Tavern we'd be playing that night. As we fielded the series of questions, the interviewer would not stop calling Ritchie "Jimmy."

OK, we're here live with John and Jimmy from the Caulfields!

I corrected him first, as Ritchie seemed a little tongue-tied wondering who the hell Jimmy was.

So Jimmy, what's it like traveling on the road and coming to a new city every night?

Does that get exhausting, Jimmy?

Thoroughly amused, my immediate thought was, *Please, please, please start talking about your gray little sick dick, Jimmy.*

From that moment on, it was official: in the confines of the van and our surrounding microverse, Ritchie was "Jimmy Sickdick."

While most of us focused on training him to answer to "Jimmy," Chuck Keith, one of our rotating cast of sound guys, preferred a more formal approach when it came to our drummer:

"Where's Sickdick?!" he'd yell in his Texas twang whenever Ritchie was nowhere to be found.

An ex-marine from Galveston, Chuck brought a militaristic bent into the Caulfields' organization during his brief time with us, moonlighting on a break from his regular sound gig with our label mates Jackopierce. Chuck had no patience for disorganization or tardiness and practically pounded holes in hotel doors to get us moving on schedule.

You ladies got your Kotex?

In spite of his being punctual, professional, and reliable, Chuck's presence in the van could feel like a cortisol spike waiting to happen. One minute he might be waxing poetic about his two favorite driving albums—*Panorama* by the Cars and *Gaucho* by Steely Dan—and next he might burst up out of a sleeping position having overheard Tony say something offensive, which, to the rest of us, was just Tony being Tony.

Goddammit, Tony! You're part of the fuckin' problem!

Jason Curtis doubled as our front-of-house engineer and tour manager during a time after Tony had been demoted by Doron for crossing the Canadian border with his one-hitter still in his jacket. Jason was something of a veteran road dog, well versed in the ways of rock 'n' roll tomfoolery and debauchery. There was a certain charm and economy in how he spoke. If an attractive woman caught his eye, he did not launch into a hyperbolic treatise or a Shakespearean sonnet; he simply blurted out variations on his signature phrase of approval:

That's so hot.

He also had a knack for finding strip clubs, not the ones populated by businessmen and dancers full of silicone and Botox but the ones with "character," like the place in Cleveland where for twenty dollars you could spend the duration of "Wango Tango" maneuvering a remote-control toy car, with a twelve-inch dildo duct-taped to the top, into the open legs of the exotic dancer of your choice. How else would you spend your evening before playing a live radio broadcast in freezing temperatures at the Cleveland Zoo the next morning?

While it all might have been tame by, say, Keith Moon standards, Jason did like to play hard, but he also worked hard and took his tour manager duties seriously, in a way that immediately put off a natural-born contrarian like Sam.

Who the fuck does this guy think he is?

Sam did not care one bit for the tour itinerary that Jason handed out to the band his first day on the job. The opening page of what I considered a pretty-well-organized presentation contained a list of rules with the words "RIOT ACT" in capital letters at the top. It was pretty standard stuff: be on time, don't be an asshole; that kind of thing. But Sam didn't like being told what to do.

"You work for *me*, not the other way around," Sam said to me, not quite ready to say anything to Jason's face.

That time would soon come. The two of them butted heads over the pettiest details of our daily routine, finding themselves up front together in the van due to one thing that put them on common ground: an addiction to nicotine. With two cigarettes burning at once, multiple times an hour, my bitching from the back seat became more persistent. Instead of smoking less, Jason put up a flimsy black curtain behind their seats, and Sam, a supposed beneficiary of this token gesture, channeled the vigor of his Sicilian father to hurl one of his favorite insults:

You jackass!

Reminding me of my own verbal diss battles in high school, the two of them waged full-on psychological warfare. Sam passed up no opportunity to undermine Jason's authority, and Jason never hesitated to mock Sam. After a time, there was no detectable trace of the playfulness in our *Shut Up, Little Man* personas when Sam clapped back at any of Jason's remarks. Things came to a head after we got into a minor fender bender just outside of Atlantic City. By the time we walked in late to a band lunch with local radio reps, Jason had double-parked on a raw nerve in Sam and poked at it with a certain sense of sadistic glee.

"The little man is sour!" he said to me from across the table, loud enough for Sam and everyone else to hear.

"Oh yeah, well, why don't you just go FUCK YOURSELF. What do think about that?"

Jason widened his eyes and puckered his lips in a derisive "Ooooooooo!"

Thankfully Sam kept it together. At that point, I would not have been shocked to see him lunge across the table at Jason's neck, because while nobody was immune from the verbal hazing that was our standard operating procedure, Sam had been on a bit of a roll as the band whipping boy. He had already endured the sobriquet "Tukeet the Eskimo" after a stolen load of laundry prompted his ill-advised purchase of an oversized Inuit sweater from a street vendor in

Madison, Wisconsin. The sweater smelled like a strange combination of motor oil and wet dog.

I recorded brief taunts into a Yak Bak, which was a little toy voice recorder I took everywhere with me.

"You stink! You smell like a *dogue!*"

Sometimes Tony got in on the Sam smackdown, proving time after time that nothing was sacred or out of bounds. Sam had just recounted the story of his near-death experience as an infant. He had been on medication that didn't agree with him, and his parents became concerned enough to rush him to the hospital. At one point his heart nearly stopped beating.

"The doctors had to pack me in ice up to my neck to bring my fever down."

Instead of saying something, you know, *compassionate*, like, "Oh, man, so glad you made it through that. Where would we be without you?" Tony took to the Yak Bak:

"Sam was a little man born with his neck packed to ice!" [*sic*]

"Fuck you, I was pronounced dead!"

As vicious as the repartee may have been at times, nobody really took it to heart. "I am impervious to your barbs!" Ritchie would always declare. We all knew it was just a way to cope. Everyone in the band had known grief and loss. Only Mike still had both his parents, but he had suffered in his own right and dealt with his own demons and regrets. He rarely got involved with the banter, cordoning himself off with a pair of headphones plugged into a Sony Discman, only occasionally making his presence felt with a loud burp, followed by the declaration: "Buck snort!"

Mike knew how high the stakes were. He knew he had to show discipline on the road in a way he hadn't during the summer we recorded *Whirligig*. He knew there would be zero tolerance for drunkenly cracking a dozen eggs into an ice tray after attempting to open a tomato soup can with a butter knife. He knew that no one else could be counted on to save him from metaphorically drowning, in the way that Tony had literally done when Mike fell asleep and almost went under in the hot tub at the band house in Larkspur. A stint in rehab had done him good. Perhaps he had turned a corner. Maybe we all had.

We all knew that our shared experience was bringing us closer in a way that was just as powerful as blood. The term "band of brothers," so often used to describe a group of soldiers bound together in battle, felt like it also applied to our little rock 'n' roll quartet from Delaware. We were David and everyone else was Goliath, and even the slightest moral victories were oh-so-satisfying.

I had five minutes before going onstage at the generically named New Rock 102.1 Fest in Milwaukee. We were the first band on and the last band to load in, allotted just enough time to run the three and a half minutes of "Devil's Diary," effectively blowing our load to the applause of the kids waiting just outside the gates to get in. The rushed soundcheck was thanks in large part to Sponge, the band that had absorbed a disproportionate amount of setup time on the "Shepherd Express" stage, which would also feature sets by the Ramones, Letters to Cleo, and the Flaming Lips. While all the bands were receiving airplay on 102.1, Sponge was riding the wave of their second of two top-5 modern rock singles. Their song "Molly (16 Candles Down the Drain)" was charting even higher than their previous single, the ubiquitous "Plowed" with its "world of human wreckage" hook line.

Backstage, there was a cooler stocked with various beverages on ice. I recognized the squat little ten-ounce bottles of Martinelli's "Gold Medal" apple juice right away. I had experienced Martinelli's only once before, in the offices at A&M, but my recollection of the taste was worthy of Samuel L. Jackson–level enthusiasm:

God DAMN, Jimmy. This is some serious gourmet shit!

I guzzled down two bottles and finished a third in our dressing room, all on an empty stomach. Having received the all-hands-on-deck signal, Sam, Ritchie, Mike, and I started making our way to the stage. As we walked, I began to lag behind, clenching my teeth from the cramp in my abdomen. This was not good.

There were just three hundred seconds left before the band would be kicking off a radio festival in front of a couple thousand people. There was no time for a proper sit-down in the restroom, so my only option was to try to fart the pain away. It was a calculated risk, and unfortunately for me, my calculations were way off. My face felt flush as I sensed wet heat in my pants.

Had I learned nothing after I bought that juicer a few years back?

The lead singer of Sponge, a tall alterna-dude with Manic Panic red hair, walked past me in the hallway with a girl on each arm. Their dressing room was empty, so I ducked into their bathroom to assess the damage.

Jesus Christ.

In spite of the horror confronting me, I realized I had lucked out. The little brown blossom in my boxers had not leaked into my jeans, so I gingerly bent at the waist to remove my steel-toed ankle boots and peeled my pant legs downward and over my feet, leaving my pants in a crumpled heap next to me as I determined the best way to remove my underwear.

I couldn't peel them back the same way I had my trousers. That would be too risky. I did my best to simply step out of them—and did so with all the grace one could expect under the circumstances of having suffered a full-blown *shart* attack. Having cleaned myself off as best I could, I put my pants back on, dabbed my forehead with paper towels, and turned to leave the bathroom.

Then I looked down at my boxer shorts, just sitting there on the bathroom floor in Sponge's dressing room. I couldn't just *leave them there*. That would be wrong. With the sound of Tony's voice yelling my name in desperate search of the lead singer due onstage, I picked them up by the elastic waistband and carried them gingerly across the room to deposit them in the garbage can by the door, muttering to myself as I walked out:

Human wreckage, indeed.

Just a few days after the Sponge incident and less than twenty-four hours after fearing for our lives but ultimately giving autographs to former Klan Wizard David Duke in nearby Slidell, the Caulfields were onstage at ZephyrFest in New Orleans. "The Zephyr" 106.1 had spun "Devil's Diary" in heavy rotation, and after playing big shows at the House of Blues and Tipitina's, this was our third time in the market.

Something felt a little different. People seemed to know who we were, and fangirls and their boyfriends were hanging around trying to meet us while we watched the opening bands. Unlike some of the other radio festivals we had done up to that point, where we often played first or second, we were scheduled deeper in the lineup, which included, among others, Adam Ant, Bush, Matthew Sweet, They Might Be Giants, Catherine Wheel, and local heroes Deadeye Dick.

There was a serious ocean of people gathered at Marconi Meadows in City Park, with some crowd estimates as high as twenty thousand.

As with most of our live shows, the gain knobs on our guitar amps were turned up just a little more than usual to give '90s alternative rock lovers their recommended daily allowance of distortion. The strategy appeared to be working with "the kids," who actually appeared to be gaining energy even six bands in with the sun beating down directly on them. The rock festival beach balls never hit the ground, and people were crowd surfing even between songs. What did they need us for?

We were in the home stretch with just a few songs left to play when "Disease" came up on the setlist. The closing track on *Whirligig*, "Disease," to my mind, was the most pedestrian song on the album, but one thing it was good for was inciting a mosh pit, especially when I sang the a cappella opening line at twice the regular tempo, forcing my bandmates to come crashing in like we were covering Minor Threat or something. As we sped through the song, I looked out over a human funnel cloud, a view that simultaneously thrilled me and scared the shit out of me.

The crowd erupted when the song was over. I took a second to wipe the sweat off my face with a towel. From the corner of my eye, I watched an anonymous arm whip a full plastic water bottle through the air, and it was flying right at my head.

Somehow, just before it made impact with my face, I managed to catch it with my left hand, like a shortstop snagging a line drive, and having saved myself from the second broken nose of my life, I did the one thing that would probably win the award for "least likely to deescalate the situation." I could have unscrewed the cap, taken a sip of water, said, "Thank you." What I *chose* to do was transfer the bottle to my right hand, and yell, "You're gonna have to do way better than that, motherfuckers," into the mic, before hurling it with all my might back out into the crowd.

Before I knew it, bottle after bottle took flight toward the stage, landing like water grenades. I had brought us to a moment of reckoning. It was either retreat or stand our ground. Ritchie clicked his sticks to count off "Rickshaw" at warp speed, and now it was us against them in what I consider the defining moment of the band. I got hit with a few projectiles but managed to deflect dozens more either with my hands between chord changes or with the body of my guitar.

Halfway through the song, Doron ran out from the wings and performed the most protective act he would ever do for the Caulfields:

IT WAS A FITTING ENDING TO THE MOST CONFUSING SHOW OF OUR CAREER. DID THEY LOVE US? DID THEY HATE US? DID IT MATTER?

he took up position directly in front of me at the edge of the stage and became my own personal human shield, swatting down every last bottle heaved in my direction, with lightning-fast reflexes like *Bernie Fucking Parent*. Nothing got by him for the rest of "Rickshaw" and the entirety of our closer, an ironic cover of Captain & Tennille's "Love Will Keep Us Together."

With some fanfare, we extended the end of the song, which degenerated into squalling feedback as I gave the crowd my final farewell:

"All right, you assholes, that's all we got. We're the Caulfields!"

Just then, our friend Mitch Cry, who worked at the Zephyr, took a running stage dive off the figurative church of the holier-than-thou and threw himself into the crowd, which appeared to part like the Red Sea as he landed.

It was a fitting ending to the most confusing show of our career. Did they love us? Did they hate us? Did it matter?

Exhilarated. Stunned. Appalled. Amused. I felt all these things, but what I felt the most was connection and comfort in the knowledge that the Caulfields *were* a band of brothers. We were together on an unpredictable journey that might put us in front of twenty thousand people in New Orleans or two people in Salt Lake, surviving it all to fight another day as we each took our place in the ecosystem of a van.

DOWN UNDA

A little past the halfway point on a thirty-eight-show tour with Del Amitri, the Caulfields found ourselves with a day off in LA, and God, did we need it. It had been almost a month since we played the first date at Club Soda in Montreal and had one of our many run-ins with Canadian border agents, who gently reminded Tony that the customs pass required to bring a trailer full of equipment over the border was pronounced "car-nay," not "carny"—although we did feel like carnies much of the time.

Our last date north of the Mason-Dixon Line was at Club Bené, an old-school dinner-and-a-show cabaret in North Jersey, where we were tasked with rocking the faces off a sit-down audience pondering whether to get the chicken or the fish. We spent the rest of the dog days of summer in the southern half of the country, with stops in Richmond, Nashville, Atlanta, Clearwater, Miami, New Orleans, Houston, Austin, Dallas, Tucson, and Scottsdale. I was fried after playing twelve shows in fourteen days and planned to sleep all day in Los Angeles in hopes I would be refreshed and rehydrated in time for our set at the House of Blues the following night.

Then Mark Mazzetti called. He told us not to make any dinner plans. We were going to have a meeting with Jay.

The head of A&M's international division, Jay Durgan was in charge of taking the label's American bands into new markets overseas. Bleary-eyed but never too tired to turn down a free meal, the four of us took the van to the given address and met Mark and Jay out in front of a door with no sign, no indication whatsoever that it was even a place of business. Moments later, the Caulfields, completely underdressed in cargo shorts and bad sneakers, followed Jay through a tiny kitchen like scruffy soldiers marching behind a general.

The six of us took seats around a solid wooden table, each place setting with a white linen napkin and the kind of silverware you could actually pawn, given the opportunity. A man we had just passed in the kitchen soon emerged with a tray full of salad plates, each with what looked like half a head of iceberg lettuce drizzled with Thousand Island dressing. *I didn't order this*, I thought.

"Excuse me, could I see a menu?"

The man's face froze in the most chilling non-expression I had ever seen in my life.

"No menus here," Jay said. "You eat what they give you."

I had no idea what was going on, but apparently Arnold Schwarzenegger liked to come there when he had a hankering for a good steak.

"I usually don't eat a wedge salad myself," Jay continued. "I like mine with a little tomato, a little basil."

The four of us shot looks across the table at one another. It was odd the way he pronounced tomato "tomaahto" and basil "baahsil"—like he was referencing some lost verse from "Let's Call the Whole Thing Off." Maybe it was some sort of intimidation thing. Sometimes people with power do weird shit just because they can. That's why the word "eccentric" exists.

The smell of sizzling meat wafted into the room, and Jay got down to brass tacks. Our record was gaining traction in Australia. "Devil's Diary" was in rotation all over the country on networks of radio stations with names like Triple J and Triple M. The single was on the actual pop chart, not just the modern rock radio chart. Even the "Devil's Diary" music video, which was largely ignored by MTV in America, had started receiving airplay.

A&M had *completely* ignored my idea for the video, which was to have the Caulfields perform on the *Gong Show*, almost making it through to the end of the song before being gonged at the very last second by Satan himself.

The clip we actually ended up making had us miming with our instruments on a rotating lazy-Susan-type device, with the loose plotline focused on a much hipper young couple driving past sideshow oddities in the desert, including "the world's largest ball of string" that director David Dobkin apparently used in all his video treatments for A&M bands. Regardless, in Australia at least, the ball was big enough.

In Jay Durgan's estimation, the reach of the song and video warranted A&M bankrolling the Caulfields to spend most of November touring with the Aussie band Died Pretty, which had been the opening act on R.E.M.'s *Monster* tour earlier that year.

As we sat in what the four of us had begun to suspect was some sort of mob-front steakhouse and dug into our no-bullshit plates of porterhouse and roasted potatoes, which I kept waiting to hear pronounced "potaahtoes," I mentally transported myself to the place lovingly referred to as the "land down under."

We spent nearly twenty-four hours in the air to get to the other side of the world. It was the longest Sam had gone without a cigarette since his first drag as a teenager. The smoking ban on international flights between the US and Australia had just been instituted in March, and he was not taking it well.

"Fuckin' yuppies!" I taunted him, referring to what had become his catchall response to being hassled by the Man. He had originally shouted this phrase on a double date with our wives at Kid Shelleen's in Wilmington, after being reprimanded by a waiter for lighting up during dessert.

I couldn't really blame him for being a bit on edge, denied the one thing that would provide him a moment's comfort in a fuselage of anxiety and claustrophobia. While most of our travel companions slept the flight away on the pharmacy-grade sleeping pills Mike passed around while supplies lasted, Sam and I toughed it out, occupying two of the worst seats on the plane, neither window nor aisle, just smack-dab in the middle of a four-passenger row in the center of the behemoth Airbus. A sudden vertical drop after hitting some choppy air over the Pacific caught Sam by surprise and he unleashed a blood-curdling *ahhhhhhhhh*, which was likely audible all the way up in the cockpit. For some reason, I just chuckled at the loss of altitude. It all felt like a carnival ride to me.

"LOOK, LITTLE MAN. IF THIS PLANE GOES DOWN, THERE'S FUCK ALL WE CAN DO ABOUT IT." THAT WAS ABOUT AS CLOSE TO THE SERENITY PRAYER AS I EVER GOT IN MY LIFE.

"How can you fucking laugh at that?" Sam scorned me, as he bore down on his fingernails with his teeth.

"Look, little man. If this plane goes down, there's fuck all *we* can do about it." That was about as close to the Serenity Prayer as I ever got in my life.

By early November, it was springtime in Australia. The air was warm and sweet-smelling as the four Caulfields, along with Tony, Doron, and our Melbourne-based sound engineer, Trevor, packed ourselves into a smaller-than-expected tour vehicle, not much bigger than one of those VW microbuses from the '60s.

Behind Trevor's scruffy goatee and gentle smile was a demeanor so ultra-laid-back, it seemed he had built an entire belief system around the phrase "No worries, mate." It was the kind of casual that high-strung East Coast Americans like us found both fascinating and infuriating, but Trevor was the one with the experience driving on the left side of the road.

Compared to the way things were in the States, we found almost everything to be a little bit "bizarro world" in Australia, far beyond a toilet flush supposedly swirling in the opposite direction in the southern hemisphere. No matter where we played, a sense of anticipation, however subtle, seemed to pervade audiences and precede us in a way we hadn't really experienced back home. Any mention of the Caulfields in America usually required one more level of explanation for someone to connect the dots.

Hey, you wanna go see the Caulfields? Who? You know …
"bigger than Jesus"? Oh, them.

In Australia, the very name of the band, famously misspelled more than half the time it appeared in print or on a marquee in the US, was already embedded in the culture, especially in Melbourne, home to a thoroughbred horse race known as the Caulfield Cup. A group of teenagers from Caulfield Grammar School, located in the suburb of Caulfield, accosted Sam the day of our first show in Melbourne. They knew him by name, noticed he had changed his hair color from the photo in the CD booklet. Sam didn't even get recognized walking down Main Street in Newark.

We made our way along the southeastern coast of the continent, going as far west as Adelaide, and up to Bribie Island, north of Brisbane, stopping for salmon rissoles in local taverns, while all four of us carried out a full docket of press and radio promotion from our hotel rooms or from a pay phone on the street corner. We did TV interviews on rooftops, taped acoustic sets for Triple J and RED, a twenty-four-hour music video channel. It became a game to find new variations on the same answers we gave over and over to seemingly every journalist in the country, as we made our way to major cities and smaller burgs in between.

Dating back to the '80s, Died Pretty had logged thousands of miles on the very roads we were traveling. Their passionate guitar-driven attack, led by front man Ronnie Pop, held its own against the younger upstarts warming up the crowds on their headlining tour. On most nights, the Caulfields played second of three, going on after an even younger new band called Rail, whose album *Bad Hair Life* was all I wanted to listen to on my portable Discman during our three hectic weeks in their home country.

A good number of shows on the tour were in hotels—the Esplanade in Melbourne, the Annandale in Sydney, the Sands at Narrabeen. This struck the four of us as odd at first, but we soon discovered that playing the Gershwin Room at the "Espy" didn't come with the same lounge-act connotation as, say, playing a Ramada Inn in Kansas City. That said, we were excited to play the one-thousand-seat Metro Theatre in the heart of Sydney. I considered it the plum gig of the entire trip. Jeff Buckley, Dinosaur Jr., and Urge Overkill had all recently played there, and now we were there, sandwiched in the middle of the bill between two great Australian bands.

The show was on a school night, a Tuesday, so my hopes for a sellout were quickly tamped down, but the enthusiasm of those in attendance at the Metro was more than enough to make it feel electric to me. Whatever jet lag I was feeling when I first arrived in the country a few days before was a distant memory. Sam, Ritchie, Mike, and I were locked in, playing with that live energy that makes every song a few beats per minute faster than the record but feels perfect in the moment. We tore through the singles and the album tracks with equal intensity, and the crowd responded in kind.

Any time there was a guitar solo or another interlude that allowed me to step back from my vocal mic, it was typical for me to turn around and play to Ritchie. I loved the interaction and the unspoken acknowledgment that we were completely in sync.

When I spun around to face Ritchie during Mike's extended solo in "The Day That Came and Went," my jaw just dropped open. Ritchie's entire face was covered in streaks of red, bleeding like Sissy Spacek in *Carrie*. He was slightly elevated on a riser, and I could see his expression change when he saw mine. Something had hit him in the head, but I never saw any projectiles fly in from the audience. Each hit of the snare drum shot crimson droplets into the air, but Ritchie kept playing while simultaneously trying to get Tony's attention in the wings. By the time I turned around to sing the last chorus, Tony was applying a mound of bar towels to a bloody gash without Ritchie missing a beat. It's funny how it never occurred to any of us to just stop playing.

At the end of the song, Tony led Ritchie offstage, leaving the rest of us to face the awkward medical moment. I still had my acoustic from the previous song, so I began to play "Fragile," which was not originally on the setlist but was our only number that didn't really have drums, except for a very sparse kick and shaker part in the bridge.

When that section came around, I was surprised to feel the thunder of Ritchie's bass drum at my back. He played the rest of the show with a blood-soaked towel clotting up the open wound, which, as it turned out, had been caused by a falling light gel holder that had plummeted from a PAR can lamp high above his head.

We spent the rest of the night in Sydney back at our hotel, which was more like an apartment, accommodating most of us in one unit. Ritchie insisted he was fine, but the rest of us begged him to get medical attention. Who knows where those bar towels had been? Doron asked Ritchie when he'd last had a tetanus shot. When Ritchie couldn't recall, Doron lit a joint and got on the phone to locate the only physician in Sydney willing to make a house call. The doctor showed up around 2:00 am carrying an old-school black medical bag. Mincing no words, the doctor asked, "Where do you want it?" With his limbs and the rest of the tour to consider, Ritchie's only option was to drop trou and take his tetanus shot in the glutes. Having put out one fire, Doron sparked up again.

Throughout the tour, Doron and Tony indulged their weed predilection with regularity, taking full advantage of the fist-sized mutant bud that a fan of the band in Brisbane just handed to Sam as a gesture of goodwill. It was pretty potent stuff, whether you inhaled or not.

At one extended pit stop, while Trevor pumped the gas, those of us with contact highs emerged from the mini-mart eating popsicles labeled "Peter's Icy Pole," giggling like fools at the juvenile comedic implications. Tony sat essentially motionless, fully baked in the front passenger seat, staring down at his shirtless chest, mesmerized and sharing his revelations:

"You know what? My nipples are *always* hard."

Tony ran his finger around his bare areola with one hand and raised his other hand to his mouth to take bites off the brick of dried fig he carried around to relieve the constipation he had suffered from since the day he got off the plane.

Doron returned from a nearby produce stall, staring at a piece of citrus fruit, which he then held in front of Ritchie's face as if he were displaying the snow globe from *Citizen Kane*.

"Look, Jimmy," he said, slurring his consonants. "Navel orange."

"I've seen an orange before, Doron," Ritchie replied.

As we piled back in the van, Trevor recited the obscure phrase from "Tie a Yellow Ribbon" by Tony Orlando and Dawn that always commenced his roll call: "Get on the bus, forget about us!"

Moving as fast as the governed accelerator at Trevor's feet would allow, we piled on thousands of miles, zigzagging about, heading north for one show, then going south for another, only to turn around and go farther north for the next. With routing like that, we all knew we were pushing our luck, driving that little van into the ground, hoping against hope it would survive the entirety of the tour. We had gone from Melbourne to Adelaide to Sydney, then Narrabeen, Brisbane, Ballina, Bribie Island, back to Sydney, then Caringbah, then up to New Castle, where we played our only college gig. Seven hours into our ten-hour drive en route to our final stop back in Melbourne, the van decided enough was enough. It conked out in a tiny town called Barnawartha, population five hundred, leaving us stranded on the side of the road with a pen of goats to one side and a brick building with a white and maroon awning called the Star Hotel just a short walk away. Sam was the first to abandon ship and in no time was bellied up to the bar and pounding five-cent drafts.

While Sam got tipsy with his loose change, Doron got on the phone with the rental company to seek a replacement vehicle. That conversation did not go well. After being denied his request, Doron raised his voice to tell the person on the other end that they could, in so many words, fuck off and come retrieve their broken-down piece-of-shit van themselves. When asked for the location of the vehicle, Doron screamed "somewhere in Australia" and slammed down the receiver.

With the knowledge that we were on foot until further notice, the rest of us ordered some fried food and broke out the nickels, fielding questions from the locals, who knew right away we weren't from around there. Ritchie took his beer onto the patio and struck up a conversation with a grizzled gent, who was smoking a cigarette and drinking a Victoria Bitter—a VB if you're nasty.

Where ya from, mate? Ya gonna spin some yarn?

That was a quaint way of asking Ritchie to tell him a story. Each one of us told someone in that bar our own version of how we ended up there that night. Strangers though we might have been, we were just as welcome, if not more so, in Barnawartha as in any other place we had visited. Amid the "g'day, mates" and the "how ya goin's" and the clinking of glasses, there was a warmth and an affinity that didn't even require us to play any music.

As word of our tribulation circulated, a man who had seen us perform on television a few days earlier informed us that he drove a tour bus and was passing through town on his way to Melbourne and would be happy to drive us and our equipment the last 185 miles to our destination. It felt like the kind of serendipitous dumb luck that could only happen to a band looking to add more yarn to its already massive skein.

Trevor asked us to spend the day of our final show in Melbourne at his sister's place. She and her two daughters lived in a house that had been transported in its entirety from its original location in St. Kilda and dropped down in the middle of a rain forest. The home was completely open-air with no windows, shaded by a thick canopy almost a hundred feet above our heads. Birds and bats flew in and out of the house at will, while the girls frolicked about, eating bowls of vanilla custard with gigantic serving spoons.

Doron, all hopped up on cannabinoids, found their trampoline out behind the house and bounced away, landing alternately on his back and belly, shouting "aaaaahhhh-ite" each time his body hit the taut canvas. The youngest daughter, Scarlett, was unamused; she called Doron "fat and stinky" after he stumbled off the trampoline, dizzy and drenched in sweat.

"Now, Scarlett, don't be rude," her mother admonished her.

"Well, he *is* fat and he *does* stink," she retorted, sounding a little like an insouciant Mary Poppins as she shoveled another spoonful of custard into her mouth.

A few of us wandered through the forest to a nearby pond, where we found Trevor and his friend Dave, who was clearly an energetic yang to Trevor's laid-back yin. Beads of water dripped from the ghost-white skin of their shirtless backs as the two of them huddled in conference beside a dusty truck parked on the grass with the hood popped open. Their hushed, secretive voices gave away that they were up to something.

I don't know if they were showing off to provide us Americans with some kind of *Crocodile Dundee* moment, but they were completely serious when they informed us of their intention to use the truck battery to set off an underwater bomb that would kill all the fish in the pond and thereby provide a meal for our small army. The rest of us stood by, amused and more than a little concerned, as Dave dove into the pond with a gallon milk jug filled with explosives while Trevor manned the truck ignition, determined to detonate their makeshift device. They tried again and again to make it work, refining their design, reevaluating their approach. Although we left the rain forest hungry that day, I admired their tenacity. It felt like the Caulfields shared the same inner motivation, the drive to do everything in our power to manifest a vision that was so crazy it just might work.

CAPITAL LIPSTICK L

In the summer of 1996, the Caulfields were shacked up in LA at the Oakwood Apartments, whose fully furnished dwellings and short-term leases were ideal for young entertainers living on ramen and Ritz crackers while chasing their dreams. Pushing thirty at this point, I wasn't exactly young anymore, not by music-business standards. I was married and had come into some money thanks to a publishing deal with Warner Chappell. Being the primary songwriter in the band had paid off, but I knew the income disparity would spell trouble, so I gave everyone in the group a taste of the windfall. Of course, it was an acknowledgment of their contributions, but part of me was also convinced I was buying something I couldn't quite define.

Personal financial cushion aside, money was a lot tighter when it came to the Caulfields' deal with A&M. We were now almost $250,000 in the red, thanks to a very costly first album and tour that did not recoup. Everything was riding on our second record, *L*, which we would have to finish in less time and on a tighter budget.

We had just spent two expensive weeks cutting basic tracks at A&M Studios, working with producer/engineer David Bianco, who had won a Grammy for his work on *Wildflowers* by Tom Petty. I never use this word, but I couldn't recall a time when I'd felt more *blessed*. Laying down scratch vocals in Studio D, in the same vocal booth where Karen Carpenter had sung "Rainy Days and Mondays," was one of those rare moments when all was right with the world. Making the entire album there was out of the fiscal question, so I would have to cut the keeper vocals during overdubs at Sound City in Van Nuys, but we emerged from A&M with the musculature of all fifteen songs that would make up *L*.

It had been no easy task even getting to that point. Our entire existing song catalog was depleted making *Whirligig* and an EP's worth of subsequent B-sides tracked with our friend Nick DiDia, who had recorded albums by Pearl Jam and Stone Temple Pilots.

Starting from an empty notebook, I submitted the first handful of songs I could come up with. Mark Mazzetti *hated* my first batch of demos, which included a song called "Big Fish Story," a snotty critique of machismo and sexual conquest. I wish I had a recording of the phone call in which Mark's opening statement set the tone for the criticisms that would fly at me like shrapnel.

"I'll be damned if any band of mine puts out a song with the word 'fish' in the title!"

He made little effort to spare my feelings, but I needed the tough love. There was no room for a sophomore slump—this was *do or die*. The new songs had to be better than the first album. My Newark roots were showing, and my writing needed something beyond local color. We had been all over the world since we made *Whirligig* and couldn't just complain about our hometown anymore. We had done and seen things, survived things. We had *lived*. That's what had to go into the record.

Sam and Ritchie came to my rescue with music to the co-writes that became cornerstone songs on the album. Contributing my lyrics and melodies to "Figure It Out," "President of Nothing," "Skeleton Key," "Tomorrow Morning," and "Born Yesterday" gave me the creative spark I needed to get my own songwriting mojo back. "Waiting to Cry," "All I Want Is Out," "Atlas Daughter," and others all flowed from a true and vulnerable place inside me. I was tapped in.

By the time the Caulfields finished the basic tracks, I already knew the album was going to be the best thing any of us had ever done. Although Sound City was no frills by comparison, it had plenty of history in its own right, much of it more recent. *Nevermind* by Nirvana was cut on the Neve console in the main room, and Weezer had wrapped up their second album, *Pinkerton*, just weeks before we arrived.

The studio was doubling as a movie set, hosting the cast and crew of *Boogie Nights* the first several days we were there. Much to David Bianco's chagrin, any noise we were making would have to grind to a halt whenever Mark Wahlberg and John C. Reilly were shooting their recording studio scenes down the hall. It was hard to get any momentum going, and we knew that the clock was ticking. In spite of the chaos, we eventually found our stride, laying down vocals, guitar solos, horns, percussion, checking off one finished song after another.

Even after ten hours in the studio, I never wanted the days to end, so I found a way to keep them going with whomever I could rope in as my partner in crime. Into the wee hours we went, driving up and down Sunset Boulevard, wasting gas and per diems on table dances and nonalcoholic two-drink minimums at so-called gentlemen's clubs. Passing over the Seventh Veil and the Body Shop, establishments well known to fans of "Girls, Girls, Girls," our preferred spot was on the fringe of the strip, just off La Cienega.

THE YIN AND THE YANG OF IT ALL

In the aforementioned Mötley Crüe song, there's a delicious moment of simulated titty bar conversation between lead singer Vince Neil and drummer Tommy Lee.

Hey, Tommy, check that out, man! What, Vince, where?

One could only assume they were laying eyes on a real stunner. With the Caulfields, the "What, Vince, where?" moments were more like this:

Wow, is that a tampon string hanging out of that girl's G-string? And what's that song she's dancing to … I'm pretty sure that's Ben Folds Five. Hey, you want another eight-dollar ginger ale?

This is what you get when you make a regular destination out of a place suggested to you after someone in your vehicle poses the question, "Hey, where do I gotta go to get an ass in my face?"

The 2:00 am shower one would require after such an evening postponed already deficient slumber. A couple of nights before we were scheduled to fly home upon completing the album, I set the alarm on the clock radio by my bed at the Oakwoods for 9:00 am. Almost two hours before the alarm was supposed to go off, a loud knock on the door woke me up, prompting me to slur as much profanity into a single sentence as I could muster.

"Who the *fuck* is at the *fucking* door this *fucking* early in the *fucking* morning," I huffed as I spilled out of bed, my body numb from sleep chemicals.

I stumbled on wobbly legs through the living room, careful to avoid the furniture on which one would be ill-advised to shine a black light. I opened the door to find a man in uniform with a chipper expression that I considered menacing for that hour of the day.

"FedEx!" he half shouted, holding up a rectangular cardboard envelope, the kind you use when something absolutely, positively has to be there overnight.

Like everyone else we had encountered in California, the guy struggled with Sam's last name. "Moooosa ... Meeeesi?"

"Musumeci," I said with zero patience. "I'll sign for it."

I scribbled my signature and took the letter. Just as I closed the door, Sam emerged from his room to investigate, bedhead and puffy eyes in full effect.

"It's for you, little man," I said before throwing the letter like a frisbee right at his face. One of the sharp corners of the envelope caught Sam full force right in the center of his forehead, causing him to shriek in pain and raise his palm to cover what was soon a serious red welt.

"OW! You asshole!" Sam yelled.

I knew it was a dick move on my part, and I immediately felt bad when I saw the envelope hit him. I felt even worse after he opened it. As he scanned the page from left to right, the color drained from his cheeks. The message was from his wife. She wanted a divorce. I had just hit Sam in the face with his own Dear John letter.

After a frantic phone call to demand the details he did not want to hear, his soon-to-be ex-wife confessed she was leaving him for the man he had, until that moment, considered his best friend. I would never wish on anyone the kind of anguish I saw wash over him. I recognized it. I had seen it in my own eyes. I had seen it in Mom's. And I had seen it before in Sam's.

When his mother, Eleanor, died just a month before *Whirligig* came out, he asked me to sing "Fragile," her favorite Caulfields song, at the funeral. The idea of musically interrogating God in a church full of devout Catholics gave me serious stage fright, but Sam faced the music with me, head on, devastated but defiantly nodding his teary-eyed approval in the front pew.

Is this the part when everyone gets on their knees for you?
I always wanted to believe in you
But you never gave me half a chance or half a reason to
Are you fragile too?

Within hours of receiving the letter, thanks to some frequent-flier miles from Mark Mazzetti, Sam was on a red-eye heading east. He needed his wife to say to his face what she had tried to get away with writing on paper. He needed her to see the pain in his eyes. During those last couple of days in Los Angeles, it was virtually impossible to concentrate, as my thoughts turned on a dime to the friend and bandmate with whom I had been through so much already.

Sam was the closest friend I had in the band. He was willing to have the confrontations I didn't have the stomach for, especially when a manager needed to be fired or a bandmate needed a talking to after the clink of the vodka bottle they had stashed in a toilet tank at the recording studio was picked up by a surreptitiously placed microphone.

Sam relished the role of the enforcer, but he was also a good sport and could take as good as he gave. I had never been easy on him, even dating back to our days in the Beat Clinic. I insisted he play at Max's on Broadway in Baltimore the same day he fell off the roof of his house and broke his leg. A half dozen Tylenol and a pair of borrowed crutches was all the medical attention he would receive that day. What was more important, after all—the outside possibility of a little gangrene or our first show ever in Fell's Point? Sam went from writhing on the ground in pain that morning to sitting in the dressing room at Max's unable to escape the Judybats' nimbus of pot smoke that same afternoon. It was probably one of many times he wanted to kill me.

I had certainly entertained thoughts of killing *him* on New Year's Eve of the following year, the only time since kindergarten that I ever came close to getting into a fistfight. The Beat Clinic was headlining at Legends in Wilmington, about to play our set, the culmination of months of hard work and planning. Chris Ryan and our friend John Ratliff had sat at the bar three, sometimes four nights a week since October, hawking tickets to our first self-promoted event. No detail had been left out: the ticket packages with discount hotel rooms, the shuttle buses to the venue, the champagne toast at midnight.

About fifteen minutes before showtime, Chris came backstage and announced in his particular matter-of-fact way: "Um, Sam's hammered."

It's funny how such a short sentence can trigger a person. When I saw Sam trip through the curtain behind the drums, I went from zero to rage in about 1.5 seconds, shoving him in the ribs multiple times with both hands and yelling in his face, nearly blacking out with fury when he told me to "calm down."

"Calm down?! Don't you tell *me* to calm down, you son of a bitch!"

I wanted to call off the show, but that was not an option. Too many people had paid good money to spend the last night of the year with us. God knows whatever possessed them. Weirdly enough, once we started the show, Sam dropped the most engaging stage moves I had ever seen him execute. He was loose and uninhibited, sweating out liquor through his pores and showing a little skin with his shirt unbuttoned below the solar plexus. Too bad you could count on one hand the number of correct notes he played. By the middle of the second song, I literally interrupted my lead vocal to yell into the mic to our sound man, Bill Craig:

"Bill! BILL! Take Sam completely out of the mix!"

As pissed as I was with Sam after that performance, we somehow found a way to get past it.

There would be no such reconciliation with his soon-to-be ex-wife. By the time the rest of us arrived back home from Los Angeles, Sam was moving out of their place in Wilmington. I invited him to live with Lisa and me for a while, and he slept on the couch in the one-bedroom apartment I had barely seen since moving to the Philly burbs after Lisa landed a teaching job at what was then known as Beaver College.

Almost every day for the next three months, Sam and I conducted walking therapy sessions on the quarter-mile track at High School Road, going around and around as I tried my best to find a positive spin. I spoke of sunny times to come—we had just turned in a record that we and everyone at the label considered worthy of going platinum. We just had to keep it together until the release date. That would be easier said than done for both of us.

Sometimes the sadness of Sam's loss was like a contagion, and it became a challenge to keep myself from succumbing to it. While I was trying to remain upbeat for my friend, I was still processing the bereavement over my estrangement from Tae Hyun. A weird, melancholic PTSD still washed over me every winter because of it.

Two songs from *L* with foundations in my sister's departure— "The Kitchen Debate" and "Tomorrow Morning," the latter written to Sam's music—were like little rock 'n' roll op-ed pieces. They felt necessary for me to write and even more so to sing.

Whether we lost loved ones to the grim reaper or to former best friends or just to a sad change of heart, how else would we be expected deal with it?

I can't forget
I'd write a song about it
It might help, I kinda doubt it
Hasn't cured me yet

Sam and I dropped close to thirty pounds each as we walked and talked our way through a winter of discontent, one lap at a time around that track. We conversed at length about the true meaning of our album title *L*. Ostensibly, it was a reference to how that particular letter always seemed to be AWOL in the frequent misspellings of our band's name, or the "capital lipstick L" on the brow of the defiant loser in "President of Nothing." But there was more to it than that.

The music the Caulfields made together was born of the love and loss everyone in the band had experienced in our own way. It was a testament to our uncanny knack for taking lemons and making lemonade. Maybe it was a nod to the biggest L-word of all, as it appeared in the last verse of my favorite collaboration with Sam:

My LIFE is mine and I'll be fine when it's over.

THE DEVIL WEARS NADA

I should have seen the harbingers of doom as they revealed themselves in the weeks leading up to the release of *L*, the album that
was supposed to catapult the Caulfields into stardom. Everyone
at the label who had heard an advance copy was in agreement: this
record was our golden ticket. There was even talk of promoting a
single at top-40. But it wasn't to be. *L* dropped like a stillborn baby,
all but dead on arrival after Mark Mazzetti was fired less than a month
before it came out.

Mazzetti's face had turned ghost-white as he took a phone call
with Bob Ludwig in the middle of *L*'s mastering session up in Maine.

"There's been a blood bath at A&M," he said at the time.

Product managers and promo people were getting their walking
papers, as rumors of a big corporate merger began to circulate, but
none of us ever thought Mark's job might be in jeopardy.

Deep down, maybe I should have known better. Doomsday
scenarios were playing out in my increasingly agitated REM sleep,
like the one in this dream: I'm in a private meeting with A&M's
president, Al Cafaro, a man I had only met once in real life. There's

an unlit Cuban cigar between his teeth as we brainstorm, trying to come up with ways to pull the band out of our huge debt to the label. Cafaro pulls a prototype cereal box out from a drawer in his desk and makes his pitch like a classic '50s ad man. "Picture it, John: in lieu of royalties … *Caulflakes!*"

Since the spring, we had been receiving a steady stream of discouraging words about the fate of *L* at radio stations. A&M had only placed a few thousand "units" in stores, a bare minimum quantity that covered their contractual ass and little else. Radio programmers who had played "Devil's Diary" and wanted to support the new record were now calling *us* to ask why A&M's promo department wasn't pushing "Figure It Out." The new track was initially serviced to the same modern rock stations that played us in 1995, along with an interlocking promotional puzzle that was, perhaps not ironically, almost impossible to figure out. The four of us joked nervously as we pictured frustrated radio programmers violently throwing our little wooden tchotchkes in the trash, with the CD single right behind it. While some stations did add the song out of the box, it was obvious there was no serious push from the label. One music director said his station was asked flat out *not* to play the song. In a word, we were *fucked.*

We all agreed to pool the small amount of money remaining from the album advance to go on the road, playing short strings of dates with nothing from A&M but a few boxes of promo posters and CDs we had to pay for up front. I spent most of my days off between April and August driving around to Tower Records and every Best Buy within a seventy-five-mile radius of my house, purchasing the two or three copies of *L* they had in stock. I practically maxed out my credit card, hoping that the SoundScan numbers, still paltry by music business standards, would somehow spark a wake-up call over at A&M, and maybe, just maybe, they'd reinstitute our tour support.

Of course, I knew on a very basic level that this was an exercise in futility, but I also knew that I wouldn't be able to live with myself if I went down without a fight.

Some of our experiences on the road supporting *L* felt like the logical continuation of the final show of the *Whirligig* tour. We had played a victory-lap New Year's Eve concert at First Night Wilmington in front of a crowd of six hundred screaming kids. It was as welcomed as we had ever felt in our home state.

Now in 1997, with our backs suddenly against the wall, we turned whatever alterna-charm we had left in the tank up to eleven, visiting the radio stations that would still play us, improvising jingles for the DJs and butchering covers we totally forgot how to play. WGRD in Grand Rapids and CD-101 in Columbus still had our backs. Even our old friend Super Frank, the guy whose radio festival in Augusta we had chartered a private plane to, was doing all he could to support the band. His Channel Z "Dare to Care" concerts, sponsored by his stations in Kansas City and Springfield, put us in prime-time slots in front of more than four thousand people over two days. An ocean of teenagers sang along to "Figure It Out" and humored us for a photo taken from the stage, with a couple thousand fingers and thumbs in the shape of an "L" on their foreheads. Some kids in Korn T-shirts defaced an ambulance with our stickers, and I autographed the dome of some guy's shaved head. The only downer of the day at the Shrine Mosque in Springfield was the premature departure from the stage by songwriting master Freedy Johnston, after being hit in the head with some flying footwear. I felt bad for him. I knew *that* feeling.

Back home from the Dust Bowl, we played the tenth anniversary of the Tower Records location on South Street in Philadelphia, reminding a small but enthusiastic crowd, who had waited in line to get their copies of *L* scribbled on by the band, that we were still alive.

Two blocks down at Jim's Steaks, a much longer line curved around the corner while side one of "Meat Is Murder" by the Smiths blasted out of some nearby apartment window.

We played the Stone Balloon in Newark for the first time in a long time, confronting the ghosts of the hometown that inspired the bulk of *Whirligig*. Ritchie emceed the benefit for the children's music foundation he had started in Rudy's name the year his brother passed away—the year that Rudy changed the trajectory of our lives.

Festival season yielded some high-exposure one-offs. The WSTW Summer Jam placed us twenty yards out to sea, as we played on a barge docked along the Christina River behind Kahunaville, one of the biggest open-air meat markets in Delaware nightclub history. There were a couple hundred actual music fans "on shore" who made the set seem somewhat worth it, but that was overshadowed by a guy in a cowboy outfit shooting somebody in the leg in the parking lot. *Home, sweet home*, as the saying goes.

I took the Doc Martens side stage at the first-ever Y-100 FEZtival in Camden, conscious that my shin-high combat boots, paid for in 1995 by our Atlanta rep, Gina Suarez, on her A&M Amex, were already symbolic of a bygone era. A&M had spent their last marketing dollar on the Caulfields. My spirits were lifted by a rowdy crowd donning complimentary red fezzes and jumping around like a mass of hyperactive Shriners.

We spent the summer solstice in Vermont, playing the Pickle Barrel in Killington, a ski resort, which appeared to be just as much fun without the packed powder. A few hours before showtime, we bore witness to a naked bicycle race, the likes of which I had never seen, except for the fold-out poster that came with every vinyl copy of *Jazz* by Queen in 1978. While the men's race was frankly a little difficult to watch, the women's race proved nearly impossible, as the width of the track went from about fifteen yards down to four, in a display of debauched ogling that delayed the start of the race for nearly twenty minutes.

Of course, no rock show could ever hope to compete with such a spectacle, and we resigned ourselves to the role of fascinated observers who just happened to be playing instruments, as our show petered out during a massive brawl involving another guy in a cowboy outfit. Once the fight was broken up by security, the winner of the men's bicycle race, plastered and still nude, raised his two-wheeler toward the heavens and screamed, "Who wants to see Daddy's cock?"

Full frontal male nudity followed us to Madison, Wisconsin, where it seemed like a good idea to invite the entire audience to "join us up here" for whatever song we were playing as an encore. The crowd at the Terrace at the University of Wisconsin was well over a thousand strong, and roughly fifty of them heeded my call to action to rush the stage, some of them deciding to get naked. You have to envy their comfort level with their bodies. One guy was motivated enough to strip down and hang from a support beam, which surely would have crushed us all had it given way.

Before driving home on the Fourth of July, we played Summer-fest in Milwaukee in a thick, soupy fog, then drove to St. Paul for "Taste of Minnesota," where we played the second stage with a band called the Dust Bunnies, who offered us organic strawberries and covered the theme from *The Dukes of Hazzard*. Not a lot of people saw either of our bands, as we essentially played to each other on the fringe of the festival grounds, while the vast supermajority of attendees were four football fields away, contorting their bodies into their best approximations of the letters *Y*, *M*, *C*, and *A*, as the Village People headlined the main stage.

We packed up our gear with the body language of the dejected. Then, in what almost came off as an act of pity, an attempt to let us know, "Hey, *I* get you," the stage manager ran up and tapped on the passenger side window. I rolled it down.

"Lemme leave you with this," he said, displaying the shirt under his hoodie. "You said you guys got some grief about your 'bigger than Jesus' song? I sell this in my shop, and I get a *ton* of flack for it."

The piece of merchandise in question was a Cradle of Filth T-shirt depicting a nun masturbating in nothing but her veil—in our friend's words, "six-packing" herself. I nodded my head in polite revulsion. He spun around like a runway model and pulled down his hoodie to reveal the back of the shirt.

The oversized lettering spelled out "Jesus is a cunt."

Taking it as our "well, on *that* note" moment, our tour manager, Chris Brown, put the keys in the ignition, and we drove off to head back east, feeling, well, *Minnesota*.

I THINK THIS IS IT

y the third week of August in 1997, about thirty-two hours
before the Caulfields were due onstage at a big radio festival
in Michigan, I was feeling worn down but hopeful when Sam,
Ritchie, and Chris Brown arrived bleary-eyed at Mom's house at the
ass crack of dawn. Everyone took a seat around the kitchen table as we
began to plot out our route to Detroit, referencing the same tattered
truck-stop road atlas that had navigated us from one American town
to another since the beginning of our major-label expedition.

Mom spoke Korean into the air: *Bap mogo!* This was my indication that it was time to put the map away and eat breakfast, even
though it was way too early in the morning for any of us to have an
appetite. Scrambled eggs cooked in sesame oil slid out of a frying pan,
and Mom started filling bowls with juicy slices of plum and nectarine.

It would be about six hundred miles to Detroit. We all gave silent
dismissive nods at the prospect of a ten-hour drive. It was nothing we
hadn't done countless times before. We were heading out to Michigan
to play Planet Fest at the fifteen-thousand-seat Pine Knob Music
Theatre.

Garett Michaels, the man in charge at 96.3 the Planet, was what you could call our "OG" program director on radio, having been the first in the country to officially add "Devil's Diary" into rotation when he was at Y-100 in Philadelphia. When I think of the time we opened for Blues Traveler at the House of Blues in New Orleans, I always think of Garett rocking out to our set in the front row. No other PD in my recollection had ever done that.

Garett had caught wind of our misfortunes with A&M and asked us to kick off Planet Fest as a late addition to the lineup. He had already put the single on the station's playlist and had been plugging our appearance in the run-up to the show. This was the act of mercy we really needed, as our resolve and our resources continued to dwindle. I allowed myself to get excited to play on the same stage with artists I genuinely liked—Michael Penn, Cowboy Mouth, Better Than Ezra, and two bands I'd adored in high school, INXS and Echo & the Bunnymen. It felt, for a moment, like we could get back to where we had been just two short years earlier.

As the "Pine Knob" jokes died down and we finished our eggs to the sound of the pendulum ticking away on Mom's battery-operated wall clock in the kitchen, someone blurted out, "Where the hell is Mike?"

The Fly was habitually the last band member to arrive for anything, so we weren't overly concerned that he was twenty minutes late. I picked up the phone and dialed his number. It rang about ten times before his answering machine picked up. I left a message at the beep.

More intervals of time went by, and I called again and again, hoping he was on his way and not even there to hear the phone ring. By the time he was an hour late, and I had made several more unanswered phone calls, Chris Brown and I got in the van and headed to his apartment in Pike Creek.

Mike drove a *black-like-your-soul* Toyota pickup truck, and there was no sign of it anywhere in the parking lot. We tapped loudly on his ground-floor window to no avail. I suggested we drive to his girl-friend's apartment, which was in a complex adjacent to the cemetery where Papa was buried. Chris asked if we should try to call her first, but we ultimately deemed this an unnecessary extra step and knocked on her door unannounced, waking her from a sound sleep. She looked justifiably ragged, with pillow marks on her cheek, when she told us she hadn't seen Mike and, with a weary, knowing expression, asked us to call her when we found him.

There was a pay phone outside Burger King across the street, so I called Mom's house to see if Mike had checked in there. Not a word. I started to acknowledge the nervous ache in the pit of my stomach that I had felt too many times before when it came to Mike. I asked Chris to drive back to Mom's, where we picked up Sam and Ritchie to join our little search mission. We decided to circle back to Mike's place, and this time we spotted the truck, the left tires askew outside of the painted white lines on the asphalt, essentially taking up two parking spaces.

There was an entire pack of unsmoked cigarettes strewn on the ground next to the driver's side door. A lot of them were actually salvageable, except for a few that looked like they'd been crushed by the soles of shoes attached to stumbling legs. The four of us exchanged suspicious glances and walked toward the building again. This time, the door to his apartment was wide open. In the wall at the bottom of the steps, there was a near-perfect-circle crater spattered with blood. It looked like a crime scene. Or something out of a GWAR concert.

I heard someone say, "He's out here!" Mike was behind the building standing next to a tree, his face dripping with blood, so much blood it actually looked fake, like the red slop dripping down Gene Simmons's chin on the cover of *Alive II*. As we gathered around him, he collapsed onto the grass.

Considering the sight before us, and the shape of the hole in the wall, we used our no-shit-Sherlock powers of deduction to conclude that he had fallen and cracked his head open. You could see the fault line as the sun started to reflect off the top of his dome, which he had shaved bald a couple of months back to placate the rest of us after several negative comments about his hair from the record company. I knew that he really didn't want to do that. I also knew he didn't want to let the rest of us down. Hair, or the lack of it, however, was the least of his problems.

I tried to push Mom's voice from my head, not wanting to hear her platitudes about perseverance and loyalty to my "team." *Work together as a team, honey. Figure it out with your team.* It was always "team" with her; she never used the word "band." I don't know if she did this intentionally or not, but it was getting harder all the time to be a member of either one.

Mike was hunched over, his legs bent slightly at the knee, where rosy patches of skin peered through frayed rips in his black jeans. He was pressing a balled-up Caulfields T-shirt, pulled in haste from the back of the van, against his still-oozing gash as I went back in the apartment to call 911. I told the operator my emergency in a cold tone of voice, like I had been rehearsing this call for years and was now tired of repeating my lines. My friend and bandmate of over a decade was bleeding from the head, and I felt nothing for him. An ambulance arrived in a matter of minutes, followed by a police car. After a few questions from the EMTs to determine his level of incoherence, Mike found himself strapped to a gurney and whisked away.

The rest of us started to follow them to Christiana Hospital, but the cop said we all needed to stay behind and answer a few questions so he could "rule out foul play." He asked if we knew anyone who might have held any kind of animosity or grudge toward "Mr. Simpson."

There was a part of me that wanted to say "Yeah, *I* do." I felt a lot of anger toward Mike—self-righteous, like, "How dare you do this to *me*?" But I didn't admit that. It was probably best that I didn't, because this cop sounded like he was just dying to accuse one of us of bashing Mike's head in. Trust me, I had wanted to do just that, more than once, but when someone is their own worst enemy, they usually end up doing your dirty work for you. I guess this was what rock bottom looked like.

Chris drove the four of us to the hospital, and we found our way to Mike, who had already been admitted and bandaged up. He was a lot more together by that point, which meant he was fully aware that he was lying in a hospital bed when we all should have been in the van, already across a good chunk of the PA Turnpike. He was being held for observation, so there was no way he would be playing the show in Michigan. His face conveyed regret with a dash of sad puppy eyes, as if to say, "Sorry I've ruined our gig."

A nurse came in to check on him, and I pulled Sam and Ritchie aside. "I still want to go to Detroit," I said.

I could see in their eyes that they were ambivalent. "That's gonna be tough with no lead guitar," Sam said.

"Plus, we can't just leave him here. Alone," Ritchie added.

"What about his parents?" I asked. "Mike, did anyone call your folks?"

He shook his head no. I suggested we call. He said he'd rather not. I overruled him and picked up the phone to dial the house in Arundel where he grew up.

His mother answered with a distant timid *hello*. I identified myself as "John, from the band" and explained the situation to her, choosing my words very carefully to avoid conveying any of my hostility toward Mike. I told her that he really needed his family with him. She told me that Mike's father was in London on business, due back the next morning. I told Mrs. Simpson she should come to the hospital anyway, but she was hesitant. I was a little taken aback by her resistance, recalling all the times she drove to Beat Clinic shows by herself to meet up with Mom, but then it dawned on me that this was a pretty long time ago. *How long had we been doing this?*

"I'll tell you what," I said. "I'll come get you."

Before she had a chance to decline, I said I'd be there in fifteen minutes and basically hung up on her. I asked Chris to come with me, and we made good time getting to the house. We both agreed that once we got Mike's mother to the hospital in the next half hour or so, we could conceivably make it to Michigan by sundown.

I tapped on the screen door. We waited. I let a few seconds go by and did it again. No answer. *Where the hell was she?* I switched to the door knocker. Nothing. I *knew* this was the right place.

I remembered sitting toward the back of the school bus in ninth grade, pulling up in front of this house every morning and watching this cool kid, a couple of years older than I was, ambling down the driveway, always carrying a black Fender guitar case.

I remembered his subtly sarcastic handshake at the year-end "mock awards" assembly, when he accepted the title of "rock star" from classmate David Muddiman, who presented him with a potato-sized igneous chunk he probably found on the side of the road.

I remembered how excited and nervous I was a decade before when Mike asked me to fill in on drums for his group, the Normandy Beach Boys, at a battle of the bands at Dickinson High School. Keith Green, Mike Neiger, and I had asked him to listen to some songs we had written during our senior year at Tatnall, hoping he would want to drop everything and join our band. He told us we had "potential and nothing else." We knew he was the missing piece, especially after we watched in amazement as he determined a mysterious F chord from an XTC song that we had spent days trying to figure out.

At the battle of the bands, we presented an eclectic setlist of covers that included "Alison" by Elvis Costello, "Take It Easy" by the Eagles, and Mike's flawless performance of "Eruption" by Van Halen. The Normandy Beach Boys ended up placing third, losing out to a band of twelve-year-olds called Purgatory, fronted by a kid in a red spandex jumpsuit who absolutely nailed a cover of "Balls to the Wall" by Accept. You can't compete with German metal. But win or lose, that's what got me my "in" with Mike Simpson and paved the way for us to play music together up until the day I stood on his front stoop pounding on the front door, shouting for his mother to answer.

"Mrs. Simpson, please come out!"

Even Chris Brown, a level-headed addition to our crew, started knocking with insistence. What must *he* have been thinking at that point? We didn't pay him nearly enough to be dealing with bullshit like this, but he was right there with me, bruising his knuckles on the door. He had given up his house-sound gig at the North Star Bar to go on the road with the Caulfields. "A big major-label tour!" Regrets, I'm sure he had a few.

Finally, we heard footsteps on the stairs. A face peeked around a half-open door.

It was Mike's mom, not at all ready to go, still dressed in a robe and slippers.

Come ON.

"Mrs. Simpson, we need to take you to see Mike. Can you get ready, please?" I asked with diminishing patience.

"I'll be right there," she said, turning around and closing the door, not quite all the way.

Minutes passed.

"Mrs. Simpson!" I yelled.

"I need to call Dave," she half shouted from the kitchen. "He'll know what to do."

Chris and I looked at each other, our mouths agape. I pulled open the screen door and shouted up the stairs.

"MRS. SIMPSON, THERE IS NOTHING YOUR HUSBAND CAN DO OR SAY FROM ENGLAND THAT IS GOING TO MAKE ANY DIFFERENCE. PLEASE COME DOWN SO WE CAN TAKE YOU TO MIKE."

I was not leaving that place without her.

"I don't understand what's happening here, man," I said to Chris, exasperated.

"Well, ever hear of agoraphobia?" he asked.

It was about one thirty in the afternoon when Chris and I arrived back at Mike's hospital room with his mother. I felt like the past several hours had aged me. I tossed a "don't ask" eye roll in Sam and Ritchie's direction as Mrs. Simpson took a seat at her son's bedside. The rest of us huddled outside the door.

"So what do you guys say?" I whispered.

"How are we gonna do this as a three-piece?" Sam asked.

"Oh, just turn up," Ritchie said, half joking, but it resonated.

Just turn up. This seemed to be the logical and correct course of action. We walked back into the room, and Mike appeared to be much more alert than before. I tried looking directly at him, but my eyes wandered toward the floor.

"Hey, man. So, it looks like things are under control here, so, we're gonna go. To Detroit."

"Wait, you're playing the show?" Mike looked surprised, disappointed.

"You're leaving?" Mrs. Simpson jumped in, as if the prospect of being alone with her son frightened her.

"We'll talk to you when we get back, OK?"

I didn't wait for a response, and I walked out of the room.

The first hour in the van was quiet, practically silent except for the hum of the engine and the sound of Sam clearing his throat. Nobody spoke. There was no music on. We were drained, each one evaporating into himself. We were all thinking the exact same thought, but no one wanted to be the first to express it. Eventually, I just blurted it out.

"I think this is it."

They all knew what I meant.

WRONG EXIT

"So what's next for you guys?"

This was the last question of the live backstage interview at Pine Knob, with about an hour to go until showtime. Ritchie, Sam, and I had done a pretty good job fielding questions from morning-show host Johnny Edwards about road life and how it feels to go from playing St. Andrew's Hall to joining all these much-closer-to-household names at the Planet's big festival. I had my super-positive, grateful-just-to-be-here, upbeat rock dude spiel down pat. I'm pretty sure I began every response with "It's amazing," using a slightly different inflection each time.

In the world that we knew the Caulfields were not long for, even if something *isn't* that amazing, it's kind of expected that you say it is. It's just what you do. Even if the van needs new shocks and smells like feet, even when flames from under the hood blow inside the vents and singe your tour manager's leg hair, even if everyone retreats into their headphones in lieu of conversation, even if the spicy grilled catfish at Cracker Barrel has lost its appeal, even if you have no particular recollection of how the show at St. Andrews Hall actually went, even if you've been the opening act at fifteen-thousand-capacity festivals enough times to know you'll be playing for closer to one thousand people, even if you're playing the show without your lead guitarist, whose wounded expression when you walked out of his hospital room is making you think you're a horrible person, it's all still "amazing" or "incredible" or "awesome."

And on some level, it still really is. Plenty of bands would kill to be playing for a thousand people and traveling in a stinky van that a record company paid for, but things can look a lot different to someone tumbling down to the foot of the mountain than to someone making their ascendance to the top.

> PLENTY OF BANDS WOULD KILL TO BE PLAYING FOR A THOUSAND PEOPLE AND TRAVELING IN A STINKY VAN THAT A RECORD COMPANY PAID FOR, BUT THINGS CAN LOOK A LOT DIFFERENT TO SOMEONE TUMBLING DOWN TO THE FOOT OF THE MOUNTAIN THAN TO SOMEONE MAKING THEIR ASCENDANCE TO THE TOP.

Although this radio banter was virtually indistinguishable from all the other promo we had done in the past three years, I still wanted to be in the moment, because I really didn't know if I would ever have such a moment again. We were going to get dropped by A&M; that was a foregone conclusion. A couple hundred CD sales at Best Buy were not going to turn any tides, and A&M certainly wasn't about to give up our expensive master tapes for us to shop to another label.

When DJ Johnny asked the "what's next" question, Ritchie looked at me and said, "You wanna take that one, John?"

I froze. Could I actually talk about this? It was still so fresh and so raw. I really just wanted to keep things light, recount the story of how this band of crazy Italian guys from Delaware got frustrated at a gig and smashed their soundboard to bits with a nearby garden tool, and how I had seen the console sitting in the corner of our local music store with a repair tag that read "shovel damage."

I had no idea what was next. There had never been a time since we signed our record deal when there wasn't something to look forward to, something new and exciting in the offing. Now there was no answer. Seconds never felt so drawn out. Time stretched into distortion like a face in a fun house mirror. I wasn't sure until the instant the words left my mouth that I was really going to say it. I turned to my bandmates as if asking for final permission, and then I spoke:

"This is actually the Caulfields' last show. We're calling it quits."

I saw jaws drop all around me, followed by a silence far more palpable than during my previous hesitation in answering the question. Maybe they'd never had a band break up on the air before. I locked eyes with Garett Michaels, who was there with us backstage. He was clearly bummed, and he was in a unique position to share in our disappointment. The two stations he led during our time on A&M served as the bookends of our two-album major-label career. He was the one person in radio who could say he was there for both our promising entrance onto the national stage and our all-too-rapid departure.

All three of us thanked the station, thanked Garett, and thanked our supporters. I always favored the word "supporter" over the word "fan." I had no problem saying "I'm a fan" when *I* liked something or someone, but I couldn't seem to say the word with a straight face when it came to my own band. I guess there was that little piece of me that still needed to be convinced I could have nice things.

I found it hard to register the disbelief among the station employees as sincere, but there was no faking their expressions. One girl even cried. It was actually quite touching. Bands come and go, but some of them leave their metaphorical stage before they've really had a chance to shine. I felt like we were one of those bands. Garett and his staff seemed to think so too.

In our little corner of the backstage area, Sam, Ritchie, and I finally got down to brass tacks, discussing how the hell we expected to play our songs without Mike. There was no way I was even going to attempt any of the Fly's parts. We agonized over every potential candidate for the setlist. Should we play this? Should we cut that? It was obvious that nothing was going to sound the way it normally would. We would just have to sing some of the solos and otherwise wing it—as loudly as possible.

Chris Brown walked into the cordoned-off green room area, took a look at Sam, and scoffed.

"Are you going to wear *that*?"

"What's wrong with it," Sam fired back. "It's just a white T-shirt."

"It's an *under*shirt, little man. You look like Pop-Pop, just gettin' home from work. What, are you gonna put a little tomata stain on there too?"

"Wear whatever you want," I said to Sam as I donned a pair of half-ironic geriatric sunshields, which I felt complemented my green polyester slacks and black Ban-Lon shirt quite nicely.

It was T-minus ten minutes. Things were starting to percolate backstage. Matchbox Twenty were milling about. Apparently, they were the very next band that producer Matt Serletic worked with after we had passed on him in favor of David Bianco to work on *L*. Serletic had made platinum records with Collective Soul and had thrown his hat in the ring for our album, but if it was between him and the guy who had produced *Grand Prix* by Teenage Fanclub and mixed *Frosting on the Beater* by The Posies, a band like ours was damn well going to pick David Bianco. It's funny how things play out sometimes. We recorded our magnum opus, which hardly anyone would hear, and Matchbox Twenty became rock stars—another twist of fate not worth second-guessing.

A few members of Cowboy Mouth came up to say hello. We had played with these guys before and witnessed what they were capable of onstage. They were one of the best live bands I had ever seen. I really respected them. Plus, they had been around. One of the guitarists had been the lead singer of the Red Rockers in the '80s, and the twelve-inch single of their song "China" was still in my vinyl collection. Their drummer and lead singer, Fred LeBlanc, who had played in Dash Rip Rock years earlier, had the ability to whip audiences into a religious fervor from behind his kit. When he saw me wave to him from about ten feet away, he walked right up to me, stuck his index finger in his mouth, and gave me a wet willy in my left ear. It was gross and beautiful and a perfect way to send me out onstage to mark the end of an era.

The show pretty much went off along the lines of what I felt were my realistic expectations. I yelled "Hello, Detroit" even though we were forty miles away in Clarkston, and we got a polite welcome from a sparse crowd still filing into the venue. We knew we were going to be loud and crunchy, and probably a little sloppy, but had resolved to channel everything we loved about one-guitar bands like the Who and the Jam. Sam and I, both tuned to drop D, cranked up our amps, and we launched into a fitting opener to our final show as a major-label band: "All I Want Is Out."

> *There's a feeling I get*
> *When I feel nothing at all*
> *And all I want is out*
> *I got nothing left but doubt*
> *And I'm almost sure I'm positive*
> *I got no plans to talk about*

We built a little momentum through the first few songs. Sam played the main guitar line from "The Day That Came and Went" on bass, revealing how much that song owed to "Blood and Roses" by the Smithereens. Chris Brown jumped up onstage during an extended breakdown in "Figure It Out" and did the same wacky dance moves that had gotten him roundly booed by the audience at our show in Columbus just weeks before. After that performance, I told him flat out he had given me one of the greatest moments I had ever enjoyed onstage. He now belonged up there with us. At this point, he was as much a member of the band as anyone.

We played "Devil's Diary" to decent recognition, even though the song hadn't been on the radio in two years. I remembered that I was the one who had written the first several notes of the guitar solo, having repurposed a melody from one of the first songs I ever wrote by myself. I tried playing it for a second, failing miserably before reverting back to the rhythm chords. Nobody noticed or cared. We were playing with what the gods of rock would call *abandon*.

When Ritchie launched into his Keith Moon freak-out on the drums in the coda of our closer "Born Yesterday," I was loving every second. This was the feeling I was going to miss—the feeling of us against the world, the feeling that when we were on, we were as good as anybody. The three of us faced each other in triangular formation.

Ritchie sounded so good playing his batshit-crazy fills that I knelt right beneath his ride cymbal and felt my whole body go practically numb as the bashing of bronze washed over me.

When Sam and Ritchie landed on their final downbeat of the song, leaving my arpeggiating guitar to fade into black, the place erupted, like the now fully engaged crowd was actually sorry to see us go. I threw my old-man glasses into the front row and walked offstage flashing devil horns with my guitar slung across my back.

We hung out at Planet Fest for the rest of the day, feeling no obligation to use the word "amazing," unless we thought it applied, as in the case of the effeminate apple bottom of the bass player in one of the bands. I remember Chris Brown and myself dying from laughter as this guy paraded his moneymaker back and forth between the front of the stage and the drum riser, all the while bursting from what appeared to be a pair of Bonjour jeans. We dubbed him the "Hope Diamond of man-ass."

Besides making jokes at others' expense, I was also savoring those little perks that make you feel special as a musician: the catering, the all-access laminate that you wear around your neck and get to take home and add to your collection, the not-so-random interactions with the crowd. I did something that almost all musicians do at least once but few fess up to. I walked out into the venue, supposedly incognito, but clearly making myself available for validation. I feigned surprise when asked for an autograph, for which I *just so happened* to have a Sharpie in my back pocket. I smiled my aw-shucks smile when greeted with raised plastic cups followed by "Great set" or "You guys are tight" or "Can you get me backstage to meet Matchbox Twenty?"

Toward the end of the show, it was time for the big guns to shoot their shots. I was mesmerized by INXS, who sounded so record-perfect it was mind boggling. The precise tone of the Fender Telecaster on the four-note riff in "Never Tear Us Apart" was flawless. Michael Hutchence lived up to my every expectation as a singer and front man. Guys like him cover the whole stage but not in a jumpy, frantic way. He slinked and slithered like a serpent in the Garden of Eden. He had a patience about him that I envied, like he'd get there when he got there, and he knew you'd be waiting. Three months after Planet Fest, that November, I heard the news that he had been found dead in a Sydney hotel room.

Echo & the Bunnymen were a band that first caught my attention in high school, when the live music video of their song "Crocodiles" was on MTV. They both fascinated and confused me. They sounded like a New Wave–y version of the Doors, incorporating the rhythmic accents from "Break On Through" into their arrangement, while their gangly, shaggy-haired front man, Ian McCulloch, hippie-danced at the mic with a lit cigarette in his hand, wearing some kind of one-piece jumpsuit with a knit sweater tied in a knot around his neck.

It was a beautiful day in Michigan, the temperature at Pine Knob hovering around seventy-five degrees, but with stage lighting being as it was in the '90s, it still felt like the heat of one hundred french fry lamps was upon you up there. It was, therefore, surprising that Ian McCulloch took to the stage draped in a full-length fur coat, particularly as a man with no water weight to spare. I was thoroughly entertained and felt like a fanboy, singing all the words to "The Killing Moon" and "The Cutter." I scowled in harsh judgment when the audience gave their loudest reaction of the set to the band's cover of "When You're Strange" from *The Lost Boys* soundtrack.

The strong desire to forestall the end of this entire experience carried over after the concert venue was empty and we were back in the hotel where the radio station put us up. While most of the acts left town for their next show as soon as Planet Fest was over, we were still there, still ready for action when we walked down to the lobby and spotted none other than Ian McCulloch. It seemed that Ian was also looking to keep the good times rolling, and after registering what appeared to be a vague recollection that he had seen us backstage earlier in the day, he approached us.

"You lads know about the after-party, yeah?"

I was dumbstruck. Ian McCulloch was talking to us. I felt a Stepford-wife smile begin to pull at the corners of my mouth and lock in place. I had five of this guy's records at home. I sang "Lips Like Sugar" in the shower all the time.

"I say you heard about the *after*-party?"

We hadn't heard. We were not really an after-party kind of band.

As it turned out, Ian had the skinny on an event at some nightclub and just wanted to find a way to get there without having to take a cab or his tour bus.

Hey! We have a van! We can get you there. We'll all go!

That's the message that somehow got communicated.

It sounded like a plan. It sounded like *the* plan. I went up to the room I was sharing with Chris Brown and announced we were hitting the town in our trusty fifteen-passenger with Echo & the fucking Bunnymen.

In short order, the now-officially-defunct Caulfields, Ian McCulloch, and a couple of his hired guns took off out of the hotel parking lot into the Michigan night with nothing to go on except a napkin with an address scrawled in Ian's drunken chicken scratch. I was riding up front with Chris at the wheel. The two of us, being the only people in the van who had imbibed no alcohol that day, were more or less on our own as far as navigation went, and it was pretty much the blind leading the blind. The club was supposedly only twenty minutes away, but after about thirty minutes of not reaching our destination, we started to hear it from the back of the vehicle.

"Take the exit for Pontiac!" slammed our ears like an eighty-proof bullhorn from the peanut gallery.

"Did you see an exit for Pontiac?" Chris whispered in my direction.

I shook my head no.

"Take. The exit. For PONTIAC!" Ian McCulloch demanded.

Chris shot me a "who does this dickweed think he is" kind of look.

We hadn't the slightest clue where we were going. At a certain point, Chris put on his signal and just got off the highway so we could turn around.

"That's the wrong fucking exit! We need to head towards *Pontiac*!" Ian shouted.

Somehow, some way, we eventually did make it to the club in Pontiac. Chris recalls it as some overcrowded three-story bro-hole with *unst unst unst* music on the top floor and a rockabilly band on another. I don't remember a thing about that. I just remember Ian McCulloch springing out of his seat before we were even parked.

Never meet your heroes, as the saying goes.

With the exhaustion of the trip finally hitting us, we knew it was best to just retire to our beds and wait for daylight so we could begin the longest ten-hour drive we would ever know. It was an abrupt ending to an otherwise, dare I say, *amazing* day, and also an apt metaphor. The final curtain fell on the Caulfields in much the same way. I was left wanting more, but the situation dictated otherwise.

To the vast majority of the listening public, we would not even be a footnote.

They couldn't miss what they never really had. For those in the know, those who gave a damn, the book on the Caulfields felt incomplete, an unsatisfying, hastily written ending. But as for me, even though I would have said otherwise at the time, parting ways with my band and losing that record deal was the best thing that could have happened to me.

PART VI

UNSIGNED AGAIN, NATURALLY

When I fall,
When I'm over
Will you stick around?

—IKE, "WHEN I FALL"

POWER TRIP

I had been looking forward to 1999 since 1982, when I was a junior in high school and first saw the MTV video in which Prince and the Revolution sang of the apocalypse and how they intended to ring in *two thousand zero zero* in a purple blaze of hedonistic glory. Listening to "1999" made me picture my own life and the myriad ways I might seize the day when that fateful year approached. Had I based any predictions on my outlook at the end of 1997, after kissing my band and my record contract goodbye, I'm not sure how convincing my game face would have been.

It's true, I had been compelled to start over many times already, but given the alternative, what else are you going to do? Your father dies—you start over. Your mother pulls you out of public school and sends you to private school—you start over. You graduate and go off to college—you start over. You form a band, some people stay, some people go—you start over and over.

After a decade of dedication to music, you're given a real shot at the brass ring, and it's within reach, and you can see it and almost touch it and almost taste it, and you're rubbing elbows with those who have it, and those who can help you get it, and you're finally there on the brink of the ultimate fulfillment of childhood wishes that are just pipe dreams for 99.9 percent of the people who harbor such fantasies. And then, it doesn't happen the way you dreamed it.

The Caulfields had once eaten an expensive dinner with Apollonia Kotero. Yes, Apollonia of Apollonia 6 from *Purple Rain*. We tagged along to a meeting between her and Mark Mazzetti, as Mark was considering signing her to a new deal. I never forgot her parting words:

Remember, fellas, there's plenty of room at the top for all of us.

I wanted very badly to believe that. I had stood at the crossroads many times and had always moved in the direction my dreams led me. But was dreaming still free? Did following *my* dreams force others to defer *theirs*? Lisa wanted a family. We had been married for close to four years, and I had yet to prioritize that contract. Subconsciously, I had tried to buy her off. My publishing money erased her student loans, bought a new car, paid for langostino dinners at Marco Polo.

I knew that Mom wanted a life of security for all four of her children, but only three of them had attained it. I was the lone holdout. People who truly cared about me began dropping hints:

You're still young, John. You could go back to school and get a new degree—something other than English this time. Maybe you could get a job teaching music; no shame in that. You'd still be doing something that has something to do with something you love. You had a good run, John.

I might have been vulnerable enough to fall in with this line of thinking, but the window through which I would have retreated in search of the security that would have set everyone else's mind at ease wasn't open for long, thanks to an unexpected pep talk from

Mom. She had taken to quoting my lyrics from "Figure It Out," the opening track on the ill-fated second Caulfields record. Though she was a woman of relatively few words, they almost always hit home, maybe not right away, but eventually. This time they hit me like the Heimlich maneuver on a choking man.

"You need to figure it out, honey. I figured out something about you: your music is not just what you do. This is part of who you *are.*"

Receiving that acknowledgment from the mouth of my mother changed how I saw her, and it changed how I saw how she saw me. She had watched, no doubt with serious trepidation, as I went off in search of myself, on a path that was surely every Korean mother's nightmare. After all, what business did a mixed-up, mixed-race kid have in the world of rock 'n' roll? Mom's words told me I had as much damn business as anybody else, whether I sold a million records or not. She had been a silent partner in my tribe all along. This was the green light for me to be OK with being unapologetically me. If the choice was to walk away or double down, I was doubling down.

"YOU NEED TO FIGURE IT OUT, HONEY. I FIGURED OUT SOMETHING ABOUT YOU: YOUR MUSIC IS NOT JUST WHAT YOU DO. THIS IS PART OF WHO YOU ARE." RECEIVING THAT ACKNOWLEDGMENT FROM THE MOUTH OF MY MOTHER CHANGED HOW I SAW HER, AND IT CHANGED HOW I SAW HOW SHE SAW ME.

On the drive back to Pennsylvania from that conversation in Newark, some words came to me in a whisper. There were so many of them, I had to pull off to the side of the road to scribble them down.

> *I crack the windows out on I-95*
> *Another midnight trip to keep my hope alive*
> *I don't ask questions, I just take the car and drive*

From the mountains to the molehills
Never know when I'll arrive
Maybe tomorrow

"Whisper at the Top of My Lungs" was the first in an avalanche of songs I wrote in 1998. Telling titles like "Cry Like a Man," "If You Could See Me Now," and "Hand-Me-Down" soon followed. I also still had my publishing deal with Warner Chappell. John Titta, the senior vice president who had signed me, and his right-hand man "Phast Phreddie" Patterson set me up on co-writing dates with some of my musical heroes. I took New Jersey Transit trains up to the Manhattan office to meet Pat DiNizio from the Smithereens and, later, Steve Wynn from the Dream Syndicate.

Beyond the initial excitement, neither one of these attempted collaborations yielded songs I considered much good. Pat seemed preoccupied and more concerned about what we were ordering for lunch, and while the session with Steve did yield a coherent song, it felt a little contrived, like we were trying too hard to write another in a string of hits about "flying away" at a time when "Fly Away" by Lenny Kravitz, "Fly" by Sugar Ray, and, of course, "I Believe I Can Fly" by R. Kelly could already be found all over the radio.

It was my third Warner Chappell co-write that proved to be the charm. Peter Case had no idea how much of an influence he had been on me as a teenager. His early '80s band, the Plimsouls, appeared in *Valley Girl*, a movie I had watched enough times to memorize most of the dialogue. Part of what may have drawn me to the film was its portrayal of two people from two very different worlds falling in love, societal acceptance be damned. It was reminiscent of my parents and of their worlds colliding to make me. I never consciously thought of that at the time. What I did think about was how much I loved "A Million Miles Away," the Plimsouls' power pop masterpiece. I had played their album *Everywhere at Once* almost every day for most of 1983. At the time I thought I did a pretty good impersonation of Peter's voice.

I revealed none of this upon meeting him at a Travelodge in Santa Monica, where he rented a room year-round to serve as his writing den. I came prepared with a lyrical idea centered around the children of immigrants and how they get stuck in a sort of purgatory between the ways of their parents and those of the new world, where they wonder how they'll fit in. Peter liked the idea and began playing a chromatic descending guitar riff that evoked both a sense of chaos and the theme from *Batman*. I loved it, and we began to craft some chords and a melody for the opening line of the song, a reflection on parental expectation lifted directly from the script of *Saturday Night Fever*.

You can't defend yourself against their fantasies

Roughly ninety minutes later, we came up with "Translation," a song that touched on race, assimilation, generational divides, and did I mention it sounded like the theme from *Batman*?

Old World crashes into New World
Do you belong now?
Will anybody take you in?
Old World, welcome to the New World
Kick off your shoes now
And join a generation
Lost in translation

Had writing with Peter Case been my only reason for being in Los Angeles, it would have been an awfully quick trip, but I was also there for International Pop Overthrow, a new music festival whose mission was to showcase musicians who worshipped at the altar of the Beatles, The Raspberries, the Knack, and *That Thing You Do!*

While I hadn't worn a skinny tie onstage in a while, I was excited to be playing in LA for the first time since the Caulfields, and for the first time under my own name.

David Bash, the founder and organizer of IPO, invited me to be part of the biggest show of the festival, at the seven-hundred-seat El Rey Theatre.

I had spent much of the first half of that year finding my rhythm as a solo performer, getting comfortable just being John Faye, or John Faye "formerly of the Caulfields" when I thought that would help. With nothing for promotion but a stack of posters featuring a new shot-at-home promo picture and the Warner Chappell logo placed far more prominently than most would consider tasteful, I embarked on a string of Sunday night shows in Philadelphia at the North Star Bar, the same club that had hosted the release party for *Whirligig* three years earlier.

As opposed to being on the main stage, my Sunday sets found me tucked into a tiny corner of the front bar, with my guitar and vocal mic both plugged into the same cube-shaped amplifier. All my new songs took shape in that room, as I ever-so-slowly learned the ropes of playing alone, exploring the space between quiet and loud, kicking on my Boss phaser pedal any time I wanted to spice things up. In the process, I was building a new little following, one Sunday night straggler at a time, and it felt like I was remaking myself from scratch, flexing new muscles in the form of new songs, performing them week after week, as healthy flesh grew around their bones.

My new confidence as a solo performer notwithstanding, I was happy to have somebody with me onstage at the El Rey. I had known Cliff Hillis as an acquaintance from the Delaware music scene during the heyday of the Beat Clinic. He fronted the bands Mystery Machine and Tisra Til, sporting a voluminous blond coif that appeared to defy the laws of gravity and likely required he spend half his gig money on styling products. In the intervening years, his hair had come back down to earth, and he was now the guitarist in a fantastic trio called Starbelly, who, as it just so happened, were also playing IPO. That lucky coincidence connected me with a musician who would color my songs in a brand-new way. Where there was once bravado and flash, there was now understatement and taste, delivered through a guitar tone from hell. The El Rey set couldn't have been more than five or six songs, but by the time it was over, it was obvious that Cliff was the guitar player for me.

I already had a drummer in mind for whatever was going to happen next. Dave Anthony, Ritchie's replacement in Matt Sevier's band, had taken a road trip with me out to Wisconsin to play a one-off college gig in Madison not long after the Caulfields' demise. Sometimes you just get a feeling about a person. Standing in Mom's driveway, loading my guitar and his djembe into the trunk of the rental we'd be driving to the Midwest, Dave let fly with an unexpected series of short, sharp, posterior bursts, pausing between each one to implore me to "check it out."

Pffft … check it out … pfft … check it out, John … pffft … hey, check it out.

Nothing accelerates a new friendship like broken wind and a thirteen-hour drive, and with nothing but time and open road, we got to know each other, listening to music and telling our tales. Dave had toured since his late teens, playing with a series of heavy metal bands. He found himself in the kinds of situations that spawned a certain strain of road story: Bandmate A moons Bandmate B in a speeding van while Bandmate C dangles a Cheeto in front of Bandmate A's bare buttocks at the very moment that Bandmate D slams on the brakes. Or Bandmate A lights a Styrofoam container of dog shit on fire in front of Bandmate B's hotel room door, and mockery from Bandmates C and D ensues.

Dave's rather blue sense of humor was in perfect alignment with my own, and with Cliff in the mix, I very much felt like I was in a band again, even if that's not really what I was looking for. Things would have to be different from the Caulfields. For better or worse, I was done with democracy when it came to making music. Opinions were OK, but the final decisions would have to be mine. I was getting ahead of myself anyway. If I was going to make another run up the rock 'n' roll mountain, I would need some help.

I was fortunate to have a few friends from the A&M years who were still in my corner. Steve Barnes, the co-host of the morning show on 99X in Atlanta, had been one of the Caulfields' most vocal supporters, always talking up our "foot-stomping pop" on the air and lobbying to play the drums on "Devil's Diary" any time we came to town. When I called to let him know I had gone solo, he brought me down to Georgia and engineered a situation to introduce me to his morning show partner Leslie Fram's husband, Lanny West.

Lanny was an artist manager who started out in radio when I was just starting elementary school. His station was the first in the country to play "Mandy" by Barry Manilow. I was immediately taken by his confident southern charm, and before long, we were on daily calls between Atlanta and Philadelphia, devising a strategy for shopping me to record companies and getting me into the studio. If I wasn't quite yet back in the saddle, at least I had a foot in the stirrup.

Lanny began setting up industry nights in New York, inviting label reps to come see my new act. Dave, Cliff, and I drove up for one such showcase at the CBGB 313 Gallery, a sidecar venue set up directly next door to the original CBGB on the Bowery. The Caulfields had played the main room just a few years before, long after the ghosts of 1977 had left the building. During our tumbleweed early evening set at 313, I thought it would be pretty punk rock to yell into the mic, "We don't need no stinking bass player!" Ironic that the only A&R person in the room to see the bass-less "John Faye Power Trio" was Nigel Harrison, then a scout for Interscope Records and previously the bass player for Blondie. Fuck my life.

It became apparent that any recording we would be doing in the near future would be *independent*—that is to say, quite dependent on whatever was left in my bank account after the down payment on my house put me in what I'd imagine is the fairly exclusive club of people who can say they burned through almost $250,000 in less than three years. Of course, that involved commissions and a lot of outstretched hands suggesting the classic Bugs Bunny line "And me, boss," but I had no time to dwell on the past. This is what it was to be in charge of my own destiny, and soon the "John Faye Power Trio" switched out one letter and took on a whole new meaning as the "John Faye Power Trip."

The first time I walked into Nickel and Dime Studios in early 1999, I wondered if I had the right address. The sampler CD containing tracks produced and/or engineered by the owner, Don McCollister, sounded like it could have been recorded at any one of the high-end facilities I had gotten used to with the Caulfields. But this was just some guy's house in Georgia. The console was located in what I guess would have been an office under normal circumstances. Drums would be set up directly down the hall in the dining room. Guitar amps were mic'd up in the kitchen.

I have to admit, I had my concerns, but the second I heard the playback from Dave's first drum take for my song "D-R-A-M-A-M-I-N-E," I knew I was in the right place at the right time. It didn't matter that there was no sound proofing. It didn't matter that there were no isolation booths. It didn't matter that Don's cat might randomly jump on the tape machine as we were rolling. It didn't matter that the lounge upstairs looked like the aftermath of a frat party frozen in time, with cigarette butts, crushed beer cans, and fossilized pizza crusts forming a pyre around a lone can of Raid. What did matter was that Don McCollister was behind the board and he made magic in that house.

Throughout the spring, Cliff, Dave, and I drove down to Decatur for marathon long weekends, recording in four-song blocks, living off sausage and peppers from Skip's Chicago Dogs next door and spending our downtime laughing and awestruck, listening to a vinyl copy of *Life*, a 1970 Christian musical that Cliff scored at the thrift store down the street. In my own nondenominational way, I felt completely reborn.

The three of us playing on every track gave the project a solid core, but there was also room for a cast of guest musicians. Mark Ross from the band Memory Dean, whom Lanny also managed, played inventive, melodic bass lines on eleven of the twelve songs. I thoroughly underutilized my friend Lee Schusterman, a learned keyboardist I knew from back in Philly, bringing him in to play just seven notes on a Rhodes piano for "If You Could See Me Now." Brandon Bush, another keyboard virtuoso, who was a couple years away from joining the band Train, played a fantastic Hammond B-3 organ part on "Whisper at the Top of My Lungs." He also nailed a Wurlitzer electric piano solo on "Miss Catch-22," a song I co-wrote with my old bandmate Ritchie Rubini, who himself added a fake theremin and synthesized bells to complement my nerdy lyrical nods to Joseph Heller's classic antiwar novel. Then there was Don, surreptitiously recording bass, keyboards, and even EBow guitar parts to complete the vivid sonic picture. By summertime, I had the finished full-length that would serve as my proof that there was life after a major label.

"Miss Catch-22" was released as a radio single in advance of the album and immediately hit the airwaves on 99X, which had played the bejesus out of "Devil's Diary" and, more recently, had catapulted independent artists like Shawn Mullins and Butch Walker and his band Marvelous 3 into major record deals.

Back home in Philadelphia, there were a few hoops to jump through when we approached Y-100, the station that had put the Caulfields on the modern rock map in 1995. Rather than adding the single outright—an admittedly *big ask* from an independent artist— the program director, Jim McGuinn, agreed to put the song into the "Cage Match."

The Cage Match was a nightly call-in vote involving two songs—a champion and a challenger. The songs were played back to back, with the listening audience acting as judge, jury, and executioner to determine which tune would survive to go another round. If we could win, and keep winning, we would be guaranteed at least one spin a day.

As fate would have it, "Miss Catch-22" went on a thirteen-victory run, which began with a surprise unseating of a great Guster song, "Barrel of a Gun," and ended on night fourteen in the agony of defeat, losing to "Nookie" by Limp Bizkit. McGuinn was impressed enough with the song's performance to add the single into medium rotation. He also offered the JFPT a spot in the station's "Big Break" contest, which necessitated taking part in a battle of the bands at the TLA on South Street. The grand-prize winner of the contest would be the opening act at an upcoming concert with R.E.M., who were touring in support of their new album, *Up*.

What R.E.M. meant to me as a teenager was beyond calculation. If I had worn out my copy of that Plimsouls album in 1983, I played *Murmur* and *Chronic Town* twice as much. After I saw R.E.M. preview a snippet of "Driver 8" on MTV a year before it came out on *Fables of the Reconstruction*, it became the first song I ever tried to teach myself on guitar. It took me years to undo my appropriations of Michael Stipe's vocalisms that had yielded so many complimentary comparisons and so much validation in my early years as a singer. I had to win this thing.

I had not played in a battle of the bands since the Energizer contest in college, and there was a big part of me that wasn't exactly chomping at the bit to do it. This Power Trip with my name attached to it would be pitted against some of the most popular young acts in Philly. Back in 1982, while pondering my future in 1999, it never once occurred to me to do the math and realize that this would be the year I turned thirty-three. That's, like, long-gone-dead in rock 'n' roll dog years. I'm thankful I never felt like I truly had a choice. If I had to win a local battle of the bands at age thirty-two and three-quarters in order to stay in forward motion, then that's exactly what was going to happen. In spite of being underestimated, in spite of my being the old guy at the club, in spite of having my stage monitors inexplicably shut off after our first song, John Faye Power Trip was the name announced as the winner at the end of the night.

We had flown Mark Ross up from Atlanta to play the TLA, but we all knew that a bassist living almost eight hundred miles away was not workable in the long term. Our bass player moving forward was actually in the crowd at the Big Break contest. It would be the only time Joann Schmidt would watch the JFPT from the audience.

Joann was a Northeast Philly girl, raised on radio, with a tough rocker chick exterior and a Suzi Quatro haircut. She had played in an earlier incarnation of Stargazer Lily, one of the bands we competed against in the contest. She had more recently been gigging with Philly singer-songwriter Nancy Falkow, whose gracious, hurricane-force personality led her to insist that Joann audition for the Power Trip, a move that would all but certainly leave Nancy without a bass player but would land her friend Joann in the band best suited for the kind of music she wanted to play. Nancy knew before any of the rest of us.

In the dank basement of my house in Elkins Park, it took three songs, if that, for all four of us to realize we were going to be a force to be reckoned with. Joann was the whole package—the chops, the looks. She had it all. Except for a car. That, she did not have. Joann's lifestyle was what you might call "off the grid." She avoided the kinds of things that might get a person called up for jury duty in Philadelphia. No bank account, no credit cards, no vehicle. I could totally respect that. And so, I would be her ride to and from her first show at Gullifty's in central PA, to her second show, opening for R.E.M. and Spacehog, and to every Power Trip show thereafter that didn't require a rental van. Double-parking my car on the sidewalk at the corner of Catharine and Queen with hazard lights flashing became part of my muscle memory.

It was overcast and drizzling at the cumbersomely named Blockbuster-Sony Music Entertainment Centre on the day of the R.E.M. show. The open-air amphitheater, typically referred to as a "shed" in the concert biz, was a stone's throw from Philly in Camden, a convenient, boozy ferry ride across the Delaware for concert goers.

Personally, I was never a huge fan of this type of place, where a large percentage of the audience seems like they're in the next county, sitting out on a general admission "lawn," beyond the covered, more expensive seats. I knew that whoever would be out there with their blankets and cheap folding chairs were in for a soggy experience that day.

What I did not know upon arrival at the "E-Centre" was that our "big break" opening for R.E.M. was never actually supposed to be on the main stage. We were slated to play out on the concourse just inside the gates, providing little more than background noise to the people walking past on their way to stand in line for an eleven-dollar beer. Because the rain posed a significant risk of electrocution on an uncovered stage, it looked as though we were simply going to be sent home without enjoying the spoils of our hard-won victory.

Lanny, who had made the trip up from Sandy Springs to see us open for a band we all knew was destined for the Rock & Roll Hall of Fame, was not taking the situation lying down. His Blackberry address book happened to contain the number for Jefferson Holt, R.E.M.'s long-time manager, who, of course, had long-standing home-state ties to Lanny and Leslie through 99X. A quick two-minute phone call later, we were given the OK to open the show on the main stage. Good news for us, not so good for the crew, who all thought they were on their dinner break. I could see the facial expressions on all the union stagehands morph into irritation as word went down the chain of command.

According to the front-of-house engineer, there were only six channels left on the mixing console. We would have to perform "unplugged," meaning no full drum kit.

Dave set up a snare drum and a tambourine on a stand. He would get one overhead mic. I would play acoustic guitar through a direct box, Joann would run her bass direct through the monitors, we'd have one mic for lead vocals, one for backup vocals, and Cliff took up the very last open input to throw an SM-57 in front of his amplifier. The four of us stood in a tight linear formation, taking up less room onstage than we normally did at the smallest of local clubs.

Even though it's not how I expected we would play, all four of us were determined to make the most of it, and that's what we did. In some ways, I think the intimacy of our acoustic set drew the audience in more than if we had bombarded them with arena-rock attitude.

We never even got an opportunity to meet R.E.M.—each band member, we were told, was holed up in their own separate tour bus— but their generosity in green-lighting our last-minute incursion onto their stage, and Michael Stipe's kind shout-out to us during their set, were indications that they were still the down-to-earth band from Athens I had fallen in love with so many years before.

1999 matched the highest highs I could have hoped for in the wake of watching that Prince video as a teenager, before I had even written my first song or played my first show. Far from being out of time, I was granted more of it, finding myself recast into a whole new tribe, with whom I would share my experiences but also make new memories.

Jerky Boys III replaced *Shut Up, Little Man* as the comic relief, but the van conversations were equally absurd, whether it was bitching about Lanny's directive

1999 MATCHED THE HIGHEST HIGHS I COULD HAVE HOPED FOR IN THE WAKE OF WATCHING THAT PRINCE VIDEO AS A TEENAGER, BEFORE I HAD EVEN WRITTEN MY FIRST SONG OR PLAYED MY FIRST SHOW.

that we cut expenses by eating tomato sandwiches on Wonder Bread or hearing stories from our new road manager, Shawn Arnold.

"Sharnold" was a 6'2" tobacco-chewin', baseball-lovin', shit-talkin' Georgia boy, full of intellectual curiosity, which we had plenty of time to explore during a string of dates on Matthew Sweet's *In Reverse* tour.

On the drive to our hometown show, back again at the TLA, Sharnold, who may very well have never been that far north, said he wanted the "full Philadelphia experience," probably expecting to get a cheesesteak at one of the tourist traps in the Italian market. Instead, I took the scenic route from Elkins Park through north Philly, down Second Street, a straight shot into the city that avoided rush hour traffic on the highway. At a stoplight, we both noticed the frame of a burned-out car just sitting there on the sidewalk, a faded bumper sticker still legible on the dented chrome.

Your school sucks!

It felt like the final scene in a comeback story, the charred remains representing the ashes of 1997 and the long road back to who I knew I could be.

This is about as Philly as Philly gets, I thought to myself, feeling more at home in my city than I had in ages.

I spent New Year's Eve at home in 1999, feeling like something was missing. It's not that I was dying to wedge myself into the human petri dish in Times Square, blowing into a noisemaker and wearing a plastic top hat from Party City. It's just that Lisa and I were drifting apart. It had been two and a half years since our last truly spontaneous act, when we drove down to the Spectrum on Easter Sunday and bought scalped tickets to see Beck on his *Odelay* tour. I knew we were no fun anymore after a recent trip to Seattle, when she chose bed over a midnight screening of *The Exorcist* I was dying to attend. She was already asleep by ten o'clock on the last day of the year.

I was left to my own devices to ponder the future. For all I knew, the very collapse of society awaited me at the stroke of midnight. The so-called Y2K bug had been the big story all year, and the panic industrial complex was predicting anarchy in the streets when computer systems, switching from "ninety-nine" to "zero-zero," would be tricked into a time warp back to the year 1900, erasing bank records and social security numbers. While there was a certain allure to that scenario, 12:00 am came and went with the electrical grid apparently still intact, and me on the couch with three cats—Mr. Misty, Gracie, and Happy Fun Sid—all purring and completely unaware that I was paying the unseen price of pursuing my so-called power trip: loneliness.

The JFPT reconvened on a quiet Sunday night in New York a couple of weeks into the year 2000. We were slated to appear on *Idiot's Delight*, an iconic radio show on WNEW hosted by Vin Scelsa, an old-school FM pioneer who began his career in the early '70s and became a giant of free-form radio, name-checked by the Ramones in their song "It's Not My Place."

Vin had seen us open for Matthew Sweet at the Bottom Line back in November and invited us to be part of his January 16 broadcast. The four of us, along with our friend Sherman, waited our turn outside the air studio while Vin got into the weeds with his first guest of the night, the very tall Tim Robbins, the actor who had starred in *The Shawshank Redemption*. We noshed on the cookies Tim had brought from a nearby deli until we got the go-ahead to come in, about an hour and a half later than we had been told.

I figured that since the previous interview ran late, we might be rushed out after a brief conversation and a quick song, but we ended up staying on for over two hours, playing nine of the twelve songs from the album and even our cover of "Coming Up," which we'd recorded for a Paul McCartney tribute due out in the fall.

Vin controlled the flow of *Idiot's Delight* like a master improviser, steering the conversation into unexpected tangents and creating clever segues on the fly—"A Good Year for the Grrls" into "A Good Year for the Roses." A fairly diminutive man, then in his early fifties, he showed zero inhibition and danced around the studio in the glow of lit candles as we played. It was one of those perfect instances when audience and artist see themselves reflected in the moment, symbiotically fueling each other.

After we went off the air around 12:30 am, he sent us back out into Manhattan moonlight with the compliment that he had not been so excited by a new band since the first time he'd seen Counting Crows. It spiked my spirit in a way that few other words of praise ever could. I hadn't considered myself "new" in a very long time, and the entire ride back to Philadelphia felt like I was floating on a cloud.

Close to 3:00 am, I arrived back at Forrest Avenue, where the last of my publishing money had gone toward a down payment on a modest house a few years earlier. I was startled to find Lisa wide awake and waiting for me in the living room.

"The Old Man died," she said with tears in her eyes.

The "Old Man" was actually not an old man at all. Our friend Brian from college was Lisa's age. His nickname stemmed from a premature shock of gray in his hair, the same issue that familiarized me with at-home hair-color kits very early in life. He was sitting in his car, stopped first in line at a red light near his parents' house in New Jersey, when another vehicle plowed through the intersection at full speed and broadsided him. He never stood a chance.

"I didn't call you because I didn't want to ruin your radio show," Lisa said as I hugged her tight for the first time in a while.

Brian had been a legendary figure during our college years: gay, but not yet out, full of catty sarcasm, obsessed with pop singer Samantha Fox and Susan Lucci from *All My Children*. Lisa and Brian had remained close after graduation. They had just emailed each other the week before. I knew he was a good friend to her, someone with whom she could talk about the things she was, perhaps, no longer sharing with me.

He was the first one from our core group of friends to go, and the tragedy of his early death on the night of one of the biggest highlights of my career both angered and inspired me in ways I could not have anticipated. The Armageddon scenario that Prince predicted had come to pass for Brian. I couldn't bring myself to write directly about it, instead channeling the Old Man's attitude and spirit into the chorus of a new song called "Revenge," in which a ghost returns from beyond with a heaping helping of the dish best served cold.

I will take my revenge
On a road that never ends
'Til I catch you unprepared for my attack
When I take my revenge
The one thing you can depend upon is
I will be the bitch who pays you back

I have vague recollections of Brian coming to visit me in my sleep, moistening his oversized two front teeth with his tongue before unleashing typically cutting remarks, reprised from insults he used to hurl at other Newark musicians to take them down a peg.

John ... John. If this whole music thing doesn't work out ... and I'm assuming it won't ... you should probably start that family your wife's been waiting for all these years.

I'm pretty sure it happened that way. But what do I know? I was dreaming when I wrote this.

AS LONG AS I'M AROUND

N atalie arrived on a Friday morning, fourteen days after her due
date, fifty-three hours into a Pitocin-induced labor. There wasn't
a doctor or nurse in sight when Lisa alerted me that it was time.
The call button on the hospital bed was useless. Maybe they were
between shifts or something, but the entire maternity ward may as
well have had tumbleweeds blowing across its antiseptic floor. We
were on our own.

My six weeks of training from the birthing class we attended that
summer kicked in like the shot of adrenaline to Uma Thurman's heart
in *Pulp Fiction*. I began barking out instructions for Lisa to breathe,
mimicking the cadence we were taught.

Hee hee hooo. Hee hee hooo. Hee hee hooo.

We exhaled together in a deliberate, hypnotic rhythm, a slowed-
down inversion of "We Will Rock You" or a high school pep rally
stomp. I dabbed sweat off Lisa's brow with a handful of Kleenex
grabbed in haste from the tissue box next to the sink.

"I have to push!" Lisa bellowed in agony.

"OK, you can do this!" I said, slurring the words together into a sound I'm pretty sure was indiscernible to a woman bearing down as her epidural was beginning to wear off.

PUSH 2, 3, 4, 5, 6, 7, 8! PUSH 2, 3, 4, 5, 6, 7, 8!

I imagine the drill sergeant urgency in my voice had to have carried beyond the confines of the birthing suite because at some point a doctor and two nurses finally ran into the room like three Kramers bursting into Jerry Seinfeld's apartment to find our daughter's head already crowning. After more pushing, a cut umbilical cord, and some misguided afterbirth jokes, I was cradling a scrunchy-faced baby girl wrapped in a standard-issue blue-and-red-striped receiving blanket.

It was love at first sight. I whispered the song I had already written for her as I watched her breathe her peaceful tiny breaths.

You'll never have to worry 'bout me loving you as long as I'm around.

I could hear that line from "Welcome Home" playing inside my head as I sat in my aisle seat waiting for my 6:00 am flight from San Francisco to take off. For the first time in my music career, I couldn't wait to get back to the East Coast from California. The Bay Area was normally the kind of place I never wanted to leave, but I felt guilty knowing my wife was back in Elkins Park without me, our baby barely over a month old. Lisa's maternity leave was ending, and she had to ask her mother to drive down from their house in Cranbury—Exit 8 off the turnpike to Jerseyphiles—so she could return to work while I was gone. Most couples we knew had extended families practically down the block, and no shortage of offers for free babysitting from grandparents or spinster aunts. After years of not-so-subtle hints to give them a grandchild, our parents were in no particular position to come to the rescue on a moment's notice, especially Mom, as driving anywhere beyond Newark city limits was a nonstarter for her by that point. The sixty miles that separated us may as well have been six hundred.

My wife left in the lurch or not, I needed to make money, and someone who had a lot of it was footing the bill for me to travel west to use my voice. It was probably the most unlikely professional situation I had encountered to date. My friend Anthony, whom I knew from the publishing and song-placement side of the music business, had been helping a guy named Bill Simon develop a pet project. Bill Simon was the new owner of Converse, the company that manufactured the only sneakers that ever mattered to me: Chuck Taylor All Stars. During high school, I owned high-tops in green, in orange, in red—I regretted buying the red ones because they looked a little too much like clown shoes—but the pair that saw the most action, that went with everything I wore outside of the Tatnall dress code, was the black pair. Yes, they were basically part of the punk rock "uniform," but I loved them, felt weirdly safe in them.

When Anthony called, offering to fly me out, telling me they were looking for someone who could sound a bit like Joe Jackson to cut a demo for a Broadway-style rock musical written by the guy who had just rescued an iconic shoe company from bankruptcy, he didn't have to ask me twice.

You mean they'll pay me AND I get free Chucks? Hell yeah, I'll do it.

I made sure to tell him I wore a size eight before hanging up the phone and immediately locating my ten-inch vinyl copy of Joe Jackson's *Look Sharp*, which I listened to pretty much nonstop for the next two weeks. Half the songs I'd ever written were a variation on "Is She Really Going Out with Him" anyway. I was born for this. I'd fly to Cali, nail the vocal, be in and out and back home with my wife and baby girl within a few days.

Anthony and I drove from his house in Mill Valley up to a little private studio in Pacheco owned by Ross Valory, the bass player from Journey. The engineer was Tim Gorman, who had played keyboards for the Who in the early '80s, and I think I recall he was personally in charge of storing the synthesizer that they used for "Baba O'Riley." Our Monday afternoon recording session went swiftly and swimmingly, and I spent more time grilling Tim for Who stories than I spent tracking the demo.

I was excited to tell Lisa about my experience and return home with some cash, which by that point was again in short supply from my end. The last vestiges of savings from my publishing deal with Warner Chappell went into the down payment on our house, and I would soon discover that stuff like diapers and formula didn't come cheap after the balances ran dry on all those Babies "R" Us gift cards from the shower.

I thought about all these things as the song I wrote for my newborn daughter continued to resonate in my internal conversation. I was proud of "Welcome Home." It was as true an expression of how I felt as anything I had ever written. And it was so damn *positive*. Who *was* I anymore?

> *Welcome home, it's so nice to meet you*
> *Got things that I wanna teach you*
> *But then it just might be the other way around*
> *I know that you're gonna change me*
> *Just like I'll do for you, baby*
> *But maybe in a way that's so much more profound*
> *And you'll never have to worry 'bout me loving you as long as*
> *I'm around.*

I loved my little girl. I loved our song and gave myself that little writer's pat on the back for using the word "baby" in reference to an actual baby and not in a Robert Plant or Vanilla Ice kind of way.

I was on the verge of dozing back into slumber when it occurred to me that the airplane I was on should have taken off at least twenty minutes earlier. Why were we just sitting there? There was no communication at all from the cockpit. People around me were becoming impatient, hoping that we weren't in for a long delay. The whole reason you wake up at four in the morning to make an early flight is so you'll get to where you're going and still have some semblance of a day left to spend with those you love. I started wondering if there was a hurricane or tropical storm messing things up for air traffic back east, but I had no idea what was going on.

Sometime around six thirty, a flight attendant got on the PA and gave a vague and infuriating announcement, canceling the flight and stating that the FAA had grounded all air traffic due to an "incident in New York."

The grumblings of already-annoyed passengers turned into loud gasps of frustration, as seat belts were unbuckled, carry-on bags were collected, and the full flight emptied back out into the United terminal at SFO, which was now buzzing with passengers from numerous other planes that never took off or never even boarded.

I reached into my backpack and took out the red Nokia cell phone I had recently purchased to make sure I was always reachable in case we ran out of baby wipes or something. Almost immediately after I turned it on, the signature Nokia ringtone, lifted from a classical guitar piece called "Gran Vals," went off. It was Lisa.

"How did you know I didn't take off?" I said, dispensing with the formality of a greeting or salutation.

"They're crashing planes into the World Trade Center," she shrieked. "And another one just hit the Pentagon!"

She sounded hysterical.

"Who's *they*?" I wondered.

Then I looked up to find the muted video screens in the terminal broadcasting network footage of a low-flying commercial jet plowing into the World Trade Center, spraying flames and concrete in all directions. Stranded passengers looked on in horror, now, perhaps, relieved that their planes had not taken off. After it began to sink in that multiple aircraft had been used to attack different cities, it felt like everyone around me began thinking the same thought:

If this was happening in New York and Washington, who's to say it won't happen here?

Terminal 3 at San Francisco International Airport now seemed like one of the least safe places one could possibly be, given the circumstances. Terrorists could be somewhere in the terminal, standing among us. It wasn't long before the vibe of the throng went from chatty disbelief to "We need to get the *fuck* out of here *now*."

People began wheeling their Samsonites with purpose toward the exits. The crowd never veered into full-blown panic mode, but I had the sense that it could flip at any second if the wrong rumor began to spread.

I made it outside of baggage claim and called Anthony, suspecting he had already made it home.

"Hey, buddy, what's up? Did they cancel your flight or something?" He had no idea.

"Turn on the television," I said, knowing I was directing him to view some of the most shocking images either of us had been exposed to in our lifetimes.

With Anthony at least an hour away and word spreading about potential bridge closures as the mass exodus from SFO continued, I made a snap decision to hop on a bus, with no regard for where it was headed. "Anywhere but here" was fine by me.

I sat down next to a young woman, and we exchanged that silent nod of acknowledgment that passes between strangers thrown together in a bad situation. I was relieved to be moving away from the airport, but I was frozen in a sense of nervous paralysis, which it felt like my seatmate picked up on when she began to make what turned out to be very comforting small talk. She had a calm about her, which made sense when she told me she was a student at a theological seminary. She seemed to have a trust in God that I was never able to muster and was certainly not feeling in that moment. I told her about Natalie and about my improbable reason for being in California.

She was generously curious about my life as a musician, and she let me ramble and babble until, almost like a miracle, we ended up getting off the bus not too far from Anthony's house, which was at the bottom of a hill overlooked by the Golden Gate Baptist Theological Seminary. Anthony picked us up in his car, and we gave her a ride up the hill. Before parting ways, I handed her the copy of *The John Faye Power Trip* I had in my bag. I felt a little lame doing that, but it wasn't so much an act of self-promotion as it was the only way I could think of to thank her for just being kind to me on a day when I was so far from the ones I love.

Back at the house on Seminary Cove Drive, I settled in with Anthony, his wife, Diane, and their dog, Cooper—all four of us on the couch, with every channel on the television showing the same thing. As the hours passed, the news networks offered dribs and drabs of new information over repetitive footage of Flight 175's moment of impact into the South Tower. It happened just three minutes after my flight was supposed to have taken off. Watching helpless people jumping to certain death from the highest floors of the soon-to-collapse buildings made it abundantly clear that we were sitting on the ultimate dividing line of our lifetimes, the spot from which all things would now be viewed: pre-9/11 and post-9/11.

Sometime in the late afternoon, after watching a shot of desperate relatives holding up photographs in hopes of locating loved ones who worked in and around the World Trade Center, Diane couldn't take it anymore and made the welcome suggestion that we turn off the TV and get out of the house. The three of us wound up at a movie theater, among maybe seven or eight other paying customers. In addition to providing the best free advice for vocal health I had heard to date, *Rock Star* with Mark Wahlberg and Jennifer Aniston served as the perfect respite from the real-life horrors we would be watching on repeat for the foreseeable future.

> WATCHING HELPLESS PEOPLE JUMPING TO CERTAIN DEATH FROM THE HIGHEST FLOORS OF THE SOON-TO-COLLAPSE BUILDINGS MADE IT ABUNDANTLY CLEAR THAT WE WERE SITTING ON THE ULTIMATE DIVIDING LINE OF OUR LIFETIMES, THE SPOT FROM WHICH ALL THINGS WOULD NOW BE VIEWED: PRE-9/11 AND POST-9/11.

Although the FAA reopened American airspace to commercial flights by September 13, the backlog of stranded passengers was huge. I wouldn't be able to get on a plane back to Philadelphia until September 16. I remember the tightness of my body on that flight, sitting upright and rigid, staring straight ahead into my tray table and eyeballing the rest of the passengers with suspicion every time someone walked by on their way to the bathroom.

When I was finally back home, it felt as if I had returned from a war. Natalie's beautiful little face looked different from when I had left her. She was already growing. I held her and rocked her in my arms, singly softly as she stared up at me:

You'll never have to worry 'bout me loving you as long as I'm around

I carried her out into the backyard and stood underneath the moon and the stars, lamenting the end of the world as I knew it and pondering just what kind of future our little family was flying into.

HIT 'EM LOW, HIT 'EM HIGH

T here's a universal piece of advice I had always heard about singing "The Star-Spangled Banner": if you do nothing else to prepare, just remember to start *low*. If you begin the song too high in your vocal range, and you are not Mariah Carey, the money note at the end of "land of the free" will either usher in a pack of howling dogs, or worse, elicit a maelstrom of deafening boos, the kind that rained down on Roseanne Barr in 1990 at a San Diego Padres doubleheader, when her utter defiling of Francis Scott Key's only hit devolved into a defiant crotch grab and a hocked loogie behind home plate.

I could not block this scenario from my brain as I sat sequestered in the bowels of the newly christened Lincoln Financial Field, which was hosting its inaugural season of Philadelphia Eagles football in the fall of 2003. I imagined Roseanne and Tom Arnold in a *Simpsons*-esque moment as she walked off the field:

> *"Tom, are they booing me?"*
> *"Uh, no, they're saying 'Boo-arr, Boo-arr.'"*

I entertained myself a lot like this in the three hours I spent in the Temple Owls trainer's room, waiting to sing the national anthem before the October matchup between the Eagles and the team formerly known as the Washington Redskins.

Kim Austin must have thought I was nuts. In her early twenties and new to the music business, Kim worked for my manager, Jim Johnson, and was assigned to keep me in line at this most unusual gig, which required us to arrive at the stadium at noon to soundcheck for a 4:15 pm kickoff.

At the time, Jim was also managing Lauren Hart, who was widely recognized as *the* anthem singer in Philadelphia. Her late father, Gene Hart, had been the broadcast voice of the Philadelphia Flyers, and Lauren was a respected local musician as well as being the go-to person whenever "Oh say can you see" was involved. This was supposed to be her performance, but fate intervened. With less than twenty-four hours' notice, there I was, preparing to sing before more than sixty-seven thousand people a song that was not written for me.

Mind you, these weren't just *any* people, these were Philadelphia Eagles fans. I knew all the folklore, which spanned decades of the team's history, from the Franklin Field snowball incident of 1968, during which a scrawny nineteen-year-old in a Santa suit was roundly pelted by angry fans during a halftime Christmas pageant, to the introduction of "Eagles Court" in 1997, which brought swift justice and a few quarters of jail time to drunk and disorderly seven-hundred-level brawlers and men's room sink-pissers, all in the confines of a basement maintenance room at Veterans Stadium. What would these Eagles fans be like at the shiny new Linc? I didn't even want to speculate. What if I forgot the words or the echo in the stadium threw off my pitch? What kind of wrath might await *me*?

I took solace in the fact that I would have the benefit of some in-ear monitors, which were provided during the soundcheck by one of the members of the sound crew, a much-needed friendly, familiar face. Brian Bricklin was a fellow musician, whose band Bricklin had also been signed to A&M some years before the Caulfields. At least I knew two people in this ocean of strangers.

I made very little conversation with Kim while we waited, only occasionally interrupting the silence to blow my opening note into the little round pitch pipe I had brought along to keep me from starting the anthem too high. It was my only safeguard to assure that the high note would land in the sweet spot of my range. I knew I was overthinking, but I couldn't help it. The mental checklist I tried to recall from the voice lessons I had taken for a few months nearly a decade earlier was causing me more stress than comfort. I could picture my instructor, Gerri Smith, a woman with formidable pipes and impeccable technique, reminding me about the breathing and the diaphragm and the vowel shapes, and then clear as day, I could see her leaning toward me to whisper the "last but not least" summation of all her words to the wise: *Don't suck.*

I was completely psyching myself out. Mercifully, a stadium employee entered the room wheeling a metal cart, atop which sat a massive deli tray with thinly sliced meats rolled into tight bite-size curls. An assortment of cheeses lay spread out like a deck of cards going full circle around the platter. It was all there—cold cuts derived from swine, fowl, bovine. The cheese selection contained white, yellow, and orange options.

I flashed back to the first performance contract I ever drew up on my own. The Beat Clinic was asked to play a homecoming dance for my old high school. The $1,500 fee was the most money we had been offered for a gig up to that point, so it was clear that things needed to be "in writing." There was no internet from which to grab a template, so I composed a document that sounded as official as I could make it, making sure to include the clause "Band shall be permitted to partake of any food or beverage at the event."

I looked down at my Eagles party tray and so began to *partake*, plunging into a full-on bout of stress eating, with no regard for one of the key tenets that any vocal coach would tell you: no dairy before singing.

As the hands of the clock on the wall moved ever closer to 4:00 pm, I blew incessantly into my pitch pipe, trying to decide whether I should start on a B or a C, trying out both keys with only the first two words of the song.

Ohhh say. Ohhh say. Ohhh say. Ohhh say.

The level of anxiety I was feeling—the cold extremities, the shivering in the pit of my well-fed stomach, the fear that I was just going to throw up all over the field—dictated that I should probably start on the B, just to be safe. I held firm to the performer's party line I had heard all my musical life: "If you're not a little nervous before going on, there's something wrong." I was nervous all right, so I told myself nothing was wrong.

Kim nudged me to let me know it was time. I followed her through the stadium tunnel, dressed in the only green shirt I could find in my dresser that morning. It was my way of pandering to the crowd, since I didn't own an Eagles jersey. I remember the moment when the dimness of the tunnel opened up into an almost blinding panoramic view of the capacity crowd at the Linc. More than 134,000 eyes would soon be looking at me; 134,000 ears would be hearing my voice.

As a series of nearly indecipherable public address announcements echoed into the open air, Brian Bricklin handed me the wireless mic and the two little earbuds that would allow me to hear what I was singing. The incidental crowd noise was already loud, due to the sheer number of voices just talking among themselves. Even though that low B should have been firmly planted in my head, I kept crouching to blow the note into the pitch pipe and sing "oh say" several more times from my position on the sidelines.

As I walked onto the field, where large men in helmets and pads would soon be pummeling the shit out of each other, I could feel the perfectly manicured Bermudagrass under my feet. I surveyed the pristine order of the white yard lines that went all the way to the end zone, where I found myself in close-up on the Jumbotron. I heard, as if in the distance, an announcer say something like "Ladies and gentlemen, please rise for the singing of our national anthem, sung today by John Faye of Philadelphia rock band IKE." That was my cue.

I brought the microphone up to my face and began to sing, fighting off the last twinges of my nerves and losing myself in the Stars and Stripes. I don't consider myself much of a patriot in the "Rah, rah, America, love it or leave it" sense, but I never felt more American than in this moment, because as I navigated the melody of the song, I knew I was connecting with my fellow Philadelphians, and my country, in a way I hadn't felt was permissible for me all those years before.

So when it came time for the money note on "o'er the land of the *free*," you better believe I held that fucker for as long as my lungs would allow, until the roar of those sixty-seven thousand people told me in no uncertain terms that they knew I had reached them. We were all Americans, singing the same song. When I cut that note off, I paused for a split second to catch my breath and felt myself smile involuntarily, not sure if I actually *was* smiling until I looked up and saw my toothy grin on the Jumbotron for all to see.

I couldn't hear much at all as I delivered the final line, but that's the thing about "The Star Spangled Banner." If you really get 'em on "the land of the free," then "the home of the brave" is just another noise in the deafening sound of people going apeshit, so I have no idea if I hit it or not. I looked up into the stands again to take in what I knew would be a once-in-a-lifetime scene, knowing instinctively that nothing else that could possibly happen that day would top this view or this feeling. I walked off the field, thanked Brian as I handed him the mic and the in-ears, and Irish goodbye'd it out of there, back into the South Philly afternoon, the sound of "Fly, Eagles, Fly" swirling in the distance.

BABY, DO YOU WANNA TAKE A RIDE?

loved Sean the second I cradled him in my arms—a déjà vu moment in the Toll Pavilion of Abington Memorial, where Natalie was born two and a half years earlier—but it was harder for me to *like* him once the night driving became a thing. Sean, like his sister, was an early teether, which made his sleep schedule not much of a schedule at all. I began to resent the fact that it was I who had to get dressed at 2:00 am and strap him into the second-row captain's chair of our Honda Odyssey, because sometimes the only way to get him to *calm the fuck down* was to drive the streets of Elkins Park for two, maybe three hours at a clip.

"House husband," which sounded to me like such a cakewalk when I willingly adopted the designation upon Natalie's arrival, was beginning to lose its alliterative shine. Lisa and I were still a team when it came to parenting, but she was the tenured professor with a class to teach in the morning, and I was the self-employed musician on self-imposed paternity leave, which meant she *needed* her sleep. I only *wanted* mine.

I was already numb from the repetition of the day; there was no beginning, no end, just a stream of semiconsciousness in which my tasks of changing diapers, measuring out scoops of powdered Enfamil, and keeping my toddler daughter alive played against an innocuous phonetic backdrop of soft-spoken foreign phrases from a Baby Einstein DVD set on repeat.

LISA AND I WERE STILL A TEAM WHEN IT CAME TO PARENTING, BUT SHE WAS THE TENURED PROFESSOR WITH A CLASS TO TEACH IN THE MORNING, AND I WAS THE SELF-EMPLOYED MUSICIAN ON SELF-IMPOSED PATERNITY LEAVE, WHICH MEANT SHE NEEDED HER SLEEP. I ONLY WANTED MINE.

Worn out as I was, I made extra sure to check the mirrors and look both ways before putting the minivan in reverse. The embarrassment of my prior lapse of concentration still irked me. I had backed out of the driveway into an oncoming car in broad daylight the week before, on four hours of sleep and half a bottle of store-brand cough syrup, guzzled down to combat the nagging cold I couldn't shake.

I was no stranger to sleep deprivation, and I was fully prepared to employ the tactics that had kept me awake and alive during many an overnight journey in my previous life. The driver's side window was all the way down, and crisp night air stung my outstretched arm, which I pulled back inside the van every minute or so to deliver the rejuvenating slap of a cold open palm to my face. Left cheek. Right cheek. Back out the window.

In between these bouts of self-inflicted violence, I spoke out loud, at times muttering to myself but primarily talking to Sean. I decided to turn our trip into a little reality tour, describing various landmarks in the voice of Butthead, while behind me, Sean served as a grunting, fidgety, non-ambulatory Beavis.

"Hey, baby, here's, like, the school you're gonna go to in, like, five years," I said as I drove past McKinley Elementary.

I made my way over to Ashbourne Road and drove by the old apartment that Lisa and I had rented the year she got hired at Beaver College.

"Hey, baby, here's, like, where Mommy and Daddy used to live."

I don't really know why I didn't address him as Sean. I just liked the sound of calling him "baby," in much the same way I had done with Natalie.

Some random turns put us on Old York Road, which, when taken south, merges into Broad Street at the northern tip of Philadelphia's city limits. I drove past Einstein Medical Center, where Mom had done her residency before I was even born.

"Hey, baby, here's, like, where Gaga became a doctor."

"Hey, baby, do you wanna take a ride into Philadelphia?" I asked, knowing full well we were already *in* Philadelphia, as we approached the bright fluorescence of the Stinger Lounge and Discotheque and the pink awning over the pickup window for Sid Booker's, known for its deep-fried shrimp.

I cut over the Roosevelt Expressway, and all the streets so often name-checked in the first five minutes of *Action News*, when anchorman Jim Gardner reports on a daily litany of petty robberies, shootings, drug busts, and general human misery.

If it bleeds, it leads.

I had never strayed this far from Forrest Avenue on any of our previous late-night excursions, but it never occurred to me to turn back. Something was pulling me toward the center of the city. I kept driving farther south, willfully ignoring the fact that we were soon just a few blocks removed from the Badlands, a part of town where no truly responsible father would be driving his only son around at the time of night my old Spanish teachers would call *la madrugada*.

I drove on, past the shuttered Uptown Theater, which appeared as the backdrop for Fat Albert, Dumb Donald, Mushmouth, and the gang on the cover of the Bill Cosby comedy album I'd obsessed over as a boy.

I was catching all the green lights by the time I drove past Temple, the only other university besides Delaware that would have me back when my only concern was keeping No Excuse intact. I remembered seeing the B-52's there the year I got my driver's license. It was their last tour with Ricky Wilson before he died of AIDS. I wondered whatever happened to my sleeveless purple tour shirt with the track listing of *Whammy!* on the back. Like so many clothes from that time of my life, it was probably either sitting at the bottom of my half of a dresser drawer, waiting for me to lose my "winter weight," or already making the rounds on the Goodwill circuit.

I drove past the abandoned Divine Lorraine hotel. It was dilapidated and windowless, unprotected from the elements. What had it been like inside there when Papa was just a boy? What was going on inside there now? My curiosity surrounding the Divine Lorraine was just a sliver of my long-standing fascination with the architecture and history of Philadelphia.

Our drive-by possibilities were endless. Maybe we would catch a quick glimpse of the Lit Brothers building on Market Street or swing by Elfreth's Alley in Old City.

Probably best to avoid the cobblestones if my goal was to get Sean to sleep. Maybe we would make our way down to South Philly, to the house on Porter Street where Philip Testa, known in mob circles as "The Chicken Man," was whacked by a nail bomb planted under his front porch—blown to smithereens and into the opening line of a Bruce Springsteen song.

What was it that kept me on this beeline down Broad Street? Was it a way to connect with Papa and contemplate his life here as a young man? With my tiny travel companion, who was already much more of a doppelgänger of my father than I would ever be, I experienced an ethereal version of the city Papa called home. I witnessed a strange beauty only hinted at through the fleeting glimpses visible from just beyond the edge of town.

It all felt like some kind of metaphor for my life. Just a few years before, I had been privy to the bright inner sanctum of the music business, witnessed fame and success up close, and sometimes got my little taste, but, like the November 21 Scorpio I considered myself, I was always on the cusp, existing in the fringe, an outsider like Sodapop and Ponyboy.

On the horizon before me, the amber glow of the north-facing clock at City Hall shone like a new moon, and once I crossed through the intersection at Spring Garden Street, I could make out the dark outline of William Penn perched atop the clock tower.

This was the magnet that drew me here. All that it symbolized shot through me like the dopamine rush from hearing a favorite song. Philadelphia Freedom was real, and I was feeling it for the first time all over again. I decided to circle around Penn Square and head back north to Elkins Park when a sing-song major-scale lullaby landed on the tip of my tongue.

Baby, do you wanna take a ride
Wanna take a ride
Into Philadelphia
Straight into the belly of a dream

IN AND OUT OF WEEKS

By the time both kids were toddlers, I had gotten used to whispering in my own home. The voice that I could throw like a Molotov cocktail into the back rows of nightclubs and concert venues throughout my entire adult life had become a shadow of itself on the brown leather IKEA couch that sat along the living room wall, a floor below the master bedroom, where Lisa slept lightly on king-size memory foam.

What had started out as a way to be considerate of my wife was putting me on the path to ultimate separation. Crashing on the couch to spare her my chronic snoring, or even the sound of a turning doorknob when coming home after a gig with IKE, morphed from the occasional into the habitual. After a time, I found any excuse not to go upstairs. It was no longer an anomaly to pull up at three in the morning, slip out of my clunky black shoes on the concrete stoop, unlock the front door in a strange real-time slow motion, then tiptoe the ten feet to the couch, where more and more often, there was a pillow and blanket already waiting for me.

I whispered song lyrics trapped in my head, attached to the names of women in their twenties, who were becoming my emotional mistresses and unwitting muses. I understood now what I used to laugh about back when I was in school, remembering my friend Julian sitting alone in the stairwell of my college dormitory, whispering to himself at the bitter end of a relationship that couldn't have lasted more than five days.

Sucks, man … fuckin' sucks … this fuckin' sucks, man … sucks …

And there I was, beginning to mourn the slow death of my own relationship—one I had been in since I was twenty. What did it say about me that I was well on my way to spending five years—more than eighteen hundred days—sleeping on that couch?

Who were these couples that stayed together "till death do us part"? I was struggling to recognize the same girl I fell in love with half a lifetime ago, the one I adored enough to cry over and charm with personalized fortune cookies. You couldn't pay Lisa to eat a cookie now; she was totally off sugar.

I wondered what Lisa's mother would think of me, so many years after I dazzled her with my command of the word "malleable," so many years after her daughter comforted me when our first attempt at making love ended in the embarrassing blink of an eye, with our friends just beyond the locked bedroom door, drinking Bartles & Jaymes wine coolers and polishing off cans of Chef Boyardee ravioli.

The "eat and laugh" credo that defined our wonder years no longer applied. Lisa had become a vegetarian. She didn't even like being awake past 9:00 pm. Maybe we had just grown apart. Maybe we should have taken it as an omen when *Seinfeld* went off the air.

Something Mom had said to me once in a private moment, which I disregarded as curmudgeonly at the time, now seemed prescient:

You know, honey, not everything in life is all just funny and laughing.

A child-worn copy of *Where the Wild Things Are* was always somewhere in the living room, often under one of the brown leather chairs that matched the couch. The book was almost always covered in tufts of cat hair once it was retrieved back into the light. How many times had I read Maurice Sendak's words to Natalie, like I was passing down some sort of holy scripture to a new generation? I had seen myself in the story's lead character, Max, for as long as I could remember. I always wanted to be the wildest thing of all.

In my imagination, I transformed the living room into my old bedroom at Mom's house. The couch became the bed, where I would lie with my eyes looking up at the ceiling, mentally projecting the stars that Casey Kasem always told us all to keep reaching for. With my headphone wire stretched taut to the jack in my stereo, I, like Max, could sail away to the place where my wild things were, the place where my rock 'n' roll dreams resided, as I drifted "in and out of weeks," as Sendak would say.

I used to love the fact that Lisa didn't fall for me because I was a guy in a band. She liked me for who I was, not for what I did. But over time, what I did became more synonymous with who I was. I was John Faye of the Caulfields, or John Faye of IKE. I didn't even see me as just John Faye anymore. So where did that leave Lisa and me? We were leading separate lives, no longer partners in crime, both feeling undesired and unvalidated. It seemed as if parenthood was our only true connection that remained.

Our youth was over, and the things that seemed so foundational in our twenties were now just memories, like so many spring break photos tucked away in a Ziploc bag.

My back felt cold against the cushions on the couch. I felt the chill of realization that words I had whispered into melody with another girl in mind, one who was way too smart to get too deeply involved with me, were far too applicable to ignore when it came to my relationship with the girl one floor above me, sleeping lightly on king-size memory foam.

In and out of weeks
Dragging my feet
Just lying dormant
In and out of weeks
Just beyond my reach
I pray for you to speak to me
And tell me it was more than just a moment

OPENING ACT

can't remember if I read it in a magazine or saw it on TV, but I
have this memory of Nick Lowe once telling an interviewer that
he didn't mind being an opening act. Not only didn't he mind,
but he went so far as to say he *liked* being the opening act: you go on
early, you play for, like, thirty minutes, and before you know it, you've
got the rest of the night to yourself. I can see the appeal of that way
of thinking, but keep in mind this is coming from Nick Lowe, the
guy who wrote "Cruel to Be Kind," "So It Goes," "(What's So Funny
'Bout) Peace, Love, and Understanding." What does he have to prove
to anybody? Not everyone in the audience may know him by name,
but as soon as he plays one of *those* classics, the switch goes off.

"Ohhhh, he's *that* guy."

It's different when you're the guy whose only charted hit would be
considered "minor" at best, and you're pretty determined not to play
it either way. I think of Nick Lowe and try to infuse his easygoing,
no-stress attitude into every opportunity I get to warm up a crowd.
But that's just not who I am.

There's a part of me that's trying to steal every show I ever play, to make the most of my short window to carry out my mission, win hearts and minds, justify to myself that it was all worth it. Did I get the great *exposure* the promoter dangled in front of me like a carrot to justify paying me what amounted to less than minimum wage? Any working musician will tell you they've done plenty of support gigs just for the chance to preach to someone else's choir.

The opening act gets no automatic respect. You know that going in. Of course, there will be those nights when the audience is courteous and welcoming, but that's the missionary position of all this. Those aren't the shows that build your character. I'm talking about the ones where your very presence on that stage elicits impatience, hostility, or even worse, apathy. For some ticket holders, you're just the half an hour standing between them and the thing they overpaid to see: the headliner. Win *those* people over and you've really accomplished something.

So is this why I like being in the opening act? Am I on some quixotic mission to tame a savage beast?

I've played the musical bridesmaid lots of times, with every band I've ever been in, dating all the way back to the Beat Clinic playing for free Miller Lite I had no use for, opening for Eddie Money at the Stone Balloon in Newark. It was about seven years after he had passed out with his body weight on his left leg for fourteen hours, destroying his sciatic nerve, and narrowly escaping full-on amputation. Members of the Beat Clinic were up in the band room at the top of the stairs after our set at the Balloon. Chris Ryan and our friend Bill Gatter, who was the drummer in Cliff Hillis's band Tisra Til, were enjoying some of our liquid compensation when Eddie Money entered the scene wearing these ridiculous-looking oversized red sneakers. Recalling his injury, I wondered if they were orthopedic or something. They were probably just Air Jordans.

Everyone was just staring at his feet, our hypnotic gaze interrupted only by the sound of his quick getaway line:

"Hey, fellas, guess I'm on in a few. Time to rock 'n' roll!"

Chris muttered under his breath, "In *those* shoes?" as Eddie Money ambled back toward his dressing room. We always wondered if he overheard that, because when he hit the stage to sing "Two Tickets to Paradise," it was apparent that those red monstrosities didn't make it through customs.

So is that the appeal? Is it all just to revel in bizarre interactions with the names at the top of the marquee? There *are* some pretty good arguments for that.

Sometime in the early 2000s, IKE was opening for the '80s band Berlin at an indoor culinary festival in Manhattan. I guess I had moved up to free food along with the free beer by then. I forget the name of the event—"Eat Out New York" or something like that—a little wink to the cunning linguists in the crowd. Berlin was known primarily for their song "Take My Breath Away," which was in the Tom Cruise movie *Top Gun*. Even way back in the aughts, that was already a pretty distant memory, which perhaps explains why Berlin found themselves accepting a gig in a giant warehouse where the attendees were more concerned with finding a good fish taco than listening to their four hits.

Since the venue was "nontraditional," the backstage area was completely makeshift, using office dividers and cheap curtains to create some semblance of order. There were no private bathrooms. I had to walk the length of a football field to the very front of the building to pee in the public men's room before going on. It was no big deal to me, but it was not a desirable scenario for Berlin's lead singer, Terri Nunn, to have to make her way through a sea of wandering foodies, any one of whom might ruin her outfit with the spill of a drink or the splash of a condiment.

I saw her spot our bass player, Joann, milling about behind the stage just before we were about to go on, and I watched in mild amusement as she cast an urgent silhouette and spoke inaudibly to Joann before retreating into her cubbyhole. Almost as if in freeze-frame, Joann stood there, arms outstretched like Jesus on the cross, ensuring that no one peeked or entered through the sheer curtain. After receiving the all-clear, Joann walked over to me, shaking her head and grinning an all-too-familiar grin that said, "Only in this band."

When she told me that she had stood guard while the lead singer of Berlin surreptitiously tinkled into what could only have been a limited number of options—a hastily emptied salad bowl or one or more plastic Solo cups—it felt as if all the bullshit we had ever endured as a band had been offset, the playing field somehow leveled. We took the stage moments later, energized and full of giddy laughter. I was bound and determined to give Joann a special intro:

Ladies and gentlemen, please say hello to IKE's bass player and Terri Nunn's Piss Tech: Joann Schmidt!

Sometimes when I'm in the opening act, it's an interaction with a member of the audience I enjoy the most. Why these anecdotes always seem to revolve around a bathroom, be it makeshift or conventional, is beyond me. When the John Faye Power Trip did the Matthew Sweet tour in 1999, there was no private restroom backstage for us at the Curtain Club in Dallas, at least not one that wasn't occupied when I needed it. A guy standing next to me in the very crowded men's room just before our showtime tilted his head toward one of the flyers hanging at eye level above each urinal.

"You know anything about this opening band?"

"Yeah, I heard they suck," I replied without hesitation as I zipped up and made my way back toward the stage, slinking through a roundup of what must have been every power pop fan in Texas.

Not long after we finished playing, the same guy came up to the merchandise table and flashed one of those begrudging I-see-what-you-did-there smiles and shook my hand. Even better, he bought our CD. Even better than that, Rahim became a friend and has been one ever since.

So yes, part of the appeal of being the opening act is that you get stories like these. There's also what I like to call the "press kit prestige"—the bragging rights. It is fun being able to say I opened for America and was invited onstage by Gerry Beckley and Dewey Bunnell to sing backups on "A Horse with No Name," or that I played before Tony Lewis and John Spinks from the Outfield in the "man cave" at my friend Steve Barnes's house. It's satisfying to have played legendary New York stages like the Roseland Ballroom, where the Caulfields opened for the Gin Blossoms and Marshall Crenshaw, or Irving Plaza, where we survived the notoriously unforgiving fans of Canadian rock royals the Tragically Hip.

Twenty years into my career, at the last IKE show of 2005, just a couple of days after Christmas, I received word of what most anyone would consider the granddaddy of all opening act opportunities. Cliff, Dave, Joann, and I were about to play the eleven-thirty slot on a Tuesday night at Grape Street Philadelphia. It seemed like everyone we knew in what had become a pretty tight-knit rock scene was there that night. Jaxon, the drive time DJ at WMMR, was the host of the

Tuesday Night Rock Show, the weekly showcase that had become the centerpiece of my social life.

IKE was riding pretty high at that point. "Into Philadelphia" had become something of a local hit. It was now in regular rotation on WMMR and was the lead track on *Jaxon's Local Shots, Vol. I*, a CD compilation of Philly bands championed by the man himself.

Being in regular rotation was a huge deal. 'MMR had not given an unsigned band that kind of airplay since the Hooters in the early '80s. For that matter, the station had not taken this kind of interest in local music since the heyday of *Street Beat*, whose host, Cyndy Drue, was the first person ever to play a song I had written on commercial radio—"Just Around the Corner" by the Beat Clinic.

It felt like "Into Philadelphia" was everywhere, not just on the airwaves. It came as a complete surprise to hear that the song was infiltrating professional sporting events, the chorus played on a loop to welcome fans coming to see the Eagles or the Flyers. Our flip phones and our Myspace pages were blowing up with messages from friends and total strangers who had just heard our song at the big game.

My friend Lexi, who was the lead singer of Head—a band whose stickers asked the question "Who doesn't like a little Head?"—walked up to me backstage with a devilish look in her eye.

"I know something you don't know," she whispered, the "nya, nya, nya, nya, nya" fully implied.

As a person with an aversion to being kept in the dark, I'm pretty sure I was unamused by her tone, which immediately prompted her follow-up:

"Don't worry; it's something good."

About ten minutes before our set, Jaxon's voice boomed through the PA:

"Can we get the members of IKE out in front of the stage. Calling IKE. Earth to IKE."

With a full bladder and my guitar still not in tune, I waddled out from behind the stage with my bandmates and found Jaxon in the middle of the floor with a wireless mic.

"Johnny, I brought you guys out here because someone has asked us to deliver a special message to you and the band."

The four of us looked at each other, bewildered, as the lights dimmed and the giant video screen, which doubled as a stage curtain, commanded our attention. Within seconds, the screen was filled with the larger-than-life likeness of Jon Bon Jovi. A hush fell over the crowded room as JBJ gave a few shout-outs to WMMR and announced that his band would be touring behind their new album *Have a Nice Day*. They would be playing a show on February 4 in Atlantic City. Then I heard him say the words that left me stunned:

"Congratulations to Philly band IKE. YOU will be opening the show for us!"

I saw his mouth continue to move, but anything he said after that was completely drowned out by the shock and jubilation that shot through the club. People were screaming, running up and bear-hugging us. I think I got kissed on the cheek about fifty times. Our friends, many of them hardworking musicians deserving of a break themselves, were genuinely happy for us. I stood there slack-jawed, still trying to process what I had just heard, when I realized that my bladder was still full and my guitar was still not in tune.

I took care of business in haste, and a couple of minutes later, the big screen went up to reveal me onstage with my hair, which was loaded with product, standing straight up on the top of my head. Without further introduction, I began to bellow *I'm Mr. Heat Miser* into the mic with my Fender Telecaster screeching at full saturation. The rest of the band bounded into their positions, and we launched into our proper show opener "Welcome Home" and proceeded to make several obvious mistakes—*clams*, as Buddy Rich would have called them. When the song ended, I asked the audience:

"How the hell are we supposed to do this after getting a bomb like that dropped on us?"

The band laughed. The crowd encouraged. I went on to flub my own lyrics, hit more bad chords, and basically lumber through our set like I was in the musician's classic recurring dream of rushing to get onstage and then completely forgetting how to play any of the songs. The beautiful thing was that none of that mattered, not one bit. We were having the time of our lives, on top of our little world, with all our friends right there with us. This was what it was all about.

HAVE A NICE DAY

IKE arrived at Boardwalk Hall in Atlantic City in the early afternoon. Our tiny entourage included Tony DeVitto and Ritchie Rubini acting as our stage techs. Tony, reprising his tour manager role from his time served with the Caulfields, piloted our rented van, which was packed to the gills with gear and the weight of the opportunity in front of us.

Cliff, Dave, Joann, and I had really come into our own as a band. We had long since outgrown the concept inherent in a name like the John Faye Power Trip. I was still writing the songs and paying the bills, but IKE had become more than me and three hired guns. We were family now. I respected my bandmates as musicians and as people, and I welcomed their input. We were almost always on the same page, and pretty much drama-free, even after Dave and Joann started dating.

Our first official album, *Parallel Universe* from 2003, as well as a follow-up DVD, *Bumper Sticker Wisdom,* had met our humble expectations, yielding a full gig schedule and respectable radio play for our song "Deathbed (Na, Na, Na)." It was our *second* full-length, however, that really felt like it had legs. Produced by Phil Nicolo at Studio 4 in

Conshohocken, *In Real Life* was cut to twenty-four-track two-inch, an expensive proposition during a global tape shortage, but making an analog record in the age of Pro Tools felt like a rebellious act.

Now here we were, a few hours from opening for one of the biggest bands in the world. It had been twenty years since "Livin' on a Prayer" made Bon Jovi a household name, but it turned out they had staying power, and even though I can't admit to having been a fan in the early days, I had gained serious respect for their ability to keep going, stay prolific, stay on top, and stay together. That is no small feat in the music business. It was also impressive that they were inviting local unsigned artists to open their shows on this tour. As far as I knew, bands in every other city had to compete for that opportunity, but for whatever reason, maybe thanks to the success we were having with "Into Philadelphia," we had been anointed.

None of our prior collective experience had quite prepared us for the treatment we were about to receive. We soon found ourselves in a veritable bizarro world, one in which every opening-act indignity we had ever suffered would be avenged seventy-seven-fold by Bon Jovi, our very own rock 'n' roll Make-A-Wish Foundation.

Being what is known as a "union" venue, Boardwalk Hall provided a cadre of helpers at the loading dock, all members of the local chapter of IATSE, the International Alliance of Theatrical Stage Employees. They were there to carry every last guitar, drum, and amplifier from the van onto the stage, placing each item in the precise spot we requested. Dave, a stagehand himself when not beating the skins, knew a couple of the guys and chatted them up as he watched them carry his road cases to a dedicated drum riser set up just for him.

I stood on the stage and looked out at more than ten thousand empty seats, picturing the sea of humanity to come. I knew I was on hallowed ground. The Beatles and the Stones had played here. Judy

Garland had played here. The building had gone up during prohibition in the 1920s and had served as Atlantic City's convention center. It was the home of the Miss America pageant *and* the world's biggest pipe organ. I had never set foot in any venue with that kind of history.

Once the gear was in place and microphones were set up, we did our soundcheck with our engineer, Dave McGuinness, running front-of-house. Knowing that he was in charge of the mix was a huge comfort, as he was one of the most respected and experienced sound guys we knew. He had toured with the Hooters and mixed at every major concert venue you could name. A big place like this would be no problem for him.

It dawned on me that we were able to run through several songs and take our time with the soundcheck. This was another aspect of the day that ran counter to the much more common MO of "hurry up and wait," busting your ass to get to the venue hours before showtime only to sit there for ages while the headliner noodles around onstage long after the engineer is good to go. There had been times when we were literally given ten minutes to plug in and run one chorus of a song before the doors opened. Bon Jovi hadn't even arrived yet, but their equipment had already been set up and soundchecked while we were still somewhere on the Atlantic City Expressway. It's times like *this* when you realize that a band like *that* is operating on a level very few working musicians can comprehend, much less get the chance to observe firsthand.

By the time Dave McGuinness was happy with our mix, we had more than two hours left before showtime—unheard of. Tony had a stack of support band credentials, satin stickers with "Bon Jovi" in big block lettering over an orange background. The sinister red smiley face from the cover of their new album stared like it was just daring me to *Have a Nice Day*.

Joann broke out a new camcorder she had just bought and began taking some random shots of what ended up looking a bit like surveillance footage. I was already feeling more like a voyeur than a participant. A little part of me was shying away like it always did whenever I was faced with the slightest vindication of my life's choices or my hard work somehow paying off. Do I belong here? Do I deserve this? Do I even *want* this?

We walked the labyrinthine hallways in search of our dressing room, with fingers and toes crossed that there would be some form of catering waiting for us. I wished out loud that we might hit the Dietz and Watson lottery and receive the recommended daily allowance of nitrates and nitrites found in tastefully arranged processed meats. Instead, the satin stickers we were now wearing on the front pockets of our jeans gained us entry into a far fancier world of gastronomic delights, the likes of which I was positive had never been seen by any opening act at any concert *ever*.

A sidewalk sandwich board sat just outside the dining room with a menu, handwritten in pink chalk, listing the day's fare: New York strip, crab cakes, grilled vegetables, baked potatoes, a pasta station, mussels, scallops, shrimp, calamari. It went on. This was the kind of spread I would ask for if I knew I was going to the electric chair. It was apparently how the crew and support acts on this tour ate every day. And the band footing the bill for all this was still not in the building.

I chose to skip the salad and went straight for the surf and turf. Who needs roughage on a day like this? The massive steaks were grilled to a perfect medium-rare and piled high in a stainless-steel banquet tray, kept warm by the flame from a can of Sterno. The crab cakes were the size of softballs, and they were the good ones—all lump crabmeat, hardly any breadcrumbs. My bandmates and I convened with our bounty like knights of the round table, each plate our own personal holy grail. I proceeded to inhale my food like it was my job. I don't even remember tasting it. Stress Eating 101.

In spite of my consuming what felt like ten pounds of cow and crustacean, my nervous energy stood its ground against the predictable food coma that would have taken me out like a wicked undertow on any other day. In the dressing room, the contrast was telling as Dave Anthony, normally IKE's resident neurotic, sat relaxed on the couch, shooting the shit and appreciating our good fortune, while I paced back and forth until the kinetic hum that was ricocheting within my skull manifested itself in an off-key mouth-trumpet version of "Gonna Fly Now," the instrumental theme from *Rocky*. This was not just a few bars for comic relief; I did the entire arrangement, segueing from the horn part into an obnoxious impression of the *wacka wacka* guitar in the song's bridge. Dave egged me on, starting his own mouth-guitar version of "Eye of The Tiger" while I played maniacal air-drums, burning up calories I should have been conserving for the stage. Ritchie finally intervened.

OK, enough of Survivor.

Like the older brother I never had, Ritchie knew I needed to take it down a notch and refocus my attention. His calm presence was a far cry from his own hyper backstage antics at Caulfields shows a decade earlier, when many a shaken-up bottle of Rolling Rock, held just below the waist at a certain angle, would spray white foam across the room as he performed the obscene pre-show sacrament we dubbed *the geyser*. Having Ritchie there on my biggest day with IKE was a comfort I could only pinpoint after the fact. Both he and Tony were connecting my past to my present, happy to support me even if our old band wasn't the one in the limelight.

I went into the bathroom and changed out of the Cheap Trick T-shirt I'd arrived in and into a black Rolling Stones T-shirt with the classic tongue-and-lips logo across the front. I slipped into a not-quite-as-black suit jacket and stood back to examine my outfit in the mirror. The jacket indicated I was taking the performance seriously, the T-shirt was a show of respect for the classics, the Chuck Taylors on my feet acted as my lifeline to punk rock, and the straight-leg Levi's blue jeans signaled my lack of pretension. The end result of these calculations was about as nondescript and un–rock 'n' roll as one could get and, in that moment, fit me like a glove.

I retreated inward, a last-ditch effort to get out from under my state of agitation and allow my cumulative experience to carry me through whatever was about to happen.

Just surrender, John. But don't give yourself away.

I knew I still had a lot more music left in me, but I also knew this might be the last time I would play it for this many people in one shot. I thought of Mom and wished she were there. The mini strokes that she was beginning to suffer made it more and more difficult for her even to leave the house, much less come to one of my shows. She probably would have been impressed by this one. I don't think she had ever seen me perform in front of more than a couple hundred people, and usually far fewer than that. This would have been a rare occasion when she wouldn't have to ask:

Is that good?

I had to fight off the urge to feel sorry for myself. Not one of us in IKE had our parents there to see us. Cliff was still mourning the death of his father just a month before, and his mom's health was in decline. As a group, we had all suffered our share of loss, and it was our connection with one another that so often made up for the absence of relatives and extended family that other bands could rely on.

My train of thought derailed when Tony burst into the dressing room with excitement in his voice.

Pierre wants to interview you guys before you go on!

One only needed to hear his first name for anyone even remotely connected to rock music in the City of Brotherly Love to know who Pierre was. Pierre Robert was Philadelphia radio royalty, a beloved personality on WMMR, a Deadhead who called everybody "citizen." He had been a DJ at the station since I was fourteen. However panicked and out of sorts I felt at the prospect of a last-minute interview conducted just minutes before going onstage, there was no way I was missing out on the chance to talk to Pierre.

> AS A GROUP, WE HAD ALL SUFFERED OUR SHARE OF LOSS, AND IT WAS OUR CONNECTION WITH ONE ANOTHER THAT SO OFTEN MADE UP FOR THE ABSENCE OF RELATIVES AND EXTENDED FAMILY THAT OTHER BANDS COULD RELY ON.

Ripped from any final moments of preparation or reflection, the entire band speed-walked back through the labyrinth in the direction of the din—thousands of human voices, intertwined frequencies, a cacophony to some ears, a symphony to mine.

Pierre stood off to the side of the stage, chronicling his thoughts through a microphone connected to a portable tape recorder. The band gathered around in a tight semicircle to better hear him over the house music blaring through the PA. Mercifully, the interview questions were gently lobbed softballs, just like those crab cakes from catering, which definitely made their way into the conversation. After several minutes of exploring every angle of our excitement and gratitude with Pierre, Jaxon emerged, ready to introduce us to ten thousand strangers.

Time is an odd thing when you live out your dreams onstage. Thirty minutes almost never feels like thirty minutes. If you're backstage anticipating the moment you've been waiting for, thirty minutes can feel like an hour. Seconds become elastic, stretching to fit the expanse of your thoughts. Once you arrive at the moment you've been waiting for, time seems to collapse, and thirty minutes is over in a heartbeat.

Maybe this is because the stage is not so conducive to thought; it exists to showcase action. If you're fully present in the moment you've been waiting for, you form a bond with the audience that enhances your own concentration.

I was not *quite* in that state of mind.

I don't know if I felt distant because of the cavernous acoustics in the hall or because the massive barricades kept even the closest audience members more than twenty feet from the stage, but the moment I had been waiting for came and went, and I walked the labyrinth once again not really knowing how to feel.

Back in the dressing room, spirits were high all around me, the general consensus being that we had "rocked." I needed to hear that from my bandmates, and from Dave McGuinness, and from Ritchie and Tony. I began to feel safe in considering the show a success. It was slightly disappointing that Bon Jovi hadn't been in the building to see us play, but I was looking forward to watching their show from the side of the stage and hopefully getting a little face time with them.

I had my angles all figured out: I'd shake Jon Bon Jovi's hand and remind him of the fact that we had met once before, when I sang the national anthem for the Philadelphia Soul, the Arena Football League team he co-owned with his bandmate Richie Sambora. Or maybe I'd mention I had co-written songs with his cousin Jody, when she and I were both publishing with Warner Chappell back in the '90s. What I thought this kind of small talk might lead to, I had no idea. Any connection, however tangential, was better than nothing, I guess.

It turned out I would not be having any in-depth conversations with Jon Bon Jovi. One of his tour managers poked his head in to inform us that Bon Jovi—the band—would finally be arriving at the venue in about five minutes and that we would have to vacate the dressing room and stay out of the backstage area for the duration of their show. We were being evicted and missing out on one of the traditional perks of being the opening act: watching the headliner from the wings. Instead, we were all given tickets to sit in the audience, with the consolation prize of a lightning-fast photo op with the band. The four of us stood interspersed between Jon Bon Jovi, Richie Sambora, keyboardist David Bryan, and drummer Tico Torres. A handful of photographers snapped away, and our friend Jeff Greene captured a telling frozen moment when multiple camera eyes vied for attention and no one in the frame knew quite where to look.

The transition from backstage to front-of-house was disorienting, jarring as the moment you're born, going from the warmth and safety of the womb to the sensory ice bath of the world just beyond. That was me up on that stage not an hour before. Now I was sitting alone, with a new perspective from twenty-five rows back, a silent observer in the din—thousands of human voices, intertwined frequencies, a symphony to some ears, now a cacophony to mine.

PART VII

IT KEEPS EVOLVING

This is why I keep on hanging around
'Cause I can't stop trying to find my soul in the sound
Perfectly imperfected
Short and sweet and profound
This is why I keep on hanging around

—JOHN FAYE & THOSE MEDDLING KIDS,

"KEEP ON HANGING AROUND"

COMFORTABLE BEING UNCOMFORTABLE

O f the many backronyms for "IKE" that I came up with after taking Lisa's suggestion to name the band after the baby on *South Park*, the one that struck the truest chord was "It Keeps Evolving." "Into Kinky Erotica" and "Irish Korean Egomaniac" weren't far behind, but I digress. Somewhere along the way, without really ever coming up for air, I accepted that nothing lasts, and I got comfortable being uncomfortable, adapting as needed to keep on doing the thing I love.

We all have our own personal connection with music. Some like to say it's the soundtrack of our lives, a rich playlist full of unique associations and attachments. My love affair with rock 'n' roll is probably the longest-running relationship I will ever have. From my earliest recollections, it's always been there, sometimes nudging, sometimes shoving me along the path that would one day lead me to my capital-*V* Voice. It's the voice that projects the me I want to see in the world, with the hope that it connects with someone who also needs to know they're not alone. Everything I ever wanted out of music and life stems from the potential of forming this bond.

It took me a while to realize I didn't have to be a household name to feel that connection. I spent so much of my young life existing in the margins of race and culture, trying to understand who I was, what I valued, and what my own value could be. My heroes were larger than life, but I looked nothing like them. As immigrants, my older sisters yearned to be accepted and fully assimilated. I watched as they took more traditional paths in search of their own versions of the American dream. Punk rock and my private obsession with shystie televangelists gave me a healthy distrust of mainstream society. I can thank Joe Strummer, Jello Biafra, and *The PTL Club* for that.

The only person I truly did not want to disappoint was Mom. She had worked too hard to help me succeed for me to pretend it didn't matter. What I finally figured out was that the definition of success was up to me.

By my estimation, 2006 was a banner year, even though I spent more money than I earned in order to keep IKE moving forward. I was already supplementing my income as an adjunct professor, teaching songwriting at Drexel University. But a decade after recording my last album for a major label, IKE had a song on the radio, opened for Bon Jovi, opened for the Hooters at the Electric Factory, and headlined "IKE on ICE," playing on a flatbed truck, high on exhaust in the center of a hockey rink after a Philadelphia Phantoms game. It was a fittingly bizarre scenario that would serve as the only time any of us would ever play the Spectrum and also as a template for the experiences I would come to seek out.

In October of that year, we recorded our only live album, *IKE Presents The Living Room Show*, at Don McCollister's new location for Nickel and Dime in Georgia. In front of a raucous and playful audience in a converted movie theater, we captured a side of the band we showcased often at private house concerts. Some of the greatest experiences of my musical life were in front of as few as fifteen people in someone's basement. At our friend Ross Albert's house in Sandy Springs, we played intimate acoustic shows with the likes of Semisonic, jamming with their lead singer Dan Wilson on Prince covers as he found the chords on the underutilized baby grand, rented specifically so he could play the opening piano part in "Closing Time."

By the end of December in 2006, both Cliff and Dave announced their amicable departures from IKE. Cliff had lost both his parents within a few months of each other and understandably decided it was time to give greater focus to his own music. Dave and Joann had come to the end of a three-year relationship, and Dave decided to move to Atlanta, where he'd find session work and touring opportunities. We were all at different points in our evolution.

In the middle of all this, Mom turned eighty and showed her first sign of declining health. It was a shock to get the call from Tae Im informing me that Mom had likely suffered a stroke. I floored it down to Newark, annoyed that I had to learn about this from my sister on the opposite coast, but Mom had downplayed it even to her, waiting until the very end of an hour-long phone call to let Tae Im know that she couldn't get up out of bed to walk to the bathroom. Mom flat-out forbade me to call for an ambulance when I got there, barely consenting to let me at least drive her to the ER, living up to the reputation that doctors make the worst patients. Maybe it was just hard not to be in control. The stroke was determined to be "mini," which meant it wasn't as serious as a full-blown stroke, and Mom recovered to the point where she could walk and even drive again.

Joann agreed to stick around for one more IKE album after Cliff and Dave left.

Brett Talley and Tommy Kristich joined the band in 2007 and helped me resuscitate and revamp yet again. Brett was the lead guitarist of Outset, one of the few pop rock groups in Philly I felt a musical kinship with. About a month before Cliff's last show, I asked Brett to fill in for him over Thanksgiving weekend, and he reproduced the guitar parts with a precision that was jarring. From the playing itself to the exact amp and pedalboard settings, it was clear how much time he'd put into his preparation. It was a foreshadowing of IKE version 2.0.

Tommy was also in another band, the Jellybricks, but he agreed to pull double duty and step in to play drums for IKE. I had known Tom since the days of the John Faye Power Trip, when my high opinion of him was sealed on a summer night in Atlantic City around the turn of the millennium. Both the JFPT and the Jellybricks had delivered lengthy sets at a twenty-four-hour Irish bar, playing impromptu Sex Pistols covers at a birthday party of sorts for our friend Lauree. After the show, a bunch of us were enjoying some ocean air on the empty boardwalk.

Tom had somehow procured a funnel cake and was drunkenly enjoying its deep-fried goodness when the type of bedraggled castaway one could only encounter on the AC boards at 3:00 am walked up and inexplicably began grilling us on state capitals. I couldn't really tell if it was just a bizarre form of panhandling, but we collectively played along and did pretty well at first: we got Trenton, Albany, Columbus. Of course, we got Harrisburg, which was the Jellybricks' neck of the woods. There was some serious pushback from our quiz master when I had to insist that Dover, not Wilmington, was, in fact, the capital of Delaware.

That's when the mood turned a little more combative and he began to stump us with some of the flyover cities.

WRONG! It's BISMARCK, not FARGO!

The whole encounter went on way longer than anyone could have expected. Finally, with enough confectioners' sugar on his face to make it look like he had just done a pound of blow, Tom decided he was over it and blurted out, "Look, dude, I'm just trying to eat my funnel cake."

"*DUDE?* Who you callin' 'dude'?!" our drifter retorted, storming off into the night, leaving the lot of us completely befuddled.

I guess you never know what's going to trigger a person. I just loved the fact that Tommy said what was on his mind as soon as he decided enough was enough. That was Tom's way—unhesitant when it came time to say "Contract over." I would have endured that guy's geographical interrogation until he got through all fifty states, and probably Puerto Rico and Guam.

Both Tommy and Brett shone on *Where to Begin*, IKE's opus for the Myspace era. The album typified the embattled spirit, if not quite the haircuts, of emo in the 2000s. We began attracting a much younger crowd with Brett's more aggressive guitar playing and a collection of songs that wore my fragile heart on their sleeves more uncomfortably than ever. "Whites of My Eyes," "A Curse Is Not Enough," "Damage Control"—these were the kinds of songs that had people coming up to me after hearing them and asking, "Are you OK?"

The answer to that question was complicated, but it was clear to me that the state of my mind and the state of my art were in cahoots, pushing me to a level of vulnerability in my songwriting that I had strived for since the beginning. I wondered, though, if I was crossing a blurry line, pushing

IT WAS CLEAR TO ME THAT THE STATE OF MY MIND AND THE STATE OF MY ART WERE IN CAHOOTS, PUSHING ME TO A LEVEL OF VULNERABILITY IN MY SONGWRITING THAT I HAD STRIVED FOR SINCE THE BEGINNING.

myself into dark places just for the sake of material. I sometimes reminded myself of the opening couplet of an old Caulfields B-side:

When does art stop imitating life
And simply start mocking you?

Whether or not I was the butt of my own joke, there was something undeniable to me about *Where to Begin*, and I really wanted people to hear it, so much so I was willing to give it away. IKE launched the album with a release party at World Cafe Live in Philadelphia, putting free copies of the CD into more than five hundred hands right out of the box. Before long, the single "We Like Sugar" was in regular rotation on WMMR, the title glowing from the station's electronic billboards along I-95 every time the song got played.

I adopted a budget-conscious guerrilla touring strategy that saved the full lineup for bigger shows, while Brett and I made in-store appearances at Hot Topic at a mall near you, or in the intimate apparel department at Macy's, or at "Amish Woodstock" in the middle of a corn field in Lancaster. It felt like the whole idea of going out and entertaining an audience was getting flipped on its head. Now *I* wanted to be entertained, and the weirder and more unlikely the situation, the more I gravitated toward it.

That was my mindset when Brittany Rotondo walked into my life. Technically, I guess I walked into hers. After months of receiving random messages on Myspace, asking for details about one upcoming show or another, I had dismissed her as a girl who cried wolf—always threatening to come see the band but never actually showing up. Sometime in December of 2008, I was hawking advance tickets for what was to be Joann's final IKE show, at Jaxon's Mistletoe Jam, an annual WMMR holiday concert I was in charge of organizing.

Brittany asked me to save a couple of tickets for her and said we should meet up on a Saturday afternoon at Dobbs on South Street. It struck me as a bit odd that she would choose a bar like Dobbs to complete this transaction when it was clear she was under twenty-one, but my main concern was collecting my thirty bucks and chipping away at the huge stack of consignment tickets I was responsible for selling. Besides, I had played at Dobbs before I was old enough to drink. The thing was, she wasn't a musician—not yet, anyway. She did, however, know the owners, Heshey and Hank, both of whom had been in the thick of the South Street scene back in the day, when Heshey cut hair at his salon on Fifth Street and Hank first started dressing in miniskirts and fishnets. The connection was through Brittany's grandfather Ray, who in 1975 had infamously called in to New York DJ Scott Muni in the middle of robbing a bank to demand he play some Grateful Dead and to discuss the hostage situation that was happening in real time.

When I arrived at Dobbs on that Saturday, I located Brittany in a sizable happy hour crowd and tapped her on the shoulder, holding her two tickets in the shape of a V.

"Hey, Brittany? Um, John Faye from IKE?" I said, inflecting everything like it was a question.

Even with the tickets right there in her face, she looked at me like I was from another planet, like she had zero idea who I was or what I was talking about. Then it clicked, sort of.

"Ohhh, right, man. John Faye from IKE. Yeah. Sorry. Uh, I just spent all my money on weed."

Then she turned around and went back to whatever it was she was doing before I got there. I stood there motionless, flummoxed.

Who the hell does this chick think she is, I thought. *The IKE "Ticket Taxi" is a privilege, not a right!*

I walked out of the building vowing never to speak to her again—another vow I would never be able to keep. Something told me I needed to know this girl with eyeliner for days, her hair pulled back in a Northeast Philly ponytail with a little extra Puerto Rican height in the front. She did show up to Mistletoe Jam; bought her tickets at the door. Maybe after seeing the show something told her she needed to get to know me, and we agreed to meet up later that night.

Provided with no street address, I followed Brittany's vague directions and pulled into a gas station at Fifth and Lehigh, parking in front of a corrugated metal fence before calling her number. She didn't answer, but she sent a text saying she'd be right out, which I didn't yet understand meant "in fifteen minutes." Eventually, she emerged from around the side of the building, smoking a cigarette, wearing a peacoat with her faded blue skinny jeans and black Chucks. She was accompanied by three tough-looking young men—her cousins, as it turned out.

I slipped on my black leather jacket and got out of my car to greet her with a quick hug in the late December chill. I approached her cousins, who gave me the once-over with arctic, icy stares. I extended my hand to one of them and felt it just hang there for an uncomfortably long time, ten seconds at least. I was just about to retract my arm when he finally reached out and shook my hand, much to my relief. With the formalities out of the way, Brittany's cousin Alex, who had attended the concert with her, gave me an enthusiastic high five and a sincere compliment.

"Johnny, you fuckin' *killed* it tonight, man!"

One of the other cousins looked momentarily confused and whispered to Alex. "Yo, you say he *killed* somebody?"

"No, man, he's a musician; he just played a show."

With that, I walked around the side of the car and opened the passenger side door for Brittany and then watched Alex open the rear passenger door and contort his body to fit among three large boxes of IKE CDs and T-shirts that permanently occupied the back seat.

I pulled out of the parking lot, and it wasn't long before Brittany was controlling the radio and pulling a pack of smokes from her coat. As she rolled her thumb down the spark wheel of her lighter, I shot her a look.

"Um, you can't do that in here," I said, peeved that she would be so presumptuous.

"Oh. Sorry, man," she apologized halfheartedly, as she dropped the unsmoked Newport out the window and shot a look back at me. I swear I heard her mutter under her breath: "What a fuckin' square."

It was an awkward way to begin a conversation about music and life that would carry us through until sunrise and plant the seed of a complicated friendship that would lead to her picking up the guitar for the first time and the two of us forming John & Brittany. It would be the most turbulent of my musical nine lives, but I wouldn't have it any other way. I guess I was just comfortable with being uncomfortable, no matter where this ride was going to end up.

It keeps evolving.

ONE-WAY TO AVALON

Mom never willingly saw another doctor again after her first mini stroke. Her blanket distrust of the medical profession sometimes made me wonder if she had some kind of inside information she was keeping from the rest of us. She didn't even like going to the dentist. When I was little, I rarely saw my DDS except for the visits required to address the cavities, which were probably the result of the bottomless glasses of sweetened milk that Tae Im was serving up with my hotdogs and corn. There was never a yearly checkup or a cleaning to be had. This was fine by me. Dr. Cox had cavernous nostrils that hovered over me any time there was a drill or a tongue depressor involved. He seemed to make a point of exhaling only through his nose, and I often pondered the horrifying scenario of a dried booger breaking loose from his nasal mangrove and floating downward into my mouth.

Mom didn't even much care for her own specialty. It was ironic to see a professional psychiatrist so averse to talking things through. "Make your long story short," she would say to me, nipping in the bud any chance of a conversation blooming into a full-on therapy session. Maybe that was just her way of not bringing work home with her—separation of church and state and all that. For her part, she took her own advice, holding fast to a long-standing policy of keeping things to herself and doling out information on a need-to-know basis.

Back in the day, Mom would quiz the girls on the address of their apartment building in Pennypack or the spelling of the word "museum" every time they drove down the Ben Franklin Parkway, but her baby bump at the age of forty was never discussed, and she and Papa left for the hospital with zero fanfare when she went into labor with me. Their justice-of-the-peace marriage at City Hall was late news to my sisters, delivered after the fact, without so much as a piece of wedding cake. Then, of course, there was Papa's funeral.

It's no wonder that by the time Mom was unable to continue living on her own, none of us knew exactly how many more mini strokes she had suffered, but it was clear that her faculties had diminished. I had been completely oblivious to the behind-the-scenes discussions between Tae Im and Tae Kyung about how best to transition Mom to a new life out west, closer to them, and essentially out of my life and out of the lives of her youngest grandchildren. Sundays at Gaga's house had become a tradition that would end abruptly.

Tae Im even bought a plot of land and approached an architect to design a house for Mom a few miles from her own in Washington State. That plan fell through, but once Mom confessed she no longer felt safe behind the wheel of her own car, my sisters decided it was time to swing into action, and both of them caught east-bound flights to get Mom prepared to put 17 Bisbee Road on the market. Essentials and keepsakes were boxed up and put into storage, and everything else was sold off at a garage sale. Even Mom saw the futility in putting up a fight at this point. The writing was now on *all* the walls, not just the basement panels where my old band graffiti lingered.

As with everything else, there was no pomp or circumstance when Mom left her home of thirty-nine years for the last time. I wasn't even there to see her off. It almost felt like she had been abducted. There was an anger inside me that I wasn't sure how to process. Part of me blamed my sisters for whisking Mom away without really consulting me, even if I knew it was in her best interest. I hated them for their efficiency, knowing they had packed up and transported an entire life in the span of just a couple of weeks, while I struggled to get through my simplest daily tasks as Mr. Mom.

Having been taught by the best, I compartmentalized my heart-break and suffered my demons in silence until, of course, they turned into songs.

I wrote "The Notion" as a to-whom-it-may-concern confession of sorts, inspired by the title of the novel *Sometimes a Great Notion* by Ken Kesey, the author who wrote *One Flew Over the Cuckoo's Nest*. Kesey had, himself, found inspiration for his title in the lines of a Leadbelly song, "Goodnight Irene."

Sometimes I haves a great notion
To jump into the river and drown

I mutated that idea into my own chorus:

If running away is part of the notion
Then what can I say, I'm making it mine
I'll ride a wave right into your ocean
And drowning's just a matter of time.

I could feel myself going under, my parallel realities washing over me. I knew Lisa and I were done, but there was no simple way of extricating myself from the ties that bound us together. We had two little kids to take care of, and there was no way I was going to abandon them the way my sisters had been abandoned by their father, the way I felt abandoned after losing Papa and now felt again with Mom's rapid departure for the Pacific Northwest.

As a teenager, I had seen the film adaptation of *Sometimes a Great Notion*, starring Henry Fonda and Paul Newman. They play Henry and Hank, the father and son of an independent logging family in Oregon, at odds with members of a striking loggers' union. Tragedy falls quite literally on their clan, as a snapped tree claims Henry's arm and he dies in the hospital while his nephew Joe Ben drowns under a massive trunk that rolls into the river. It's a sequence of catastrophes I never wanted to see again, but I could watch the final scene of this movie on an infinite loop. While bucking the odds to transport four giant rafts of logs around seemingly unnavigable river bends, Hank attaches Henry's severed limb to the mast of their tugboat, the middle digit extended as a final one-finger salute to the naysayers watching on the shore. It's a gold-standard depiction of stubborn defiance, the same kind that's laced into my own family's DNA.

Four months under Tae Im's roof in Richland proved more than enough for Mom. She had gone from having an entire house to herself to feeling trapped in a single room. As her health improved, she wanted to take back control of her life—get a place for her stuff, as George Carlin would have said. She had only brought a few things with her to Washington, one of which was Papa's gun, ostensibly his retirement "gold watch" from his years as a Philly cop. Tae Im was mortified that Mom brought a sidearm into her home, whether it was a bygone relic or not. She didn't like that her son Michael was captivated by it. She didn't like having to overhear hushed-voice complaints about the living conditions while Mom was in the next room airing her grievances on the phone to Tae Kyung.

Everyone knew that Mom needed her own space. It all came down to the very last facility on a long list of old folks' homes that Mom visited and rejected one by one. The Stafford was nestled in the quiet town of Lake Oswego, just outside Portland. It had only been open for six months. Mom could get an apartment that had never been lived in. The food looked good. She could have breakfast in the mornings and stroll on the walking path at Luscher Farm right down the road. Most important, the Stafford was in Oregon, a state that had a decade-old "Death with Dignity" law, one that allowed the terminally ill to take a medically prescribed lethal dose of barbiturates to end their suffering on this mortal coil. Mom had spoken openly for years that she didn't want to "live too long," making all us kids promise never to resuscitate her or keep her on any kind of life support should things go drastically south. I always thought she just liked being morbid to get under my skin, but she was serious about it. She needed to know she had options.

NONE OF MY OPTIONS WERE GOOD. THE ONLY THING THAT MADE ANY SENSE AT ALL WAS TO KEEP WRITING.

As Tae Kyung and Tae Im settled Mom into her new place, it hit home that I was the only person in my family left on the East Coast. Every last one of them was gone. So what were *my* options? Stay in a loveless marriage indefinitely? I had practically lost count of how many years I had slept on the couch. It wouldn't be long before I'd lose count of how many beers or shots or packs of cigarettes I'd buy for Brittany, getting her into Doc Watson's without an ID then burning with jealousy when she paid attention to anyone other than me. None of my options were good. The only thing that made any sense at all was to keep writing. I wrote of losing what I once had, yearning for what could never be, and, of course, coming to grips with starting

THE YIN AND THE YANG OF IT ALL

over one more time. The second verse of "The Notion" summed it up pretty well:

Can I tell you something that's been sinking in
Between the cracks of wondering why
My lot in life is to begin again
Hello.
Goodbye.

For weeks after Mom moved into the Stafford, I kept a title on an otherwise blank page inside one of my notebooks: "1-Way to Oregon." It was a song I knew I had to write. Mom had come to that point in life when the concept of the roundtrip ticket becomes obsolete. She was at the place that flight attendants refer to in their closing remarks as "wherever your final destination might be." I tried to sing my lonely song title fifty different ways with no luck. "Oregon" wasn't exactly the kind of word that rolled off the tongue. I tried to think of something else that would fit the idea but sing better, running through a series of rhyming word associations:

Oregon ... born again ... bored again ... Billy Corgan ... carry on ... amazon ... Babylon ... Avalon.

Avalon. For years, Mom kept a tattered paperback copy of *The Legend of King Arthur* alongside her leather-bound "New Concise" English-Japanese dictionary between the two sets of pillows on her bed. Whenever I thought of King Arthur, my mind always turned to *Monty Python and the Holy Grail* and the sound of clacking coconuts. Mom took a more scholarly interest in Celtic mythology, in which Avalon refers to the island where King Arthur is taken after being gravely wounded in the Battle of Camlann, his final epic stand.

I came to realize that Lake Oswego was Mom's Avalon. She had battled hard her entire life, and now she needed to heal. She had never been one for coddling, giving, or receiving, but she had earned some rest in a place that was just for her. I knew that deep down. It was just hard to accept that from where I was on the other side of the country.

Everything I know means nothing now
Trees are falling but they make no sound

The song felt like a last goodbye for the one true heroine of my life, a bittersweet send-off into the sunset of her golden years.

Tell me one more
Time it's all for
Everybody's good you're moving on
One last look
Was all it took
To realize that you're already gone
1-Way to Avalon

ODYSSEY

A detached normalcy settled in once Mom got used to life in Lake Oswego and I got used to life without her. My Sunday visits to Newark with the kids were now replaced with a weekly phone call from Forrest Avenue, as we engaged in rote exchanges, indistinguishable from one conversation to the next. With my phone on speaker, I'd motion for the kids to yell, "Hi, Gaga," and watch them scamper off, out of earshot before Mom even had the chance to respond with her usual:

"Goosie! Seanie! Are you being good for your father?"

Once the phone speaker was off, it was just me and Mom going through the motions of asking how the other was doing.

"I'm making," she'd say.

"Me too," I'd say.

Sometimes I'd make a little small talk about my teaching gig at Drexel. Of all the things I had accomplished in my life, landing an unexpected job as a part-time college professor seemed to please Mom the most. By that point, I took what I could get. Plus, offering banal details about taking the SEPTA train into the city with all the other working stiffs was a convenient way to avoid letting Mom know where my head was really at. I knew better than to do that. Mom had absorbed too much pain over too many years for me to throw my midlife crisis into her lap. I felt like it was my turn to shield her, perhaps in the way she had tried to shield me when the news was less than sunny. I didn't talk to her about sleeping on the couch or how the bond I'd shared with Lisa for over twenty years had slowly eroded into little more than a sense of obligation.

My connection with Mom, and her connection with her grand-children, were bordering on that same sort of erosion. I wanted her to see how Natalie and Sean were growing, but I couldn't FaceTime her or text her a photo through her stubborn landline. She refused to get a cell phone, refused to get a computer, wouldn't even accept one as a gift. She walked around Luscher Farm taking pictures of trees and vegetation with a disposable camera, the cardboard kind that people put out on guest tables at wedding receptions. When it came to tech-nology, Mom never made it beyond the VCR she reluctantly bought for the TV in her den back in the '80s, and even then, I was the only one who really used it, mainly for after-midnight viewings of the sort of VHS cassettes that lived in the back rooms of local video stores.

I didn't get the sense that Mom used her CD player much in Oregon and wondered if she would ever listen to another recording of one of my songs. Maybe it was better if she didn't. Music, for me, had fully morphed into my only source of therapy, holding a mirror to the things I couldn't speak out loud but somehow felt the urge to sing in full voice over guitar, bass, and drums.

IKE would evolve through two more iterations after Mom moved away. Our drummer, Tommy Kristich, who had replaced Dave Anthony, would stay through a couple of albums before returning full-time to the Jellybricks, making way for our third drummer, Jason

Miraglia, who would ride out our musical wave to the shore. Brett's wife, Susie Steen, stepped in on bass after Joann left the band at the end of 2008, practically writing her parts as she recorded them on *Tie the Knot with All That You Got*, an album that, compared to its raw predecessor *Where to Begin*, was even more emotionally haunted.

In another sense, it felt *literally* haunted. During a recording session at Philly Sound Studios, which was housed in a converted church, Tommy and our engineer, Ron DiSilvestro, both felt an inexplicable tug on the bottom of their pant legs while setting up the drums. I watched through the thick glass window in the control room as the two of them exchanged bewildered, freaked-out looks. Both Ron and Tommy swore they could feel the pull of something invisible.

Equally disquieting was Ron's discovery of playful high-pitched children's voices on the isolated room mic tracks at the beginning of the song "Forgiven." There were no kids anywhere near those microphones when that song was recorded. It felt like some kind of supernatural sign, but of what? If nothing else, it made me ponder the song where these voices appeared.

I realized that I wrote "Forgiven" as a permission to finally speak up and talk with Lisa about ending our stalemate.

Can you see the sunlight shining down into the well?
We've been living in the shadows of our former selves
Where do we go from nowhere
And how are we going to get there in time
To say what's on our minds
It's all forgiven

The two of us were alone, driving in our Honda Odyssey, the very symbol of our partnership as parents, when I initiated what ended up being our easiest and most soothing conversation in years. I would move out. She would keep the house. I would keep my key and see the kids without restriction. Neither of us wanted lawyers involved, so we jointly hired one just to do the paperwork. In one sense, I was free, but in another, I felt an all-too-familiar sense of seclusion.

I gave Mom the news over the phone, providing no more detail than necessary. I couldn't talk to her about feeling alone, not in the way I wanted to. She, of all people, would understand that feeling, having lived by herself with grace and aplomb for over twenty years, but I didn't expect her to suffer my complaints about it. After all, this time I had asked for it. I certainly didn't talk to her about the ways I was trying to fill the void, gallivanting around Philadelphia in dimly lit rock clubs with my newfound muse.

My new home was a studio apartment on the third floor of a house in Fox Chase, a few miles from Lisa and the kids. It was just one bedroom, a kitchen, and a bathroom with a shower, but everything in it was new, completely remodeled with hardwood floors and fresh paint. It was just what I needed for what I saw as a minimalist clean slate. The kitchen window opened up to the roof above the second floor, providing me a makeshift deck to strum my guitar under the stars, with a romantic view of the Dunkin' Donuts and the German butcher shop down the block. It was a place to go to make the day last just a little longer.

There's a lot I liked to criticize about the culture I grew up in— the rapid-fire, high-intensity, short-attention-span, action-movie mentality, where every orifice of every minute must be filled, and people will do anything to avoid the quietude at the moment every-thing stops. My tinnitus had been there for years, but it wasn't until I was alone, staring up at the ceiling from my new IKEA bed—no babies crying from the floor above me, no television beaming some Time-Life infomercial as I drifted off—that I realized I could hear the ringing in my ears for the first time in ages. It was crazy, but I welcomed it.

I realized something about myself: I was someone who had avoided the quietude, who couldn't handle the idea of getting off the ride. That's why I never afforded myself a single break or vacation in twenty-plus years of rock 'n' roll pursuits unless it was under duress or for the benefit of somebody else. The Suburban Lizards, No Excuse, the Beat Clinic, the Caulfields, John Faye Power Trip, IKE, my new band with Brittany, aptly named John & Brittany—these were all different heads on the same relentless beast.

What that beast was in pursuit of was never something I explicitly spelled out in any sort of mental mission statement. Validation? For sure. It definitely wasn't money, at least not after a certain point. A sense of belonging? Of course. In the end, I guess when you know the thing you do best, you just do it the best way you can, with purpose.

There was a short-order cook that Brett and I once encountered at a Waffle House on the outskirts of Atlanta. This man epitomized the definition of the culinary term mise en place—"everything in its place." He was a marvel to watch, knew his every move before he even made it. We stared in awe as his arms whirled around him, almost like an octopus, cracking eggs on the rim of a metal bowl with one hand, loading slices of white bread into toasters with the other, then moving on to pour perfect portions of batter into multiple waffle irons. It was like a late-night ballet, and he performed all of it without seeing a thing he was doing. No, he was not blind. He was a full-on hunchback, with a spine as severely curved as one might think humanly possible. His only sightline led straight down to the brown tile floor, but perhaps this only served to sharpen his concentration on the tasks at hand. Any time we returned to Atlanta, I always wanted to go back to that same Waffle House, in hopes of seeing him again.

On one occasion, we actually did, and I tapped Brett on the shoulder to whisper, "Look who's on the grill."

In a way, I was just like that short-order cook. I had navigated my personal odyssey with a similar kind of tunnel vision, focused on my own tasks at hand, never deterred, never bored, if only because I never stopped long enough to allow for the possibility. I guess it was in my blood. Without ever speaking her intent, Mom had raised me to push through, to keep going even in circumstances when it might be understandable if I didn't. Like all of life's trade-offs, that kind of perseverance comes at a price, and now I thought I knew what it was.

I still had no idea.

WALK THE WALK

Although I never cared for the term "hump day," by the spring of 2012, Wednesday definitely represented a mid-week protuberance that I had to "*make it* over." It was sandwiched between my two lecture days at Drexel, during which I'd teach three consecutive eighty-minute sections of Songwriting 323—9:30 am for the morning people, 11:00 for the artist types who can't function at 9:30, and 12:30 for the ones who are there under protest, merely fulfilling a requirement to graduate from the music industry program. It was like playing three shows a night for a contemptible amount of money, except these performances required you to wake up at 6:30 in the morning, and the club owner made you fill out a W-9.

Luckily, the Fox Chase regional rail line was only a two-minute jog from my place. The ten-minute breaks between my classes were barely enough time to dip into a baggie of apple slices or walk up a flight of stairs to speed-shit in the third-floor men's room. If there's one piece of advice I can give to aspiring adjuncts: never take a crap in the bathroom on the same floor where you teach. The last thing you need is to emerge from a handicapped stall the second the dubstep kid, who sits in the back row, comes in to fix his hair.

I had all weekend to prepare for Tuesday's classes, but Wednesday took the full brunt of the prep time for Thursday. And then, of course, there was Dobbs. I had recently become the host of the Wednesday open mic night at the first club I ever played in Philadelphia. Sipping on a dusty six-ounce can of pineapple juice from behind the bar, I'd put the sign-up sheet out at 8:00, start the music at 9:00, and eventually hit the pillow at 2:00 am, with just a handful of hours to sleep before waking up to do my three shows at Drexel, with all-new Thursday material.

It was midmorning on the first Wednesday in May, and the walls were already closing in on me. I had sixty assignments to grade and still needed to go over what the hell I was going to talk about the next day. Everything started sounding like bullshit—the assignments *and* my lecture. I had to get out of the apartment. I drove up to Montgomeryville to walk in the mall with the AARP track-suit crowd, lapping the geezers as *Riot!* by Paramore blasted in my tinny earbuds.

For a while, I could forget about Drexel and take a brief respite from thinking about the knock-down-drag-out argument with Brittany that had been weighing on me since the weekend. It was the latest round in a fundamental disagreement we were having over cocaine and its place in our band. I had flipped out on her at Dobbs a few months earlier after learning she had done a line or three up in the green room on a night when we debuted some of the songs we had written for our as-yet-to-be-recorded full-length follow-up to our debut EP.

The ongoing tension surrounding this topic was boiling over as we approached the launch of a risky $10,000 Kickstarter campaign to offset our studio expenses. I needed Brittany to be fully present for us to successfully beg for money, but she didn't particularly see going through life with her "head in the clouds," as she liked to put it, as that big of a deal. Coke, weed, whiskey, cigarillos were, after all, just part of walking the walk implied by our chosen album title: *Start Sinning*. I told her about the role that Mike's alcohol addiction had played in the demise of the Caulfields and that I was never, *ever* going through that again. I sadly hadn't given much consideration to the inner pain that she or my former bandmate might have been trying to fend off when turning to their illicit substance of choice. That would be a subject for a more enlightened version of me to worry about.

My worry on that Wednesday in May over what would become of John & Brittany turned out to be nothing compared to the moments after "crushcrushcrush" was interrupted by a ring tone, incoming from the main phone line at the Stafford. I stopped walking and veered off down a long hallway that led to the restrooms before accepting the call. An administrator named Matt asked for me with a nervous edge in his voice. I confirmed that I was indeed "Mr. Faye" and listened as he informed me that there had been an accident. Mom had been struck by a car while she was out for her morning walk. He didn't have any details other than the fact that she was alive and had been rushed to the hospital in Portland.

I ran out of the mall and threw myself into my car. As I sped down Route 309 fumbling with my phone, I managed to call both Tae Im and Tae Kyung. They had received calls from the Stafford as well and had already gone into their own separate "fixer" modes, muting their distress with pragmatism as we discussed what needed to be done. Tae Kyung would fly up right away from San Francisco, putting a pin in the birthday celebration for her husband, Jim, that day. Tae Im and Randy would drive to Oregon that afternoon, and I would need to find a seat on the next flight out of Philly. I wanted so badly to call Tae Hyun, as scenes from the car accident we both endured so many years before flashed in my mind, but that was just a bridge too far. Instead, I hit speed dial to let Lisa know what had happened, and she responded with kindness and sympathy, offering to talk to the kids after school and to help me find a same-day nonstop to Portland.

As I was making my way through midday traffic, something compelled me to call Brittany, not knowing how she'd react to my abrupt ending of the silent treatment I'd been giving her the past few days. I didn't even know if she would pick up, but she did without letting it ring too many times. I barely got the words out about Mom before I started bawling at a red light. Within minutes of arriving back at my apartment, Brittany and her mother, Anna, were at my door with a pot of soup and the hugs I so desperately needed. For the time being, all was forgiven.

By midafternoon, Lisa had found me a flight, but there was no way she could take me to the airport, so on very short notice and with very little time before the evening rush hour would jeopardize my trip, Susie Steen whisked me and my backpack of bare essentials off to Philly International, with her and Brett's infant son, David, drifting off in his car seat to the sounds of "Octopus's Garden."

I landed at PDX after midnight and soon found myself in the hospital at Oregon Health and Sciences University. Tae Kyung and Tae Im were wide awake, attending to Mom, who was awaiting a five-hour operation on her fractured hip. I wasn't at all prepared to see her like that. Her tiny frame had absorbed the impact of a moving car, driven, we came to find out, by another elderly woman, who didn't see Mom enter Rosemont Road at an unofficial but well-traveled crosswalk by Luscher Farm. Considering the extent of her injuries— the broken hip, two broken ankles, broken ribs, and the fact that she was thrown over twelve feet in the air before hitting asphalt—it was something of a miracle that she was still among us. She had even lost a small piece of her skull, leaving an actual hole in the back of her head, which no one noticed until later.

She had been days away from making what she figured would be her last trip back to Seoul. Her bags were already packed. Tae Im had driven down the Saturday before to help her get ready, ordering Chinese takeout and placing the shoes Mom would wear on the plane atop her bulging suitcase. The brief privilege Mom had been born into back in Kyung-joo didn't amount to much by the time she landed in that hospital bed. The sight of her was the heartbreaking physical embodiment of the metaphor that defined Mom's life. She had taken another hit and survived, just like she survived the Japanese occupation, the Korean War, abandonment by the father of her girls, the tragedy of a child with polio, the death of her second husband, the estrangement of her youngest daughter, the breakup of two of her children's marriages, and perhaps most draining of all, the prejudice she faced as an Asian and as a woman who refused to play to either stereotype.

In the hours after her surgery, we all felt there was reason to be optimistic. The doctors had considered the procedure a success and gave reassurance that Mom could make a recovery. My sisters, my niece and nephews—we all gathered around Mom, heaving into the universe our hope that she would pull through. It was a sobering feeling, watching her struggle to sip ginger ale through a bendy straw or chew on the tiny piece of a bean that Tae Im tried to feed her. To Mom's credit, she never broke character, making sure to grill me on what I was doing with my life and informing me I had gained weight.

"Like a true endomorph," I said, thrilled to be the butt of any joke that might lighten the mood.

While Mom rested in a medicated haze, the rest of us felt our appetites kick in. The café on the third floor served the best hospital food I had ever tasted. It felt like I was at Thanksgiving dinner, eating with family, full of gratitude and hope. I returned to Philadelphia on the following Monday, picturing Mom's triumphant return to the Stafford, where she would share her war story with her neighbors Harriet and Alma.

It took only one physical therapy session, however, for all our collective optimism to come crashing down. Making Mom try to walk, less than a week after the accident, felt premature. She couldn't put any weight on her legs without squealing in excruciating agony. Mom's legendary stubbornness kicked in right away, but not in the direction we all would have wanted. She demanded to return to her room. She was done. Her mind was made up. Instead of fighting to recuperate, she was now fighting to run out the clock. Mom wanted to *go*, and she wanted to exercise her rights under Oregon's Death with Dignity Act, a law with roots in the early '90s "right to die" movement, when Jack Kevorkian was a fixture on the evening news.

Even knowing what Mom's attitudes were, having bristled for years at her open talk of not wanting to linger after her expiration date, it still felt like a bombshell when Tae Kyung called to tell me that Mom had initiated a request to voluntarily end her life with a fatal cocktail of drugs. My sisters were moving her to Legacy Hopewell House, a hospice in Southwest Portland, where Mom would ride out the legally required waiting period to finalize her request. The hospice would provide a more peaceful atmosphere and what they called "palliative care," which I came to learn was a fancy way of saying "morphine, and lots of it."

I flew out to Oregon again at the end of the following week after teaching my classes and hosting at Dobbs. I could have asked

Brittany to fill in again, as she had on the day of the accident, but I needed to be around music, and more important, other musicians. It was a welcome diversion to sing along with Bunny Savage on "Go Back to New Jersey," a song he played every week, lambasting the "cock-sucking retards" who loiter around South Philly cheesesteak joints like Pat's and Gino's.

I arrived at Hopewell House, where my sisters kept vigil pretty much around the clock at Mom's bedside. The fifteen-room sea-foam-green building had been the final stop for AIDS victims and stage IV cancer patients since the turn of the 1990s. I'm quite sure this was the first time they had seen a case like Mom's.

Mother's Day was that Sunday. The weather was beautiful outside, and Tae Kyung convinced the nurses to let us wheel Mom's bed out into the courtyard that was visible from her room. Mom's face lit up at the sight of the healthy trees standing tall against a cloudless blue sky. Beams of light filtered through the web of branches and found Mom as she reclined, her face shaded by a canopy umbrella. I wished for her that she could spend the rest of her time on earth in that precise moment, surrounded by nature and people who loved her, as close as she could now get to feeling sunshine on her shoulders, like in that John Denver song she'd loved since I was a little kid. Such moments can't last forever, or even long enough for someone to pass away perfectly within them.

Back inside with my sisters, their husbands, and their children, we celebrated through the sad recognition that this would be Mom's last Mother's Day. We took turns crowding around her, trying to rouse her senses with fragrant yellow and purple flowers. In quieter moments, Tae Im, Tae Kyung, and I sat with her stroking her white hair and dabbing her chapped lips with a wet cloth to keep them from cracking. I hoped Mom was present enough to understand me when I took her hand to say what I believed would be my last goodbye before leaving to catch the red-eye back east.

"Mom. It's been my honor to be your son. Thank you for everything you did for me. I love you."

She didn't speak, but she gave me a tiny nod that I recognized. It looked just like the one she gave me when I was six after she told me that Papa had died, and I told her I thought I was going to cry. I took the nod to mean she loved me, too, which of course I knew, but "I love you" was not a common exchange between the two of us. She always complained that people said it too much out of habit, rendering it meaningless. Words were nothing without action to back them up, and Mom always knew what spoke louder. I don't know if hearing "I love you" more often from her would have made a difference in our relationship, but maybe not hearing it is part of what pushed me so deeply into music. Maybe it's part of what drove me as a songwriter and a singer. If that's the case, there's no room for regret.

Back home, I immersed myself even deeper into a life already stretched thin. My self-imposed mayhem contrasted with the solemnity I knew I'd left behind in Portland. The mood ring that was my mercurial state of mind adapted to the gravity of the situation. While I could picture Tae Kyung trying to keep Mom hydrated with ice chips, I fumed with a figurative chip on my shoulder. How could Mom just give up like this? Where was the steadfast stoic drive that was now manifesting itself in me as I continued to power through my days and deliver my lectures and song deconstructions to dozens of college kids, not a single one of them with the slightest inkling of what I was compartmentalizing behind my facade? I didn't tell a soul in that world what was going on with me as I came to grips with the hard truth that Mom hadn't given up at all. She was fighting with all her might to get what she wanted: peace. I had left and returned to my life in the middle of that fight, while her two oldest daughters sat with her in a hospice waiting for some doctor to sign off on a fistful of horse tranquilizers.

It wouldn't even be that simple. As it turns out, there's a lot of red tape when it comes to state-sanctioned suicide. Mom wouldn't be allowed to take the meds at the hospice; she would have to check herself out and go back to the Stafford, but she couldn't take an ambulance, which would be some sort of unethical collusion. How were they going to move her broken body in a regular car? Mom would also have to self-administer the drugs with no outside help. None of us were even sure she'd be able to swallow the pills. Tae Kyung was desperately trying to build up Mom's strength with homemade liquid concoctions laced with protein powder from the local health food store. Talk about filial dedication: a daughter doing everything possible to make her mother strong enough to kill herself.

It turned out not to matter. Well before the fifteen-day waiting period was up, word came that Mom's request had been denied. Her condition was not considered "terminal," according to the law. Broken bones were technically survivable, so if she wanted to die with dignity, the state of Oregon would be no help. With her future quality of life as an eighty-five-going-on-eighty-six-year-old looking seriously bleak, Mom summoned what remained of the fire in her shrinking belly and resolved to go out the hard way, refusing any further care beyond the morphine. No food, no water, no IV; nothing that might prolong her life even another minute.

From that point on, we all knew it was just a matter of time. How much time was the question. Even without eating or drinking, Mom's body, which was ninety pounds soaking wet when she was healthy, was slow to break down.

Although she was getting weaker by the day, she was still urinating, still able to communicate, still herself. To their credit, my sisters barely ever left her side for thirty-two grueling days at Hopewell. Tae Kyung was committed to staying parked next to Mom's bed, monitoring her every need and communicating that need to the staff, like the squeaky wheel she had always been. Toward the end, she and Tae Im even rented out a room on the second floor of the hospice and spent the night in lieu of returning to Mom's apartment at the Stafford.

My sisters encouraged me to fly out one more time the first week in June, when it was obvious the end was near. By then, the effects of Mom's decision had finally become noticeable. She was only occasionally drifting *into* consciousness as she floated along on the maximum allowable dose of morphine. I told Tae Im on the phone that I couldn't fly out there again. I had just enough in the bank to come out for the funeral. I had said my goodbye to Mom, and I knew that she'd heard me. What would be the point of my being there now, when she probably wouldn't even recognize me?

Four days before she died, I caught a lucky break and communicated with Mom in a brief, clear moment. While Tae Kyung held the phone, Mom spoke softly and told me she was watching the French Open on TV. Tennis had always been her favorite sport, and it felt like a gift to have one more exchange with her, one that felt like everyday conversation without the weight of a final farewell. My memory went back to the tennis racquet she'd given me when I was eleven and all the power chords I'd played on it.

Mom would have one more lucid moment with Tae Kyung and Tae Im even closer to the end. Almost like she had awakened wide eyed from a long dream, Mom looked into my sister's eyes and said, "Tae Kyung, where have you been?"

"Mom! I've been right here!" Tae Kyung said, giddily surprised and somewhat perplexed.

Tae Im chimed in nearby:

"Mom, it's me, Tae Im! I'm right here too."

"Oh. Whatever," Mom blurted out before drifting right back into the opiate slumber that would carry her to eternity.

LAST LETTER TO AN 8 × 10

You took your last breath exactly six weeks after the accident—a collision that, statistically speaking, should have killed you right on the spot. I guess I wasn't really that surprised. Everything about how you lived defied the odds, so of course how you died would too. If I wasn't feeling surprise, I also wasn't allowing myself to feel much of anything else. Not at first. I got the news on another Wednesday morning and wrote a thirty-six-word Facebook post, prompting more than three hundred people to offer their thoughts and prayers. Then I hosted my open mic that night and received more condolences, all for the grief I could not yet feel.

When I think about it, I guess there was one thing I could feel burning behind my stiff upper lip: anger. I was angry at the old woman who hit you. I was angry at the Lake Oswego cops who didn't do shit to at least get her license revoked. I was angry at myself for not being there at the very end, which of course I projected onto Tae Kyung and Tae Im, who barely let you out of their sight for six weeks. I felt like a shitty son, and that all the years I looked after you, when I was your only kid who hadn't bolted for the left coast, had somehow been erased. I was even mad at you for having the massive balls to end your own life in the most stubborn way imaginable: by not eating. I still have these split-second panic attacks whenever I think about dying and glimpse a mental picture of total nothingness. You went willingly and steadfastly right into the darkness.

It made me think of my teenage obsession with Bobby Sands, the guy from the IRA who went on a hunger strike in 1981. I spent most of the spring of that year quietly making sure I was on the couch next to you to watch *World News Tonight* and wait for Peter Jennings to give the count: day sixteen, day twenty-nine, day forty-four, all while Bobby Sands slowly withered away in a prison cell at Long Kesh. It took him sixty-six days to die. You were over three times his age, full of broken bones, and still lasted thirty-two days, which, by my calculation, made you indisputably tougher. Maybe that's part of why I felt angry.

You were more Irish than I ever was.

I had gone most of my life considering the combination of Irish and Korean to be off-kilter; unnatural, even. But in one defiant act, you showed me how much the two have in common and make sense within me. Granted, that commonality includes their long histories of suffering and cultural coping mechanisms, which take untold amounts of unprocessed pain and crush that pain into little diamonds of delusion. Maybe that's an apt metaphor for how I write my songs. The best ones come from a place of pain or longing or loss—some negative feeling that needs a change of shape. "It's cheaper than therapy," I always used to say, relying on it time after time to convince myself I was exorcising my demons, when maybe I was really just holding them at bay with my little sonic diamonds of delusion.

I turned to songwriting in the aftermath of 2012, as someone hanging off the edge of a cliff would cling to an outstretched arm. It took me a year to write "Church and State," the song I now sing in the shower whenever gallows humor and incongruity seem like the best way to start the day, which, to be honest, is pretty often. I have this love/hate relationship with the song. I love it because it depicts the way I always wanted to talk to you, the way I'm doing now, and I hate it because it's a reminder of never really having that rapport while you were alive.

For a psychiatrist, you sure had an aversion to talking about any of our family's past or present hardships. Maybe you just didn't want to trigger long-suppressed memories from your own life, the life you had before any of us came along, the life that no parent's child can truly comprehend until they start digging into their own. But maybe all that circumvention is why I was so much in search of connection and catharsis through music. "Church and State" was practically my entire grieving process writ large in the key of E-major. The simple ascending-then-descending riff felt like the ups and downs of who we were: what we share versus what we keep to ourselves, what we accept versus what we deny, the ringing in our ears versus what we actually hear and take to heart.

> I TURNED TO SONG-WRITING IN THE AFTERMATH OF 2012, AS SOMEONE HANGING OFF THE EDGE OF A CLIFF WOULD CLING TO AN OUTSTRETCHED ARM.

> *Whatcha say, whatcha say, I'm listening*
> *Whatcha say, whatcha say, I'm listening now*
> *I'm listening now.*

I thought about all the chances I wanted back, like our only trip to Korea, which I'm sure I would have appreciated so much more at any age other than thirteen. And what I wouldn't give to hear you quote Lao Tzu one more time and actually absorb the wisdom of what you were attempting to pass along, like the most enlightened member of a relay team, trying to hand off a baton to someone whose fist was clenched tight.

When I let go of what I am, I become what I might be.

Writing "Church and State" helped me feel, for the first time, like I could present myself to you as the flawed, complicated person I am, and maybe give a glimpse into the possibilities of what I might become. It allowed me to see your complexities the same way.

The dichotomy of how you lived in your house on Bisbee Road morphed from a frustration into an oddly cherished memory. You were such a neat freak in so many ways, always dusting things and spraying them down with Lemon Pledge. Your bedroom was immaculate, everything in its place, blankets never ruffled. Your ice box, on the other hand, was a house of refrigerated horrors that I marveled at for years until I finally got the opportunity to go scorched-earth on it during your last trip to Korea before you left Newark. I showed no mercy for the Handi-Wrapped bowls of unidentifiable leftovers and the *jangjorim* jar with its rusty lid and its little lily pads of mold floating atop a black brine pickling chunks of beef and discolored hard-boiled eggs. The two boxes of ShopRite melon balls in the freezer were carbon-dated back to the late 1970s. Out of sheer curiosity before chucking them in the trash, I opened up the containers to find the spherical pieces of cantaloupe and honeydew, pictured in "actual size" on the packaging, shrunk down to these tiny dehydrated pellets resembling something that astronauts would eat in outer space. It was like the bittersweet ending to a long scientific experiment.

Whether it was cleanliness contrasted with filth, or who you present yourself to be contrasted with who you really are, I started to see the yin and the yang in just about everything. Things that seem incompatible somehow coexist. I think about your memorial service. The girls insisted on calling it a "celebration," much to my annoyance at the time. I suppose I was superimposing my own thoughts on how a funeral should be run. I've often envisioned my own with a lot of hysterical weeping and gnashing of teeth, while my exes and near-missus all throw themselves at my open casket. Then again, I've also stated on more than one occasion that maybe I'd rather be made into a human piñata so the children in attendance could take a whack at me with some Wiffle Ball bats after the eulogy.

Of course, many tears were shed in the main meeting room at the Stafford, where we gathered to remember you, but there were also moments of laughter and levity, lending balance and contrast to the full, rich picture of our collective psyche. The solemn sounds from the harp played by a woman in the corner were juxtaposed with the sight of a floral arrangement full of orange tiger lilies, yellow roses, pink carnations. The handmade walking stick you took on hikes leaned against the front of a lectern.

Your white sun hat was perched at an angle atop the grip. Dried ornamental onion stalks you picked off the ground at Luscher Farm stood close to four feet high in a tall thin glass vase. On the carpeted floor at the foot of these items sat your once-white walking shoes, which had likely not been pristine since the first time you wore them out on a trail. Three orange roses, wrapped in a pink cellophane bow, spanned their laceless tops, as if beckoning you to step into them one more time.

Two poster-size photo tributes captured a few dozen moments of joy from the long and winding road of your life: pictures with relatives and all your kids and grandkids, pictures of you out in nature, smiling your gentle smile against casually stunning backdrops of foliage and fire pits, mountains and waterfalls. In a few of these shots, you're holding one of those green point-and-shoots that you never left home without. The girls placed your last half dozen or so, still sealed in their reflective silver wrapping, next to a stack of remembrance cards out on a guest sign-in table, perhaps hoping someone might carry on your passion for disposable camera photography.

Natalie and Sean had flown out with me. You would have thought they looked so grown up—Goosie, almost eleven, in her pink floral dress, and Seanie, all of eight years old, dressed up in his khaki pants and button-down shirt with clip-on tie. They were gamely manning their posts by the door, handing out programs bound together with single strands of burgundy yarn. The well-intentioned but condensed *Reader's Digest* summation of you, printed in oversized typeface on the heavy card stock, is what gave me the first inkling that I should write out these memories, that maybe by recollecting what I could about me, it might somehow pay the smallest of tributes to you. For the time being, there were just the basic facts: CELEBRATION OF LIFE in all caps, the antiseptic version of your name, "Dr. J. S. Faye," the dates serving as the bookends of your time on earth, and the date of the service, Wednesday, June 27.

What was it about Wednesdays? Or June 27, for that matter? It's crazy to think how many times that date has come up on our family roulette wheel, all bets on 27 red. June 27 is the day in 1964 that the girls first arrived on US soil to join you in a new life as you were finishing your residency at Einstein. It was the date that you came to discover was your lunar calendar birthday. It was the date that Papa died, which I wondered many times how long you would have kept from me if I hadn't pressed you on his whereabouts. Finally, it became the date we all eulogized you.

I was the first to go up after the pastor's opening remarks. Our tiny Korean contingent of core family and relatives I hadn't seen since

I was a teenager occupied the front row, with a sea of mostly white-haired Anglo octogenarians populating the rest of the forty or so chairs. It was a respectable crowd for a Delaware expat in Oregon. As I looked out at Tae Im and Tae Kyung's attentive faces, Tae Hyun's face was conspicuously absent but surely in the front of all our minds, just as you were. I think about it all the time—how you might have felt, marching with purpose toward your own demise, knowing there was this loose end, an unmendable tear in our familial fabric that never had to be that way. Or maybe you were at peace with it. Tae Hyun had made up her mind a long time ago that she wasn't coming back, and my songs about that had already been around for fifteen years. If you look at old pictures of all of us before Papa died, you'd have thought we'd forever live this idyllic, carefree life. How quickly that changed for me, but maybe there was a piece of you that still held on to those images of the collective dream we all shared at one time.

I don't remember a word I said about you as I stood next to the podium, but I had something more than oration to share. Dating back to the days when I would peruse the seven-inch singles at Woolworths, "Sunshine on My Shoulders" was the epitome of uncool, in part because it was "my mom's favorite song," one that I'm fairly certain you ranked high above anything I ever wrote, but also because I just couldn't wrap my head around such unabashed sincerity. Deep down, I guess I envied it. John Denver had no use for irony or sarcasm or any of the obfuscations I leaned on as a songwriter. He wrote simple tunes with simple words that spoke to his elemental appreciation of beauty in this world. No wonder you loved him. He was a kindred spirit. As I sat in a chair and accompanied myself with just a quiet bass line played on an acoustic guitar, I stepped into the stream of those lyrics as I glimpsed down at your empty shoes, and I was there with you on the plane of enlightenment you worked so hard to reach and so hard to share with me.

In that moment, I felt a connection with you through music that I never managed to achieve while you were alive. When I finished singing the song, I felt like my voice was complete, devoid of the need for any further validation. Your old stock reaction of asking "Is that good?" any time I played a song for you was no longer applicable. I knew that it was good.

The rest of the celebration felt like we were all joined together in a new dream.

Speaker after eloquent speaker shared their stories about you. Your grandchildren extolled your virtues and your impact on their lives. Even Natalie got up and spoke confidently from her young heart. Sean was in charge of releasing two clusters of pink balloons, and when he pulled the string from the netting that held them, my eye followed the last one into the air and out of sight, as it floated off to survey the world's wonders from above. *Isn't that beautiful*, you would have said.

The following day, when our family and a few friends and relatives arrived at Luscher Farm to scatter your ashes at the foot of a new copper beech tree planted in your honor, I could feel the summer sun bathe me in its warmth. My natural inclination to run for shade was overruled by the urge to bask in the light, just as you would. I suppose I had acquired your taste for it. Sunshine, nowadays anyway, almost always makes me high.

ACKNOWLEDGMENTS

I want to express my eternal gratitude to the people who encouraged me throughout the years-long process of writing this memoir. From the casual comments from friends along the lines of "This kind of thing only happens to you, John. You should write a book" to the moral and financial support to be able to focus on what sometimes felt like several full-time jobs, I have a lot to be thankful for.

First and foremost, I want to thank my sisters Tae Im and Tae Kyung, not only for having faith that I could pull this off but for the countless hours of conversation about our mom and her story, which is inextricably tied to my own. "Im-pel" and "Kim-pel"—I love you both dearly. And Tae Hyun, I miss you and hope you and the girls are happy in all you do.

Huge thanks to Lisa and my beloved children, Natalie and Sean. LB— all these years after we parted ways in marriage, you are still my closest friend and my emergency contact. It couldn't have been easy for you to read some of the things in this book, but you had nothing but kindness and encouragement for me throughout the entire process.

I want to thank every person with whom I've ever had the privilege to share a stage, a studio, a rehearsal space, or a fifteen-passenger van. My fellow musicians are my tribe in this world and even if we no longer talk or we had a musical or personal falling out, we were part of something together that has meant more to me than just about any other set of experiences I've had in my life. Music saved me, showed me I could have a voice in a world that has many times left me feeling otherwise silenced, and I sincerely appreciate everyone who has played or sung a single note with me.

I want to especially thank my long-time bandmates and musical brothers Sam Musumeci, Ritchie Rubini, and Brett Talley. You have been my closest confidants and cheerleaders, even when you weren't part of a particular band or project with me. Our friendship goes beyond our rock 'n' roll connection, which is, no doubt, strong. You guys are quite simply the people I enjoy being around the most. I can't walk into a room with you without immediately cracking up at the thought of the utter stupidity that is bound to ensue. Bands come and go, but when you can truly be yourself with people, especially those you play music with, you've really got something, and I am beyond lucky to know you.

I also want to acknowledge and thank these musicians, who have colored my musical world: Mike Simpson, Mike Neiger, Keith Green, Chris Ryan, Scott Kohlmorgen, Tom Marks, Rich Stevens, Cliff Hillis, Dave Anthony, Joann Schmidt, Tommy Kristich, Susie Steen, Jason Miraglia, Brittany Rotondo, Mike Vivas, Steven LaFashia, Michael Leavy, Michael O'Brien, Carl Bahner, Greg Pinney, Joey DiTullio, Ken Herblin, Sarah Herbert, Ron DiSilvestro, Kara Lafty, Josh Mayer, Brianna Sig, Larry Kennedy, Bryce Connor, Garrick Chow, Reece Ratliff, Madalean Gauze, Andrea Nardello, Robbie Rist, Sean Slattery,

Alexis Dundovic, Richard Chodak and my Bluebond Music School family, and the fellow musicians from every music community or town that has welcomed me. There are no doubt more who belong on this list, but please know that if we ever spent any time making music together, you are in my heart.

Thanks to my long-time friend John Ratliff, who has always, *always* had my back on every level, from my earliest musical days in college with the Beat Clinic up through the release of this memoir. John, I have you to thank for so much of my ability to pursue the creative life I've always wanted. Your friendship, support, and acceptance into your family means the world to me. I flat out would not be able to do *any* of this without you. I appreciate you, Lynne, and the kids beyond words. Thanks also for generously giving me access to align-Space and connecting me with the amazing team there, who have all been nothing but kind and helpful. The opportunity to write, record, and create at the space has been a godsend.

I want to thank my editor, Louis Greenstein, who came into my life at a time when I didn't quite yet know I actually had a real book and not just a bunch of ramblings on my hands. Louis, your vast experience, knowledge, honesty, and wonderful humor has made me feel so validated in these final stages of getting my story out into the world. Your reaction to the memoir has given me so much confidence that my story could resonate with someone who didn't know me already. I also want to express my gratitude to the amazing team at Advantage Media, whose enthusiasm and expertise have taken this book across the finish line.

To quote Hunter S. Thompson: "The music business is a cruel and shallow money trench, a long plastic hallway where thieves and pimps run free, and good men die like dogs. There's also a negative side."

The music business *is*, indeed, a tough world, one that I fully discourage anyone from getting into if they can avoid it, but through all the many, many challenges, there have been enough bright lights to help me move forward, even against the odds and my better judgment. There are certain people I encountered on this journey without whom I would never have had many of the opportunities and experiences that I got to recount in these pages. Some of these folks are no longer with us, and some I haven't spoken with in many years, but I wish to thank them all from the bottom of my heart (in no particular order): Rudy Rubini, Doron Segal, Mark Mazzetti, Tony DeVitto, Jonathan Ehrlich, John Titta, Bert Padell, Trevor Baptiste, Jake Fine, Vikki Walls, Bill House, Al Marks, Kevin Moloney, Tracy Chisholm, David Bianco, Bob Ludwig, Garett Michaels, Lanny West, Leslie Fram, Steve Barnes, Matt Pinfield, Vin Scelsa, Rob Acampora, Jim McGuinn, Dan Fein, Shawn Arnold, Cyndy Drue, Paul Jaxon Miller, Pierre Robert, Preston Elliot, Steve Morrison, Bill Weston, Chuck D'Amico, Sara Parker, Mark Rogers, Mike Rossi, Johnny B., John Wilson, Pete Booker, Wendy Rollins, Jessie Marley, Paul Barsky, Brian Bereznak, Jim Johnson, Rich O'Halloran, John Luneau, Don McCollister, Butch Walker, Pat DiNizio, Peter Case, Steve Wynn, Phast Phreddie Patterson, Jon Bon Jovi, Del Amitri, Lauren Hart, Jesse Lundy, Bryan Dilworth, Steven Van Zandt, Dennis Mortensen, Kevin Walsh, Phil Nicolo, Hal Real, Laura Wilson, Jason Curtis, Chris Brown, Randall Butler, Chuck Keith, Beth Tallman, Terry Dry, Jay Durgan, Anthony Cordova, Rick Neidig, Mark Hershberger, David Bash, and anyone else in the music biz who let me know that I wasn't invisible.

In addition to the music lovers from all over the world, who have kept my rock 'n' roll flame burning for over three decades, my eternal thanks goes to these close friends and super supporters: Vince Watchorn, Jonathan Hunt, Ross Albert, Mariano Mattei, Greg Styer,

Kirk Waldrop, Sean McCloskey, Robin Little, Lauree McArdle, Bob Baylis, Lauren Lyons, Suzanne Hiscock, Michael Magoolaghan, and thanks Matt Kurland for connecting me with your cousin Louis to edit the book.

Finally, thank you, Mom and Papa. I hope I've lived my life in a way that makes you proud wherever your souls watch over me.

Final thought: On the eve of the final editing of this book, I was contacted by and was able to meet my half brother Jon David McCormick Faye, thanks to the efforts of his daughter, my niece Faye Jeffries, who is only three months younger than I am. I want to thank them for connecting with me and welcoming me onto a new branch of the Faye family tree.

Jacket Design: Michael Leavy